CANADIAN WRITERS AND THEIR WORKS

Cumulated Index, Poetry Series

CANADIAN WRITERS AND THEIR WORKS

Cumulated Index, Poetry Series

Edited by Donald W. McLeod

ECW PRESS, 1993

CANADIAN CATALOGUING IN PUBLICATION DATA

Main entry under title;
  Canadian writers and their works cumulated index : poetry series

Supplement to: Canadian writers and their works : poetry series.
ISBN 1-55022-143-4

1. Canadian writers and their works : poetry series – Indexes. 2. Canadian
poetry (English) – History and criticism – Indexes.* 3. Poets, Canadian
(English) – Biography – Indexes.*
1. McLeod, Donald W. (Donald Wilfred), 1957–

PS8141.C32 1993 016.811'009 C91-095094-6
PR9190.2.C32 1993
74620

Design and imaging by ECW Type & Art, Oakville, Ontario.
Printed and bound by Hignell Printing Limited, Winnipeg, Manitoba.

Distributed by General Publishing Co. Limited, 30 Lesmill Road,
Don Mills, Ontario M3B 2T6.

Published by ECW PRESS, 1980 Queen St. E., Toronto, Ontario M4L 1J2.

PREFACE

THE IDEA FOR THE *Canadian Writers and Their Works* series was first put forward in 1980. It was a big, original plan — nothing less than to produce an authoritative, well-researched, and well-documented critical series covering the development of Canadian writing over the past two centuries. Other critical reference books on Canadian literature had already appeared, but there was nothing of this depth or magnitude. From its inception, *Canadian Writers and Their Works* was envisioned as a bold new approach to the study of Canadian writing.

The project editors assembled a team of Canadian literary specialists to write individual essays on Canadian writers. Each specialist devoted an essay to *one* particular author. In addition, much time was spent in editing and updating the essays and in performing independent verification of facts and sources. This attention to detail necessitated publishing the series over a period of years — almost ten years elapsed between the appearance of the first volume, in 1983, and the publication of the final volumes, in 1992. The result is that *Canadian Writers and Their Works* is the most comprehensive and accurate commentary to date; it also includes a wealth of previously unknown information about individual Canadian writers.

The essays have been combined in twenty volumes that are arranged chronologically to present Canada's literary history as it has evolved over the last two centuries. Ten of these volumes are devoted to writers of fiction, and ten to poets. Each volume, in turn, contains four or five essays that are unified in a general introduction by George Woodcock. Each critical essay includes a brief biography of the author, a discussion of the tradition/milieu influencing his/her work, a critical overview section that reviews published criticism of the author, a long section analyzing the author's works, and a selected

5

bibliography listing primary and secondary material. Each essay includes an original illustration of the writer by Isaac Bickerstaff, and each volume is fully indexed.

The project editors of *Canadian Writers and Their Works* wish to acknowledge the contributions of the many people who have played an important role in creating this series. First, we would like to thank the critics who prepared the essays for these volumes (complete listing on pages 8–10), as well as George Woodcock, for his incisive Introductions to each volume. Don Evans (a.k.a. Isaac Bickerstaff) drew the marvelous illustrations of the authors. We are indebted to the following people for their editorial and verification work: Edna Barker, Matthew Carnicelli, Graham Carr, Val Daigen, Jamie Gaetz, Bob Hilderley, Jeff Jones, Ken Lewis, Ross MacKay, Don McLeod, Scott Mitchell, Nanette Norris, Tom Orman, Holly Potter, Carole Turner, Anne Williams, Mary Williams, and Jean Wilson. We are also pleased to acknowledge the production and design teams of Paul Davies of ECW Type & Art and Tim and Elke Inkster of The Porcupine's Quill, and the keyboarding skills of Debra Burke, Pat Kenny, Wiesia Kolasinska, Stephanie Termeer, Jennifer Trainor, and Hilda Keskin Weber. Special thanks to Tom Orman for his help in keying the cumulated indexes.

Robert Lecker/Jack David/Ellen Quigley
Project Editors
Canadian Writers and Their Works

A NOTE ABOUT
THE CUMULATED INDEX

THE PRESENT VOLUME is an edited, slightly revised cumulation of the indexes that appeared with each of the *Canadian Writers and Their Works* volumes. This index lists all proper names mentioned in the volumes, excluding place names, academic institutions, names of characters, and names of relatives mentioned only in passing. All critics named or quoted in the text or in explanatory notes are indexed. All titles of poems, stories, articles, books, etc., that are discussed in the text are indexed, as are the titles of periodicals and critical works about which substantive remarks have been made.

The index is arranged alphabetically, word by word, and chronologically if there are separate entries for different editions of the same work. Names beginning with McC are indexed as McC, not Mac. Abbreviations such as St., No., and Mrs. are indexed as they are spelled, not as if spelled out in full. Where titles are identical or are similar to works by other writers, the author's last name is also listed, in parentheses. Pseudonymous names are listed under the pseudonym (e.g., Twain, Mark), with the person's real name listed in parentheses afterwards (Samuel L. Clemens). Newspapers are indexed by city, and the titles of college publications cite the name of the school in parentheses. Continuous pagination (e.g., 47–49) is cited only if the discussion of the topic is also continuous.

LIST OF CONTENTS: POETRY SERIES

*Each volume contains a critical
introduction by George Woodcock.*

Volume I:

Isabella Valancy Crawford by Robert Alan Burns
Charles Heavysege by George Woodcock
Charles Mair by Fred Cogswell
Charles Sangster by W.D. Hamilton

Volume II:

William Wilfred Campbell by George Wicken
Bliss Carman by Terry Whalen
Archibald Lampman by L.R. Early
Charles G.D. Roberts by Fred Cogswell
Duncan Campbell Scott by Gordon Johnston

Volume III:

Raymond Knister by Joy Kuropatwa
Dorothy Livesay by Paul Denham
E.J. Pratt by Peter Buitenhuis
W.W.E. Ross by Don Precosky

Volume IV:

Robert Finch by Susan Gingell
Leo Kennedy by Francis Zichy
A.M. Klein by Noreen Golfman
F.R. Scott by Sandra Djwa
A.J.M. Smith by Michael Darling

Volume V:

Earle Birney by Peter Aichinger
Louis Dudek by Terry Goldie
Irving Layton by Wynne Francis
Raymond Souster by Bruce Whiteman
Miriam Waddington by Peter Stevens

Volume VI:

Margaret Avison by David A. Kent
Ralph Gustafson by Dermot McCarthy
Jay Macpherson by Lorraine Weir
P.K. Page by John Orange
Anne Wilkinson by Christopher Armitage

Volume VII:

Milton Acorn by Ed Jewinski
Alden Nowlan by Michael Oliver
Al Purdy by Louis K. MacKendrick
James Reaney by Richard Stingle
Phyllis Webb by John F. Hulcoop

Volume VIII:

bill bissett by Karl Jirgens
George Bowering by John Harris
Daphne Marlatt by Douglas Barbour
bpNichol by Douglas Barbour
Michael Ondaatje by Nell Waldman

Volume IX:

Margaret Atwood by Jean Mallinson
D.G. Jones by E.D. Blodgett
Patrick Lane by George Woodcock
Dennis Lee by T.G. Middlebro'
Gwendolyn MacEwen by Jan Bartley

Volume X:

Leonard Cohen by Linda Hutcheon
Robert Kroetsch by Ann Munton
Eli Mandel by Dennis Cooley
John Newlove by Douglas Barbour
Joe Rosenblatt by Ed Jewinski

Index to Canadian Writers and Their Works, Poetry Series, Volumes 1–10

"A l'Ange Avant-Gardien" IV 191

ABC: the aleph beth book VIII 298

A.J.M. Smith Award VI 89 IX 232

A.M. Klein V 281, 310–11, 315

A.M. Klein Research and Publication Committee IV 132, 133

"A-N & Etc." VII 219–20

Abbey Theatre IV 252

Abel, Darrel VI quoted 98

"About a New Anthology Again ..." VI 50

"Abracadabra" III 87

Abrams, M.H. IV 42

"Absences" V 318

Absinthe Drinker, The (Degas) IX 140

"Absinthe Drinker, The" (Lane) IX 140

"Absolute" VI 61

Absolute Smile, The VII 181

"Absolution" VII 109

Abstraction and Artifice in Twentieth Century Art VIII 304

"Absurd Prayer" X 38

Academia Brazileira de Letras VI 224

"Academic Literature" V 80, 87, 98

Acadie II 90

"Accessions" IX 203, 222 n.33

"Accustom the grey coils" VI 304

"Acid Sibyl, The" IX 31

Acis in Oxford and Other Poems IV 32

Acorn, Milton V 112, 151 VII 6, 7, 10, 11–12, 85, 136, 138, 139, 140–41, 195 VIII 134 IX 2, 135, 137, 138, 139, 231, 236 X 8, 339, 342, 343

Acquisitive Society, The IV 173

"Acrobat, The" IX 203

Across My Path II 245, 280 n.45

"Across the Mary River ..." VII 180

"Act of the Apostles" IX 151

Acta Victoriana III 19 VI 26, 66 n.5 IX 2, 189, 192, 222 n.33

Acton, Lord IX quoted 3

"Acts, The" VIII 142

Adachi, Ken VIII 371

"Adam and God" VI 303

Adamov, A.G. VII 254, 266

Adams, Ansel VI 214 n.47

Adams, John Coldwell II 199, 225 n. 7

"Adam's Rib" VI 303

Addison, Joseph II 35

"Address to a Maid" I 140

Adeney, Marcus VI 92, 93

"Adolescence" III 94 VI 246

"Adonais" III 65 V 20 IX 205

Adorno, Theodor X 245

"Advance of an Army" V 261

Advice to My Friends X 74, 110, 130–41, 144, 147–48, 150, 154, 157, 165, 166, 170

"Advice to My Friends" X 130

"Advice to the Young" V 301–02

"Advocate" I 80, 81, 84, 86, 88, 89, 108

Aeneid III 142

Aeschylus VII 262

"Afloat" II 215, 221

"Afloat on Waters" VII 252

"AFTER BIRD (improvising)" VIII 335, 338

"After Breughel" IV 52–53

"After Donne" VI 261

"After Exile" III 20, 35

"After Great Shock" VI 295, 298

"After Jaynes" IX 57, 63

"After Rain" VI 254

"After Reading *Albino Pheasants*" VI 261

"After Reading Kafka" VI 292

"After the Ballad 'Lord Randall, My Son'" VI 292–93, 303

"After the Flood, We" IX 33–34

"After the Rates" VII 150–51

Afternoon Moon VII 205

"Afterwards" IX 66, 77 n.67

"Again the Concrete Is Best" VI 153

Against a League of Liars VII 23, 44–46 VIII 134

"Against a League of Liars" VII 45

Agee, James VIII 225

"Agonizing Search for the Elusive Title, The" VIII 389

"Aguirre: The Wrath of God" X 268

"Ah Rats!" V 214 n.64

Aichinger, Peter V quoted 18, 21

Aiken, Conrad IV 235, 241 VI 44

Aikman, Audrey VI quoted 282–83

"Aim of Life Is Life, The" VII 65

Ainsworth, William Harrison VI 279

"air canada whats th storee" VIII 85

Aitken, Sir Max (Lord Beaverbrook) II 192

Al Purdy VIII 138

"Al Purdy" VIII 146

"Alaska Passage" V 55

Albers, Detlev VII 198

Alberta X 73

Albino Pheasants IX 143–44, 167

Albion, The I 84, 169, 171

"Alcazar, Cecil, Belmont, New Fountain, names stations of the way, to" VIII 224

Alcorn, Douglas V 269 n.44

Alcyone II 136, 143, 144, 145, 146

"Alcyone" II 153–55, 156, 159, 164

"Alden Nowlan: Autobiographical Sketch" VII 77, 79, 80, 86

Aldington, Richard V 79

Aleph Unit VIII 302

Alexander, D. VIII 190, 212

Alexander, W.J. VII 199

"Alexander Trocchi, Public Junkie, Priez Pour Nous" X 48

Alexandra (wife of King Edward VII) II 29

Alfieri, Vittorio I 83, 99

Alfred de Vigny et l'Angleterre IV 31

Alfred the Great VI 86, 97, 100

Alibi X 73, 83

"Alice" I 140 VI 250

"Alix" III 47

"All Bread" IX 56–57

"All Fool's Eve" VI 30, 44, 45, 56

"All men delight in you" X 44

"All That Is in the World" VI 118, 121

"All the Fine Young Horses" IX 236

"All the Spikes but the Last" III 150

"All There Is to Know about Adolf Eichmann" X 47

"Allegory # 3" VIII 299

"Allegory # 10" VIII 299

"Alleluia" VI 294

Allen, Carolyn IX 73 n.50 quoted 70 n.23

Allen, Donald IV 261 V 242 VIII 192

Allen, Moira III 121

Allende, Salvador III 92

Alligator Pie IX 10, 191

Allison, Susan III 62

Allison, W.T. III 21

Allophanes VIII 136, 150, 151–53, 160

Almon, Sophie Louise II 225 n.9

Alphabeings & Other Seasyours V 30

Alphabet VI 174, 175 VII 195 IX 135 X 202, 203

"Alphabet, The" VII 209, 214

"Already the Lies" X 294

"Altar, The" X 359

Altieri, Charles VI 125 quoted 124, 125, 126, 161–62 n.76

Altman, Robert X 22

"Aluroid" V 52

"am or" VIII 38

Amabile, George IX 144

Amalrik, Anrei V 197

"Ambition" II 167–68 III 29

American Mercury, The IV 69, 193, 235

Amhertsburg Courier I 83, 99

Among the Millet and Other Poems II 136, 143, 144–45, 146

"Among the Timothy" II 151 VI 146

"Among the Wheatfields" VI 145–49

"Among These Beings Not This at Least" X 223

"Amor Vitae" II 162

"Amphibian Shores" VI 302

Amprimoz, Alexandre L. IX quoted 145

Ana Historic VIII 249

"Anagogic Man, The" VI 187

Anansi *See* House of Anansi Press

"Anarch" V 166

"Anatomy of Angels, The" VII 101

Anatomy of Criticism VI 184 VII 232 IX 191 X 200

"Anatomy of Melancholy" VI 152

"Anchor, The" IV 44

"ancient lord laydee uv th univers, th" VIII 76

"Ancient Maps of the Real World" VIII 290–91

"Ancient Myth and Poetry: A Panel Discussion" VI 17, 176

Ancient Near Eastern Texts VI 200

"Ancient Slang or a Modern, An" X 287

"And Dreamers, Even Then, If Dreaming" X 128

"And He Wept Aloud, So That the Egyptians Heard It" VII 107

"And in Our Time" VII 287

Andersen, Hans Christian VI 278 VIII 208

Anderson, Mia VI 38, 50–51

Anderson, Patrick III 68 IV 8, 38, 176, 177, 202 V 2, 80, 240 VI 88, 92, 223, 229, 231, 247 VII 265

Anderson, Sherwood IV 80, 103, 106, 235

"Andrew Marvell" IV 76

Andy VIII 274, 307

"Angel Guest, The" I 193–94

Angel Guest and Other Poems and Lyrics, The I 163, 174, 193–94

"Angel's Drop" X 385

Anglo American Magazine, The I 160

"Anglosaxon Street" V 40, 41, 43–44

"Anima" IX 192

Animal Farm III 45

"Animal Rhythm" X 362

"Animal Syllables" IX 240–41, 262

Animals in That Country, The IX 22, 30, 36–40

"Annabel Lee" I 140 VI 279

"Anne Frank" IV 215

Anne of Green Gables V 36

"Annex Elegiac" IX 202

"Annexation of Savoy and Nice by Napoleon III, 1860, The" IV 173

"Anniversary" VI 134–35, 163 n.94

Annotated Edition of the Correspondence between Archibald Lampman and Edward William Thomson (1890–1898) II 171 n.1

"Annunciation, The" V 36

"Another April" V 266

"Another 'Child of Promise' " I 194

"Another Christmas" VI 33, 46

Another Mouth VIII 136

"Another Space" VI 258

Another Time IX 197 X 74, 168, 175, 177, 190, 193, 194, 199, 206, 250–51, 254, 264

"Another Week in the East" VIII 160

"Answer from Vermin, Prague May 27, 1942" V 262

"Answers to a Grade-School Biology Test" V 45

"answring servis" VIII 84

"Antenna" VII 175

"Anthem" VII 113

Anthology (CBC) IX 136

Anthology of Canadian Poetry (English) VI 87, 156 n.4

"Anthology of Up-To-Date Canadian Poetry, An" IV 197

Anthology of Verse, An IX 189

"Antibes: Variations on a Theme" IX 107

"Anti-Christ as a Child" VII 214, 215

"Anti-Narcissus" VII 104–05

"Antisong" VII 301 n.35

Antler River VII 197, 207–08, 231

Antoinette de Mirecourt; or Secret Marrying and Secret Sorrowing I 81

"Ape and the Pharisee, The" V 173–74

"Apex Animal, The" VI 39, 40, 41, 49, 52, 53

"Apocalyptic?" VI 51, 53, 56

"Apocalyptics" VI 44, 52, 53

"Apollo Twelve" IX 240, 261

"Appeal to a Lady with a Diaper" V 49, 54

"Apple Jelly" IX 56

"Application for a Driving License" VIII 375

"April Eclogue" VI 111

"April, Radio, Planting, Easter" IX 55

"Arab King" III 47

"Arabian" V 317

Arabian Nights I 167

"*Arc* in Conversation with P.K. Page" VI 258

"Archaeology of Snow" VII 154–55

"Archaeopteryx" IX 177

Archer, The IX 207, 208

"Archer, The" IV 259–60, 267

Archilochos VII 9–10

Archimedes VI 45

"Arctic Rhododendrons" VII 8, 163

Arendt, Hannah VI quoted 81 X 33

Argyll, ninth duke of II 28

"Ariobarzanes" VI 131

"Aristocracies, The" IX 240, 247–48

Aristotle IX 198, 206

"Ark Anatomical" VI 186, 187

"Ark Astonished" VI 1

"Armageddon" IV 201, 211

Armies of the Moon, The IX 232, 238, 240, 241, 256–61

"Armies of the Moon, The" IX 240, 256–57

Armitage, Christopher VI 15

"Armorial" VI 118

Arnason, David III 26, 27, 31–32, 33, 39, 44, 49 quoted 26, 32, 33, 39, 44 VIII 206 X 196, 200, 202–03, 217, 220, 246, 261

Arnold, Matthew I 136, 146 II 13, 82, 97–98, 138, 139, 141, 142, 148, 150, 156, 170, 239, 240–41, 243, 252 quoted 240–41 IV 192, 213, 215 V 91, 95, 123 VI 279 VII 264 VIII 114 IX 9, 195, 204, 205, 208, 215

"Arnulph" II 168

"Arp's Randy Rant in the Comfy Confession Box" IV 258

"Arras" VI 251, 252–53

"Arrival, The" X 295, 296

"Arrogant, Unkind" X 297

Ars Poetica IV 254

"Ars Poetica" V 315

Art and Society IV 98–99

"Art, Entertainment and Religion" V 123

Art of the Kwakiutl Indians VIII 221

Artaud, Antonin VII 254, 266 VIII 29, 40, 55

"Arthur Miller and 'The Misfits'" V 110

"Artifact" (Purdy) VII 176–77

"Artifact" (Webb) VII 296

"Artificial Hand, War Veteran" V 260

"Artists and Old Chairs" V 301

Arts and Letters Club (Toronto) poetry prize V 280

"As a Comment on Romans 1:10" VI 57, 58

As Elected: Selected Writing VIII 275, 302, 304–05

As for Me and My House IX 1 X 6

"As I Left" IV 164

"As One Remembers a Death" VI 263

As Ten, as Twenty IV 163 n.43 VI 223, 231, 236, 242, 250

"As Ten, as Twenty" VI 247

"As the Mist Leaves No Scar" X 57 n.61

As You Like It IV 206

"Ascendancy of Impersonalism, The" III 143

"Ash Wednesday" VI 176

Ashbery, John IV 261 X 217

"Ashtoreth" V 163

"Ask for No Promise" IV 46

"Aspect of a Cut Peach" VI 151–52

"Aspects of Some Forsythia Branches" VI 131

"At a Fireside" IV 241

"At Evergreen Cemetery" VII 154; (1968) 157

"At Gull Lake: August 1810" II 256, 258 IX 217

"At Hamlet's Grave, Elsinore" VI 110

"At Lac En Coeur" V 113–14

At Marsport Drugstore VII 171

"At Midnight" V 317–18

"At Moraine Lake" VI 126–28

"At Mycenae" VII 180

"At Roblin Lake" VII 150; (1968) 157

"At Sea" II 253–54

"At the Athenian Market" VII
169–70
"At the Bay" IV 65
"At the Belsen Memorial" V 191–92
"At the Cedars" II 259
"At the Chaudière" I 194
"At the Edge of the Jungle" IX
165–66
"At the Long Sault" II 149, 151,
169 X 343
At the Long Sault and Other New
Poems II 143, 145, 146, 149, 163
"At the Mermaid Inn" II 17, 28, 29,
135, 137–38, 140, 141, 161,
162–63, 166–67, 237, 250
At the Mermiad Inn: Wilfred
Campbell, Archibald Lampman,
Duncan Campbell Scott in The
Globe 1892–3 II 143, 239
"At the Movies" VII 162
"At the Ocean's Verge" VI 118,
121–22
At the Ocean's Verge: Selected
Poems VI 89, 108
"At the Turning of Leaves" VI 153
"At the Wayside Shrine" II 226 n.15
"At the Window: Late November"
IX 102
"At This Time" X 287
"At Victory Square" VIII 134
At War with the U.S. VIII 135, 150,
160
Atala I 147
Athenaeum, The I 84
"Atlantic" X 316
Atlantic Advocate, The VII 83
Atlantic Insight VII 83
Atlantic Monthly, The I 75 II 27,
79, 145 VI 88
Atlantis V 10, 11, 21, 78, 83,
89–90, 91, 97, 115–18, 122, 123

"Atlantis and the Department
Store" VI 30, 53
Atwood, Margaret I 14, 90, 96
quoted 90 III 3, 66, 71, 78, 116,
119–20, 142 quoted 78, 142 IV
179, 183, 209, 234, 261 V 112,
125, 238 VI 97, 105–06, 174–75,
177–78, 183, 185, 210–11 n.15,
211 n.16, 225, 229, 241 quoted
174, 179, 185–86, 189, 241, 242
VII 24, 28, 29, 45, 85, 94, 195,
201, 210, 213, 225, 255, 275,
295, 302 n.42 VIII 8, 15, 31, 92,
114, 154, 162, 170, 370 quoted
6, 33–34, 370, 371 IX 1, 2, 5–8,
13, 137, 139, 166, 167, 174, 189,
192, 197, 201, 208, 231, 233,
235, 236, 239 quoted 5, 11, 239
X 13, 24, 181, 213, 233, 287–89,
292 quoted 11, 288
"Aubade" VII 211
Aubert, Rosemary IX 147 quoted
147
Auden, W.H. II 12, 17, 98, 262 III 4,
12, 65, 74 IV 6, 13, 21, 23, 61
n.56, 74, 128, 133, 139, 177,
181, 201, 211, 212 V 1, 2, 31, 34,
57, 59, 79, 80, 240, 250 VI 29,
36, 88, 90, 91, 92, 98, 111, 154,
157 n.15, 228, 229, 245, 247 VII
138, 198, 263 VIII 139, 151, 296,
369 IX 8, 20, 21, 88 X 118, 191,
208, 213, 246, 251
"Auguries" VIII 317–18
"August" I 141
"August Evening on the Beach,
Lake Huron" II 31–32
"August Reverie, An" II 33 V 238
"Aurora Borealis" III 186 n.12
"Auschwitz: Poetry of Alienation"
X 245

Austen, Jane VI 278

Austin, Alfred II 162, 175 n.49
quoted 162

"Author of *Saul*, The" I 75, 77, 78,
85

"Authors Are in Eternity, The" VII
264

"Autobiographical" IV 134

Autobiographical Fragment
(Sangster) I 159, 160, 167, 171,
193

Autobiology VIII 10, 126, 135, 138,
141–45, 146, 148, 161, 165, 167,
170, 174

"Autochthon" II 214

"Auto-da-fé" IV 162 n.23

"Autumn" I 182 III 40

"Autumn Ode" I 189

Auxier, Peter VIII 192

"Ave" I 142 II 197

"Average" VI 247

Avison, Margaret II 268 III 13, 68
quoted 68 IV 233, 262 V 152–53,
280 VI 7, 10, 16, 18–20, 178,
229, 258 quoted 189, 283 VII
201, 266, 301 n.31 VIII 114, 129,
132, 160, 173, 192, 264, 271,
298, 371 IX 9, 19–20, 88, 193,
215–16, 235 quoted 215

"AW 1–7" VIII 148

awake in th red desert VIII 21, 38,
89

Aylward, David VIII 264, 293

Ayscough, Florence III 181

B.C. Monthly VIII 125, 126

Babel, Isaac V 150, 163 quoted 163

"Baby Face" III 47

Bach, J.S. VII 198, 218

Bachelard, Gaston VII 214, 217 IX
219

"Back at York University" V 324

"Backdrop Addresses Cowboy" IX
40, 73 n.48

"Backwards Journey, A" VI 258

*Backwoods of Canada, The: Being
Letters from the Wife of an
Emigrant Officer, Illustrative of
the Domestic Economy of British
America* I 57, 58

Badlands VIII 366 IX 235 X 73

"Bahaman" II 120

Bailey, A.G. II 198

Bailey, Philip James I 83

Baillie, Joanna I 89

Baker, Howard V 160, 212 n.60

Baker, R.P. I 86, 172, 181, 190,
191, 198 quoted 86, 172, 181,
190, 191, 198

Bakhtin, Mikhail VIII 172, 207, 280
X 79, 83–84

Bakunin, Mikhail II 15 VIII quoted 7

Baldoon VII 196, 207, 229–30

Ball, Hugo VIII 11, 23, 37, 40, 60,
269, 274 X 358

"Ballad" (Cohen) II 258

"Ballad" (Wilkinson) VI 303

"Ballad for Brave Women, A" I 150

"Ballad [My lady was found
mutilated]" X 35, 36

"Ballad of Kootenay Brown, The"
V 57

"Ballad of Me" III 93

"Ballad of the Revenge" V 145

"Ballade un peu banale" IV 264

Ballads and Lyrics II 96

Ballads of the Restless Are VIII 292

Balls for a One-Armed Juggler V
188, 189

Balzac, Honoré de V 7

"Bands and the Beautiful Children,
The" VI 246

"Banff" VI 40

"Banff: The Magic Mountain" X 194

"Bangkok" IV 209, 215

"Bangkok Boy" V 20, 43

"Bank Strike: Quebec — 1942" VI 248

Barbara Ladd II 199

Barber, Marsha III 72

Barbour, Douglas V 90, 99, 212 n.56 quoted 90 VI quoted 107, 284 VII 93, 217 VIII 11, 27, 32, 38, quoted 202, 371 IX 91, 197 quoted 87, 142, 143 X 88, 171, 206, 286, 291 quoted 11, 33, 86, 203, 204, 346, 347

Barbusse, Henri III 65

"Bargain" V 181

"Baritone, The" III 145

Barker, George V 2

Barker, Terry VII 35

Barnes, Djuna III 20

Barnes, William VI 29 IX 166

Barreto-Rivera, Rafael VIII 265, 270, 280 quoted 279

"Barricade Smith: His Speeches" IV 138, 153, 161 n.14

"Barriers" VII 148

Barros, Paul de VIII 190

Barsley, Michael VII 299 n.4

"Bartail Cock, The" IV 207

Barthes, Roland VII 268, 274, 285–86, 287, 298 VIII 48, 277 quoted 46–47, 249, 285, 334 X 79, 83, 259, 314, 391 quoted 260, 261

Bartley, Jan IX 10, 11, 240–41 X 284, 285, 299, 314, 317 quoted 289, 290, 291, 318, 322

Bartok, Béla VI 213–14 n.43

"Bartok and the Geranium" III 70, 89

Barzun, Jacques V 81, 82

Baseball: A Poem in the Magic Number 9 VIII 135, 139

Basmajian, Shaunt VIII 27

"Basque Lover" VI 113

Bates, Ronald VI 182, 280 quoted 99 VII 269

"Battle, A" I 47, 48–50

"Battle of Lundy's Lane, The" II 267

"Battlefield at Batoche, The" VII 173–74

Baudelaire, Charles II 13 IV 127, 139, 141, 145 V 150 VI 226, 227, 243 VIII 6, 11 IX 8, 140, 212 quoted 105 X 17, 24

Baxter, F.W. IV 276 n.80

Baxter, Marilyn VII 94, 100

Bayard, Caroline VIII 36

Beach Head VIII 265

"Beach Sunday" III 67, 95

"Beachcomber" VII 261

Bear II 220 X 36

"Bear Hug" VIII 391

Bear on the Delhi Road, The V 30 X 343

"Bear on the Delhi Road, The" V 20, 46

Beardsley, Aubrey X 17

Beardsley, Doug IV 72 IX 146

Beardsley, M.C. VII 268

Beat poets V 40, 52, 151 VII 140

"Beating the Bushes: Christmas 1963" IX 120

Beattie, Munro II 150 quoted 150 III 29, 69, 76, 170 quoted 29, 69, 76, 170 IV 12, 40, 80 V quoted 254 VI 100, 109 quoted 100

Beaumont, Francis I 99

"Beautiful Land by the Sea, The" I 140, 141

Beautiful Losers IX 190 X 16, 17, 21, 24, 25, 28, 29, 30, 34, 38, 45, 47–50

Beautiful Rebel, The: A Romance of Upper Canada in 1812 II 29

"Beauty" II 138–39 IX 85

Beauty and Life II 238

" 'Beauty and the Beast' and Some Relatives" VI 184

Beauty, History, Romance and Mystery of the Canadian Lake Region, The II 29

"Beauty My Fond Fine Care" IV 43–44

"Beavers of Renfrew, The" VII 173–74

Beckett, Samuel V 260 VII 266 VIII 268 IX 192, 193 X 78, 98, 313

Beckmann, Susan III 121 quoted 121

Beckwith, John VI 174 VII 193–94, 195, 197, 206, 219 IX 189, 209

"Become That Village" IV 34

Beddoes, Thomas Lovell I 83, 87, 89 VI 29

Bedingfield, Dolores X 27

"Bed-Sitting Room" VI 242, 247

Beer, Gillian VI quoted 237

"Bees" III 31

"Bees Are Flies with Gland Trouble" X 360–61, 362

"Bees, Thistles and Sea" IV 29

"Before I Go" V 322

"Before the Big Bend Highway" X 297

"Before the Dawn" II 43, 45, 47

Begg, Alexander I 125

"Beginning" VII 101, 105 VIII 291

"Beginnings of a Canadian Literature, The" II 104

"Behind the Arras" II 102–03, 104

Behind the Arras: A Book of the Unseen II 82, 95

Behind the Log III 113, 146–48

Behrman's Jewish Book House IV 125

"Being a Writer in the Thirties: An Interview with Dorothy Livesay" III 71–72

Being Alive VII 137, 170, 175, 178

Being There V 164

"Belatedly, for Carol on St. Valentine's Day, 1945" VII 104–05

Belford, Ken IX 140

Belford's Monthly Magazine I 161

Bell, Marvin V 290 quoted 290

"Belle" VII 43, 62

"Belle Dame sans dormi, La" VI 292

Belloc, Hilare IV 104

"Below Quebec" IV 196

Bemrose, John X quoted 206

Ben Hur VIII 380

"bend ovr so we can see whats in yr asshole" VIII 99

Benda, J. V 81

Benét, William Rose III 117

Bennett, Donna VIII 206, 248 IX 196

Bennett, Joy V 161

Benson, Nathaniel III 27

Bentley, D.M.R. I 173 II 143, 151, 246 IV 133, 240, 249

Beowulf I 138 III 138

Béranger, Pierre-Jean de I 25, 36–40

"Bereaved" VI 63–64

Bergson, Henri IV 173, 188, 191, 192, 196, 197, 206, 211 VII 86

Bering, Joy V 161

Berliner, Lilo VII 256–57, 271

"Bermudas, The" IX 53

Bernstein, Harriet V 147, 163

"Berry Picking" V 157

Berryman, John VI 101, 233 X 373

Bersianik, Louky VIII 195

Berton, Pierre III 150

"Bertram and Lorenzo — a
    Dramatic Fragment" I 183, 197

Bertram Warr Award VI 224

"Beside One Dead" IV 245–46

"Beside the Winter Sea" II 221

Bess Hopkins Prize IX 68 n.1

Bessai, Diane X 89, 94–95

Bessai, Frank I 30, 31, 32, 55, 56,
    61 quoted 31–32, 55, 56

Best American Short Stories VI 88

Best of Leonard Cohen, The X 22,
    31

"Bestialities" VI 50

"Bestiary" V 33

"Bethuniverse" VII 60

Betjeman, John IV 39

"Better Day, The" II 158

Betts, Lorne V 39

"Between" IV 53

Between Tears and Laughter VII 83,
    92–93, 111, 112–15

"Between the Rapids" II 138

"Between the Sheets" VIII 160

Beutler, Bernhard III 30 quoted 30

Bevington, Stan VIII 369

Beware the Months of Fire IX 2,
    135, 141, 142–43, 157, 163,
    165–67

"Beware the Sick Lion" X 267

Beyond Even Faithful Legends VIII
    39, 50, 62, 63, 72, 78

*Beyond Good and Evil: Prelude to a
    Philosophy of the Future* V 217
    n.81

"Beyond the Gamut" II 100, 104

Beyond the Hills of Dream II 28,
    33, 59

"Beyond the Hills of Dream" II 33

"Beyond the Photograph" IX 112

Bhagavad Gita I 25

Bialik, Chaim Nachman IV 129,
    131

Bible I 25, 50, 77, 82, 83, 102, 104,
    159 II 39, 140 IV 11, 30, 188 V
    166, 170, 171, 174, 180, 184,
    189, 197–98, 200, 204–05, 217
    n.81, 223 n.102, 224 n.105, 225
    n.106, 306–07, 315, 316–17,
    321, 322 VI 25, 27, 32–33, 36,
    59, 61, 63, 64, 121, 180, 181–82
    IX 96, 97, 98, 210

"Bible to Be Believed, The" VI 49,
    62

Bid Me to Live VIII 193

Bieman, Elizabeth VII 94

*Big Bird in the Bush: Selected
    Stories and Sketches* V 30, 38

"Big Leagues, The" VIII 155

"Big Mirror" X 328

"Big Saw, The" VII 57–58

Bilan, R.P. IX 197

"Billboards" VIII 384

"Billboards Build Freedom of
    Choice" V 53

Billy the Kid *See* Bonney, William

Biographia Literaria VI 30

*Biographical History of Philosophy,
    A* II 175 n.48

"Biography" VI 117

"Birches, The" IV 243

"Birches at R.M.C." IX 101

"Bird, The" IV 247 IX 161–62 X
    364

"Bird of Paradise, The" VII 216

"Bird on a Wire" X 42

"Birds, The" VII 297

Birds, Beasts and Flowers IV 176

Birney, Earle I 142 II 13, 244 III 2,
    12, 14, 27, 28–29, 31, 74, 84,

116, 117 quoted 29, 117 IV 21,
37–38, 131, 133, 162 n.22, 163
n.43, 175, 179, 180, 233, 234,
236, 239, 262 V 2, 3, 4, 10,
18–21, 82, 87, 93, 98, 125,
154–55, 239, 244 quoted 19–30,
87 VI 10–11, 87, 92, 93, 107,
116, 229, 247 quoted 231, 233
VII 13, 17, 29, 52, 138, 140, 262,
265 VIII 21, 25, 27, 30, 31, 121,
122, 125, 127, 131, 189, 269 IX
97, 135, 137, 138, 140, 201, 235
X 28, 343, 344, 359, 388 quoted
171

Birot, P.A. VIII 40

"Birth of a Disorder" X 375

"Birth of a Voyeur, The" X 387

"Birth of Mood and Moodlets,
The" X 364, 365

"Birth of Tragedy, The" V 180

"birthmark:" X 261

Bishop, Elizabeth VI 33

bissett, bill V 53, 54 VII 23–24, 29,
52, 255 VIII 6, 11, 15–16, 19–22,
147, 269, 270, 333 quoted 19,
20, 26–27, 42, 51–58, 61, 65,
67–68, 71, 75–81, 83–87, 90–99
IX 20, 135, 137, 140, 234 X 343,
359, 388

"Bite deep and wide, O Axe, the
tree!" I 29

Black and Secret Man X 224, 266

"Black and White" VI 305 IX 255

"Black Bottom" IV 103–04, 108

"Black Colt, The" IX 160, 165

"Black Filly, The" IX 160

Black Huntsman, The V 154, 173

"Black Huntsman, The" V 173

Black Mountain poets III 66, 72, 89
V 1, 3, 30, 35, 39, 40, 51–52, 54,
66 n.44, 207 n.4, 243 VI 33, 94

VII 6, 29, 87, 138, 267 IX 87,
137, 139

Black Mountain Review, The V 52,
207 n.4, 238, 247

Black Night Window X 282, 289,
297, 298, 303, 306–12, 313

"Black Thread" VII 104, 113

Blackfish VIII 137

"Black-White under Green: May 18,
1965" VI 40–41, 42–43

Blake, Edward I 25

Blake, William I 25, 35, 50, 88
quoted 88 II 101, 139, 142, 150,
162, 166, 214 quoted 202 III 65,
131 V 150, 167 VI 10, 18, 31, 37,
45, 52, 181–82, 183, 190–91
quoted 10, 194 VII 138, 200–02,
211, 215, 218, 281 VIII 6, 15, 23,
24, 27, 28, 33, 35, 72, 94, 114,
135, 154, 159, 282, 312, 319 IX
191, 192 X 202, 257, 343

"Blanchisseuse, La" I 36, 39

Blaser, Robin VIII 125, 126, 133,
quoted 132, 159–60

Blasted Pine, The: An Anthology of
Satire, Invective and Disrespect-
ful Verse, Chiefly by Canadian
Writers IV 174, 180, 215–16

Blau, A. VII 299 n.4

Blavatsky, Madame Elena Petrovna
I 25 IX 10

blewointment VI 68 n.56 VIII 6, 21,
30, 35, 264 IX 135

Bligh, Katherine (Dorothy Livesay)
III 102 n.80

"Blind Date" X 377

"Blind Girl" IV 87–88

Blind Photographer X 340

"Bliss Carman" (Roberts) II 77, 111

Bliss Carman (Shepard) II 89, 124
n.65

Bliss Carman (Stephens) II 92–93

Bliss Carman: A Portrait II 90–91

Bliss Carman and the Literary Currents and Influences of His Time II 89–90

Blodgett, E.D. VII 287 IX 3, 92, 93, 200 quoted 3, 4, 92 X 92

Bloom, Harold VII 259–60, 263, 265, 281 X 79

Blostein, David VI 203

"Blowing" VI 254

"Blowing Boy" VI 246

"Blue Blossom, A" II 213–14

Blue Propeller, The V 156

"Blue Valley Night" IX 172

Bluebeard's Castle VI 213–14 n.43

"Blueprint for a Monument of War" IV 161 n.14

"Blues" VIII 287

"Blues on Green" VIII 289

Blur in Between, The VII 136, 152–53

Bly, Robert VII 13, 14, 94, 104, 309 n.130 IX 20

"Boardwalk at Verdun" V 184

Boas, Franz VIII 199, 221

"Boastful Songs" VI 304

Boatman, The VI 7, 17–18, 174, 175, 177, 179, 180–85, 186–92, 192–95, 196, 198, 207, 209, 211 n.16 VII 218–19 IX 191

"Boatman, The" VI 188, 195

"Bobby Sands" VII 122

"Bobolink, The" II 271

Bodin, Lars-Gunnar VIII 28

Bodin, Svante VIII 28

"Body, The" VIII 144

Boehme, Jacob IX 236, 241, 243 quoted 243

"Bohemia" II 216

Boileau, Nicholas IV 42

Bolden, Charles (Buddy) VIII 13, 365, 368, 370, 387–89

Boller, Paul F., Jr. II 30 quoted 31

Bolt, Carol VIII 369

"Bond, The" V 308–09, 313

Bonnard, Pierre V 40

"Bonne Entente" IV 209

Bonney, William (Billy the Kid) VIII 378–79

"Book" VI 189, 195

"Book of Ancestors" IX 54

Book of Canadian Poetry, The: A Critical and Historical Anthology I 14, 28, 86, 87, 134, 181, 190, 192 II 11 IV 8, 17, 22, 32, 34, 39, 78, 233, 236, 238, 244, 260 V 154, 240 VI 7, 34, 46, 68–69 n.39, 156 n.5, 231, 265 n.9 IX 19

"Book of Common Prayer" VIII 317

"Book of Days, The" VIII 309

Book of Hours IX 108, 109

"BOOK OF HOURS, A" VIII 335, 336–37

Book of Job I 95

Book of Mercy X 23, 25, 30, 48, 50–51

Book of Roberts, The II 205

Book of Samuel I 92

Book of the Native, The II 206

Book of the Rose, The II 197

"Book II: 65" X 310

Bookman, The II 87 IV 70

Books in Canada VIII 155 IX 133, 136, 143, 147, 197 X 88, 282

"Boquet and Some Buds: A Stable Anthology" III 45–46

"Border Incident" VII 146

Borders VIII 11, 265, 272, 288, 292

Borduas, Paul-Emile IX quoted 209, 210

Borestone Mountain Poetry Award
VI 88

Borges, Jorge Luis VIII 370 IX 252
quoted 252 X 78, 262, 318, 355

"Borrowed Plumes" IV 53–54

Boston Transcript, The II 79

"Bottle of Chianti, The" V 257

Boundary 2: A Journal of
Postmodern Literature X 73

"Bouquetiére, La" [sic] (Crawford)
I 39

"Bouquetière et le croque-mort, La"
(Béranger) I 40

Bourinot, Arthur S. I 181 quoted
181 II 143, 171 n.1, 245

Bovey, Wilfred VI 97

Bowering, George III 170, 171
quoted 171 IV 236, 261 V 86, 91,
238, 243 VI 37 quoted 28 VII 34,
48, 143, 182, 200, 206 VIII 5,
7–9, 10, 31, 192, 195, 196, 197,
206, 208, 232, 238, 264, 268,
369 quoted 9–10, 25, 40,
114–15, 118, 121–23, 127–29,
131–33, 138–47, 149–55,
160–61, 165–67, 169–71, 198,
222, 278–79, 301 IX 88, 93–94,
97, 99, 112, 116, 124 n.11,
137–38, 194, 233 quoted 11, 29,
90, 93, 94, 115–16, 194, 234,
236, 237, 238 X 9, 132, 148, 164,
167 quoted 21, 28, 92, 204, 289,
292, 318

Bowering, Jabez Harry VIII 9

Bowering, Marilyn IX 144 quoted
144

"Bowl, The" VII 296

Bowman, Louise Morey III 32

Boxer, Avi V 151 VII 265

"Box-Social, The" VII 194

"Boy and Girl" I 194

"Boy in the Lamont Poetry Room,
Harvard" IX 110

"Boy with a Sea Dream" VI 250

Boy with an R in His Hand, The
VII 197

"Boy's Beauty, The" X 40

bp VIII 11, 265, 272, 283–84, 288,
297

bpNichol: What History Teaches
VIII 276

Bradbrook, M.C. IV 160–61 n.11

Bradley, F.H. VII 211

Bradshaw, Leah IX 197, 199

Bradstreet, Anne VIII 172

Brahe, Tycho VI 45

Brain's the Target, The VII 23,
41–44, 46

"Branches" VI 32, 57

"Brass Box. Spring. Time." X 310

Brautigan, Richard X 379

Brave New Wave VIII 38

Brazen Tower, The: Short Stories VI
156 n.8

"Brazilian Fazenda" VI 254

Brazilian Journal VI 226, 234

Bread, Wine and Salt VII 82, 92, 95,
107–08

"Breakdown" V 190

Breakfast for Barbarians, A IX 232,
234, 235, 237, 239, 240, 241,
242–43, 246, 247, 250, 253, 256,
257, 259

"Breakfast for Barbarians, A" IX
243

"Breaking" VII 287

"Breaking Bread in Jerusalem" V
316

"Breaks, The" VIII 142

"breath th" VIII 81–83

Brébeuf and His Brethren III 5, 112,
113, 119, 120, 141–45, 148

Brebner, J.B. V 81

Brecht, Bertolt VII 285

Breton, André VI 227

Brett, Brian IX quoted 143

Breughel, Jan IV 52–53

Brewster, Elizabeth IV 182–83, 189, 216

"Brian Fawcett" VIII 145

Brick: A Journal of Reviews IX 191, 197

"Bridegroom, The" IV 256

"Bridegroom Rises to Speak, The" X 131

Brides of the Stream X 340, 345, 375, 377–81, 382

Bridge, The V 262 VII 81

Bridges, Robert II 17, 239 IV 72

Briefly: The Birth/Death Cycle From The Book of Hours VIII 266

"BRIEFLY: The Birth/ Death Cycle — Hours 11, 12, 13 & 14" VIII 336

"Brigadier" IV 264

Brigadoon V 260

Briggs, William I 130, 148

"Bright Eyes" I 160

"Bright Swan for My Daughter, A" IV 71

Bringhurst, Robert IX 200

Brinnin, John Malcolm IV 238

"Brisbane" X 168

"Britain" II 33

"Britain Street" VII 109, 114

British American Magazine, The I 161

"Briton to Briton: An Appeal" II 66

"Broadcast from Berlin" III 77–78

"Broadcaster's Poem, The" VII 117–18

"Brock" I 191–92, 193, 198

Brock, Gen. Isaac I 8, 142, 145, 152 n.13, 191

Brockington, Leonard II 235, 240, 245

"Broke" VIII 229

Broken Ark, The: A Book of Beasts VIII 366

Bronfman, Samuel IV 125–26

Brontë, Emily III 64

Brontë Sisters, The VII

"Brontës, The: Gothic Transgressor as Cattle Drover" VII 197

Brooke, Rupert II 81, 239, 241–42 IV 98 VII 80

"Brooklyn Bridge" II 216

Brossard, Nicole VII 258 VIII 195, 203, 249

Brown, Audrey Alexandra II 242

Brown, E.K. I 14, 28, 29, 30, 61, 87, 133, 135, 151 n.1, 172, 183, 199 quoted 28, 87, 135, 172–73, 199 II 137, 143, 149, 151, 236, 239, 243, 244, 246, 247–49, 250, 252, 257, 261, 262–63 quoted 248 III 68, 117 quoted 68 IV 77, 92, 96, 109, 130, 131, 132, 237–38 V 35 quoted 87 VI quoted 97 VII 15, 204

Brown, Norman O. VII 255 X 251

Brown, Russell VII 11 IX 27, 196 X 77, 85 quoted 90, 91, 112–13

"Brown-Eyed Jane" I 194

Browning, Robert I 25, 32, 61, 83, 89, 136 II 37, 78, 82, 89, 162, 197, 239, 242, 258 III 23, 125 V 45, 150 X 284

Bruce, Lenny V 52

Bruce, Phyllis IX quoted 93

Bruno, Giordano VIII 373

"Brunswick Avenue" IX 213–14

Bryant, William Cullen I 139, 167

Bryce, George II 61

Bryden, Ronald VII 207

"Bubble Dancer and the Wickedest Man in Carleton County, A" VII 81, 82

"Bucket Had Not Really Been Meant for Flowers, The" VI 14

Buckler, Ernest VII 87

Bucolic Comedies IV 246

Buddha V 189

Buffalo Republic I 169

"Buffalo Stones" IX 175

"Building a Skyscraper" V 99–100

"Buildings" V 54, 55

Bukowski, Charles VII 137–38, 139, 140, 145 VIII 168

Bukowski/Purdy Letters, The VII 137

"Bull Calf, The" V 15, 16 VI 33 X 343

"Bull Moose, The" VII 14, 93, 103, 105

Bumblebee Dithyramb X 340, 343, 357, 359–63, 370, 376

Bunting, Basil V 91

Buñuel, Luis VI 228

Bunyan, John I 77 VI 29 IX 219

Burgess, Anthony V 51

Buri, S.G. VII 145

"Buried Life, The" II 240

Burke, Edmund II 160

Burnham, Clint VIII 281

"Burning Bush, The" V 197

"Burning Hills" VIII 385

"Burning Remnant, The" V 196, 199

Burning Water VIII 9, 134, 138, 155–59, 171 X 167

Burns, Robert I 25, 35, 40, 167, 183, 197 II 258

Burns, Robert Alan I 16

Burns, Walter Noble VIII 379–80

Burpee, Lawrence J. I 85 II 35–36

quoted 35–36

Burroughs, William IV 207 X 24

Bursting into Song VII 137, 175, 178

Burton, Dennis III 165

Burton, Jean IV 103

Burton, Robert VI 281, 301

Bush, Douglas IV 84

Bush Garden, The X 200

"Bushed" VI 93 IX 201

But We Are Exiles X 72

Butler, Joseph I 25

Butler, Samuel III 3 IV 10

Butling, Pauline VIII 281 quoted 162

"Butterfly Bat, The" X 358

"Butterfly Bones, or, Sonnet against Sonnets" VI 40, 48

"Butterfly on Rock" V 190

Butterfly on Rock: A Study of Themes and Images in Canadian Literature II 246 IX 3, 4, 86, 94–98, 99, 103, 235 X 286

"By Ecstasies Perplexed" V 180

By the Aurelian Wall, and Other Elegies II 119

"By the Church Wall" X 305

"By the Fire" II 43, 44

"By the Sea: For A.M. Klein" V 315

"By the Shore" II 251–52, 268

"By Word of Tongue" VI 304

Byron, George Gordon, Lord I 82, 83, 95, 136, 167, 175, 184 II 139, 140, 239 IV 176, 194 V 114, 150, 221 n.95 VI 27, 31, 47, 50, 72 n.91

"Byzantium" VII 264 VIII 149

CBC *See* Canadian Broadcasting Corporation

CBC New Canadian Writing Contest IX 232

CCF *See* Cooperative
Commonwealth Federation
CIV/n V 85, 247 VII 254 IX 2, 86 X
21
CV/II III 63, 66 IX 144 X 88
"Cab Driver" III 20, 21
"Cabin, The" VIII 137
"Cabinet Secrets" X 254
Cabot, John X 134, 180
"Cachalot, The" III 112, 118,
131–33, 134, 148
"Cadence, Country, Silence: Writing
in a Colonial Space" IX 190,
191, 196, 205
Caedmon V 322
"Caesar's Wife" I 65 n.65
Cage, John VIII 23 X 251
"Caged Bird, The" V 221 n.95
Cain I 82, 83, 95
"Cain" V 157
"Calamities and Crystals: Fate and
the Unconscious" VII 256
"Calgary City Jail" IX 152, 153
Call, Frank Oliver III 167 VI 86
"Call in December, A" VII 97
Call My People Home III 85
Call Them Canadians V 281, 288
Callaghan, Barry III 6, 165, 166,
167, 169, 171, 172 quoted 6,
165, 169 X 340
Callaghan, Morley III 20, 26, 27, 95
IV 103, 106, 107, 114 n.89 V 39
VI 48
"Callaghan Revisited" VI 29, 48
"Calling Eagles" IV 75, 99–100
Calvino, Italo VIII 370 X 78
"Camera" IX 34–35
Cameron, A. Barry X 204, 205
Cameron, Donald X 94 quoted 113
Cameron, Elspeth V 162
Cameron, George Frederick II 152

Campbell, Alexander I 161, 162
Campbell, Joseph VI 238, 240
Campbell, Roy III 115
Campbell, William Wilfred II 7, 8,
11, 12, 16–17, 23, 81, 82, 135,
200, 237, 240 III 23 IV 72, 178,
234, 236 V 238
Campion, Thomas VIII 390
Campos, Augusto de VIII 28
Campos, Haroldo de VIII 28
Camus, Albert VII 266, 304 n.77
Canada II 29
"Canada" X 311
Canada Council V 149 VI 225
Canada Council awards V 239, 281
VI 89, 225 IX 136, 232
Canada Council Medal III 113
Canada First association I 8, 122,
123, 126, 127, 151
Canada Foundation Fellowship V
143
Canada Gazette X 108
Canada Gees Mate For Life VIII 29,
83, 85, 96
*Canada in Flanders: The Story of
the Canadian Expeditionary
Force* II 192
Canada Speaks of Britain II 198
"Canada to England" I 25
"Canada to the Soviet Union" III 78
*Canada Today: A Study of Her
National Interests and National
Policy* IV 174–75
"Canadian, Th" VIII 89
*Canadian Accent: A Collection
of Stories and Poems by
Contemporary Writers from
Canada* VI 87
Canadian Anthology IV 40
Canadian Author & Bookman IV
70, 82 VII 136 IX 145

Canadian Authors Association II
80–81, 192, 196, 238 III 1, 115 IV
70, 110, 177–79, 232, 236 V 154
VI 222

"Canadian Authors Meet, The" IV
190, 193, 199 VII 283

"Canadian Boat Song" I 191

Canadian Bookman IV 111 n.11

Canadian Broadcasting Corporation V 28, 78, 110, 280 VI 28,
89, 155 n.3, 222 IX 136

Canadian Brothers, The VII 197,
203, 208, 233

Canadian Council of Teachers of
English V 78

Canadian Dimension IX 194

Canadian Encyclopedia, The IV 17

"Canadian Folksong" II 44, 46

Canadian Forum, The I 87 II 37,
91, 148 III 68, 112, 115, 167, 170
IV 8–9, 14–15, 32, 70, 73, 76, 84,
103, 105, 106, 108, 111 n.11,
124, 130, 131, 175–76, 196, 197,
232, 233, 236, 238, 239, 243,
254, 259, 271 n.13 V 28, 31, 152,
170, 239 VI 9, 26, 36, 38, 48, 88,
223, 231, 279 VII 135, 194 VIII
35, 121 IX 135, 146, 190, 194,
196, 197, 231 X 86, 88

Canadian Girl V 280

"Canadian Girl, The" III 25, 26

Canadian Jewish Chronicle IV 125,
126

Canadian Jewish Congress IV
125–26

Canadian Jewish News, The V 163

Canadian Journal of Political and
Social Theory IX 191, 197

"Canadian Letter" III 10, 23, 24, 34

"Canadian Literati" III 23, 24, 26,
43

Canadian Literature I 88, 90 II 22
III 70 IV 7, 10, 15, 181, 236, 239,
262 V 86 VI 7, 9, 19, 35, 95, 96,
102, 183, 286 VII 136 VIII 12,
206 IX 136, 142, 143, 145, 146,
194, 195, 197 X 88

"Canadian Literature: A General
Impression" III 26, 44

Canadian Literature Club I 132

Canadian Literature in English X
292

Canadian Magazine, The II 35, 87,
245–46

Canadian Mercury, The III 116, 166
IV 5, 11, 69–70, 73, 74, 82, 84,
85, 104, 105, 124, 175, 193, 195
VII 253

Canadian Monthly and National
Review, The I 85, 161

Canadian Packing House Worker,
The V 112

"Canadian Poetry: A Criticism" II 87

Canadian Poetry Magazine III 4,
62, 112 IV 32, 111 n.11, 131 V
155, 244 VI 222, 298 VII 135, 194

Canadian Poetry: Studies,
Documents, Reviews II 143 IV
184, 240

"Canadian Poetry: The
Interregnum" III 31, 33, 44

Canadian Poetry: The Modern Era
X 283

"Canadian Poet's Predicament,
The" VII 199, 200

"Canadian Publishing: Answers to a
Questionaire" V 56

Canadian Review of Music and Art
VII 92–93

"canadian sasquatch sitid in
nicaragua fighting against u.s.
backd contras" VIII 96

Canadian Short Stories III 21, 25

"Canadian Short Story, The" III 24, 25

Canadian Singers and Their Songs: A Collection of Portraits and Autograph Poems I 168

"Canadian Social Register, The" IV 207

"Canadian Tradition and Canadian Literature" V 288

Canadian Who's Who II 192

"Canadian Winter" VIII 170

Canadian Writers and Their Works II 144

Canadian Writers Foundation II 238

Canadian Young Judaea IV 124

"Canoe, The" I 31

Cantor, Aviva V 180

Cantos IV 268 V 6, 10, 83, 99, 262 VI 94, 131 VIII 331 IX 2, 85, 175

Capilano Review, The VIII 190, 238

Caplan, Usher IV 133

Cappon, James II 89–90, 97, 197, 198, 201, 202 quoted 89

Capra, Fritjof IX 127 n.50

Caprice VIII 171

"Captain Cook" V 50

Captain Neal MacDougal & The Naked Goddess VII 25, 66

Cardwell, Ann VII 197

Carew, Thomas IV 181

"Caribbean Kingdoms" V 47, 48–49

Cariboo Horses, The VII 6–7, 137, 143, 158–62, 174

"Cariboo Horses, The" VII 162

"Caring" IV 207, 209

"Carleton University: January 1961" X 228

"Carlo" III 125

Carlyle V 82

Carlyle, Thomas II 235, 241 V 82, 109, 110, 167, 178, 219 n.87, 221 n.95

Carman, Bliss I 167, 169, 187 II 7, 10, 11, 13, 15, 16, 22–23, 29, 31–32, 38, 189, 195, 200, 201, 206, 213, 220, 226 n.21, 238, 240 quoted 22, 31–32 III 1, 3, 23, 114, 150, 151 IV 32, 177, 178, 196, 236, 241 V 39 VII 6, 28, 47, 49, 55, 90, 145–46 VIII 121 X 284

Carnal and the Crane, The VI 175

"Carnations in Winter" II 79

"Carnival" III 87

"Carnival Man, The" IX 148

"Carol" VI 295

Carpenter, David X quoted 86

Carr, Emily II 236 III 64, 65 VI 87 X 132

Carrier, Roch IX 211

Carroll, Lewis (Charles L. Dodgson) VI 278 VII 199 VIII 23, 95

Carruth, Hayden V 245 quoted 245

Carry on Crime and Punishment VIII 366

"Carter Fell" VIII 164

Cartier, Jacques IV 156

Caruso, Barbara VIII 302, 303

"Case Supervision" III 96

"Cassandra" X 227

Caswell, E.S. I 168 quoted 168

"Catalpa Tree" V 299–300

Cataract V 210 n.40

Cataraqui Review, The VII 254

Catch, The VIII 137, 148–50

Catch-22 V 62, 260

Cathay III 181

"Cathedral Dusk" VI 110

Catullus V 150 VII 138 VIII 304

"cause of doubles:, the" X 262–63

"caut in yet anothr fixd fuck" VIII 89

"Cautionary Tale, A" VI 301

Cavafy, Constantine V 150

Cavalcanti, Guido VI 132

Cave, The X 282, 289, 298, 312–18, 324

"Cave, The" V 303–04 X 318, 325

"Cave Painters, The" VII 148–49

"Caverned Woman, The" VI 187, 193

"Cedars" III 40

"Celebration" X 39

Céline, Louis-Ferdinand V 150 IX 12, 13, 141, 157, 158 quoted 141

Cenci, The I 82

Centennial Commission Prize IX 68 n.1

Centennial Medal V 239

Century, The II 27

Century Has Roots, A IV 31

Cerberus V 77, 84–85, 87–88, 239, 250, 254, 269 n.51, 270 n.53 VII 85, 268

"Cereals for Roughage" VIII 148

"Ceremony for Rosh Hashonah" X 216

"Ceremony Is Called For" VI 150

"Certain Kind of Holy Man, A" VII 120

Cervantes, Miguel de VIII 7 X 80

Cézanne, Paul IX 89

Chadwick, Charles VI quoted 227

Chagall, Marc V 17 VI 294 VII 277 IX 89, 110

Chambers, Jack VII 195

Champlain, Samuel de X 134, 180

"Chandelier, The" IV 59, n.17

"Change" III 40

"change (changing)" VIII 296

Change-Up: New Poems V 262, 269 n.45

Chanson de Roland V 42

"Chant to the Fire-Fly" VIII 304–05

Chap Book, The II 79

Chapman, George I 120

"Character and Poetry of Keats, The" II 139, 141, 173 n.15

"Charcoal" II 271

"Charity" V 313

Charles, Ray X 49

Charles G.D. Roberts (Keith) II 199, 200

Charles G.D. Roberts and the Influences of His Time II 197

"Charles Heavysege" (Burpee) I 75, 76, 77, 79, 81, 82, 84, 85, 103

"Charles Heavysege" (Lanman) I 75, 85

"Charles Heavysege and the New Edition of Saul" I 85, 168

"Charles Isaac Mandel" X 223, 224, 225

Charles Mair: Literary Nationalist I 8, 11, 15, 120, 124–25, 128, 129–30, 131, 133, 134, 137, 145, 146

Charlesworth, Roberta IX 189

"Charlottetown Harbour" VII 11, 47

Chastelard I 83

Chateaubriand, René de I 147

Chaucer, Geoffrey II 101, 114, 258 IV 124, 128, 131 V 2, 27, 29, 39, 40

Chekhov, Anton III 24

Chesterman, Robert VII 256

Chesterton, G.K. IV 74, 82, 99, 100, 103, 109 VII 86, 89

"Chestnut Tree — Three Storeys Up" VI 72 n.94

Chetwynd, Tom X 163, 170 quoted
   143
"Chiaroscuro" VII 147
Chicago Review, The IX 136
"Chicken Poems, The" IX 176–77,
   178
Child, Francis II 78
Child, Philip III 27
Childe Harold's Pilgrimage I 175,
   185 IV 134
"Childhood Musette" VII 212
"Children" (Page) VI 245
"Children, The" (Campbell) II 33, 34
"Children's Coloured Flags" V 284
"Child's Prayer at Evening, A" II
   226 n.15
"Chimères, Les" VI 110
"China Poems" IX 177–78
Chinada: Memoirs of the Gang of
   Seven IX 177
"Chinese Boxes" VI 261
"Chinook" IX 171
Chocolate Moose, The IX 232
"Choice, The" II 168
Chomsky, Noam X 82, 159
Chopin, Henri VIII quoted 34
"Chopping Onion" VII 122–23
Choyce, Lesley X quoted 87
"Christmas" VI 52
"Christmas: Becoming" VI 64
"Christmas Eve" VI 295, 296
"Chronic" VI 30, 41
"Chronicle of Karn" VIII 314–15
"circa 1955 me n my middul sistr
   wer lookin at moovee
   magazines" VIII 85
"Circe/Mud Poems" IX 6, 26–27,
   30, 40, 48–50, 70 n.23
Circle Game, The IX 18, 19, 24–25,
   28, 31, 33–36, 52, 55, 64, 68 n.1,
   77 n.68

"Circle Game, The" IX 34, 53
Circle of Affection, The II 237, 238
"Circle of Affection, The" II 272
"Circuit, The (Phil. 2, 5–11)" VI
   39, 59
Cirlot, J.E. X 152, 156, 166, 170
   quoted 143
"Cities of the Mind Interred" IX
   202
"Cities We Longed For, The" X 325
Citizen of the World I 159
"City" III 183
"City Enforces, The" III 183–84
"City Girl" IX 20
City Hall Street V 255
City of Dreadful Night, The II 18
"City of the End of Things, The" II
   18, 147, 148, 201 III 184
City of Toronto Book Award V 239
   IX 68
"City Park in July" VI 61
"City Park Merry-Go-Round" X
   222
"City Street" V 306
City to Last, A VII 83
"City Wife" III 61, 76–77, 81
"City's Life, The" V 16–17, 307
Civil Elegies (1968) VIII 34 IX 190,
   194–95, 201, 205
Civil Elegies and Other Poems
   (1972) IX 9, 190, 195–96, 201,
   204, 205, 207–10, 213, 214, 222
   n.39, 233
"Civility a Bogey, or, Two Centuries
   of Canadian Cities" VI 41
Cixous, Hélène VIII 172, 195, 203
Claire, Paula VIII 28
Clare, John III 10 IX 166
Clark, David VIII quoted 333
Clarke, George Herbert II 245 III
   quoted 28 V 35 VI quoted 98

"Classic Canadian Poetry and the
Public Muse" I 47, 90, 91, 173
Classic Shade, The IV 243, 246, 260
"Claude Glass" VIII 395
"Clay" IV 153–54 n. 27
"Clean as the Grass" X 44
"Clearer Self, The" II 158–59
Cleveland, John IV 184
Clever, Glenn I 23, 56 II 247 III
120, 146 quoted 146
"Climate of the Brain" VI 293
"Climbers" V 47
Clinton, Martina VIII 21
Clinton Special, The VIII 366
"Closed Door, The" II 270
"Cloth of Gold" IV 215
"Clotheslines" IX 119
"Cloud, The" (Shelley) I 141
"Clouds" (Nichol) VIII 317, 319,
334
"Clouds, The" (Reaney) VII 212
Cloudshadows VII 197, 233
Clough, Arthur Hugh II 239, 250,
251
"Clute Boulay" II 273
"clyde dunkobbs" VIII 85
Cobbing, Bob VIII 28, 264, 265
"Cobra, The" V 255–56
Cochrane, C.N. VII 225
Cockburn, Robert VII 92
Cocteau, Jean VIII 25
"CODA: Mid-Initial Sequence" VIII
281, 325–27, 330
"Coelacanth" IV 186–88
Cogswell, Fred I 9, 10, 13, 14, 15,
16, 30, 61 quoted 9–10, 13, 15 II
20, 247 quoted 10–11, 19, 20 IV
142, 150–51, 152 quoted 151 V
150 quoted 156 VI 233 quoted
281, 283 VII 31–32, 43, 52,
81–82, 84, 86, 90, 92, 269 IX 195

X 197, 203 quoted 345
Cohen, Leonard I 37 II 86, 258 IV
34 V 77, 151 VI 29 VII 26, 27, 85,
140–41, 265 VIII 173, 366, 370
IX 190, 219, 235 X 8, 12, 16–18,
22–65, 192 quoted 25
Cohn-Sfectu, Ofelia VII 143–44
"Cold Eye and Optic Heart:
Marshall McLuhan and Some
Canadian Poets" IX 99
Cold Green Element, The V 143,
156
"Cold Green Element, The" IV 262
V 180
"Cold, Heat" X 328
"Cold Stone" VI 192–93
Coldwell, Joan VI quoted 286
Coldwell, M.J. IV 217
Cole, Christina VIII quoted 202
Coleman, Victor V 86, 238 VIII 27,
125, 135, 197, 264, 369 IX 234 X
346 quoted 345
Coleridge, Samuel Taylor I 95, 133,
136, 139, 167 II 30, 139, 249 VI
30, 48 VII 307–08 n.112 VIII 114,
149, 159, 162, 164 IX 54 quoted
210 X 43, 51
Coles, Don IV 38 VI quoted 108
"Collar, The" IV 151, 152
Collected Later Poems (Williams) V
269 n.51
Collected Poems (Birney) V 30, 38
Collected Poems (Layton, 1965) V
158, 204, 213 n.63
Collected Poems (Pratt, 1944) III
117, 123
Collected Poems (Purdy) VII 7, 137
Collected Poems (Smith) IV 14–15,
233, 239
*Collected Poems of A.M. Klein,
The* IV 132 V 315

Collected Poems of Anne Wilkinson and a Prose Memoir VI 7, 277, 281, 284–85, 286, 288, 301–04

Collected Poems of E.J. Pratt, The (1958) III 3, 113, 114, 118, 121, 123, 124, 127

Collected Poems of F.R. Scott, The IV 6, 18, 19, 174, 189, 218 X 283

Collected Poems of Irving Layton, The (1971) V 144, 151–52, 204, 213 n.63

Collected Poems of Isabella Valancy Crawford, The I 23 II 170

Collected Poems of Raymond Knister IV 22, 27, 28

Collected Poems of Raymond Souster (1980) V 269 n.48

Collected Poems: The Two Seasons (Livesay) IV 63, 65, 69, 70, 74, 85–86

Collected Poetry (Dudek) V 78, 93–94, 96, 121

Collected Works of Billy the Kid, The: Left Handed Poems VIII 12, 272, 365, 368, 369, 370, 372, 373, 374, 378–84, 387, 389, 393 IX 190, 199, 222 n.50, 235 X 24, 224

Collected Works of E.J. Pratt, The III 122

Collerye, Roger de I 36

Collin, W.E. II 148, 241 III 67 quoted 67 IV 5, 69, 76, 77, 79, 80, 90, 92, 94, 96, 110, 130, 179–80, 182, 237, 239, 246, 252, 253

Collins, Aileen V 85 VII 300 n.23

Collins, Judy X 21

Collins, Robert G. III 142 quoted 142

Collins, Wilkie II 243

Colombo, John Robert III 6, 9, 163, 175 V quoted 60, 93–94 VI 50 quoted 36 VIII 272

Colony and Confederation: Early Canadian Poets and Their Background II 143

Colour of God's Face, The ("Zambia") III 63, 89–90

"Colour of the Light, The" VII 276

Colour of the Times, The/Ten Elephants on Yonge Street V 259

Colour of the Times, The: The Collected Poems of Raymond Souster V 239, 245, 257, 259, 269 n.48

Colours in the Dark VII 15, 196, 202, 204–05, 206–07, 216, 225

"Colt, The" III 29

Colum, Padraic II 90

Columbus, Christopher X 134, 137, 142

"Columbus Poems, The" VIII 216, 219–20, 241

Colville, Alex VII 14 IX 4, 89, 119, 213

Combustion V 242, 243 VII 85

"Come Away, Death" III 127–28

"Come Not the Seasons Here" III 127

"Comedians, The" X 230

"comédie humaine, La" V 7

"Comet, The" VII 146

"Coming Days" I 46

"Coming Home" (Lane) IX 171–72

"coming home" (Marlatt) VIII 220

"Coming of the Messiah, The" V 191, 203

Coming through Slaughter VIII 13, 365, 366, 368, 369–70, 387–89, 393

Commentaries of Pius II, The X 321

"Commentary, The" X 48

"Common Man, The" IV 257

"Commoners, The: He and She" III 93

Commonweal, The II 90 IV 70, 87

Communist Manifesto, The IV 188

"Community" VIII 135

"Company" X 319–20, 322

"Compass, The" IX 253, 54

Compleat Angler, The X 379

Complete Poems of Sir Charles G.D. Roberts, The II 225 n.7

Completed Field Notes: The Long Poems of Robert Kroetsch X 74

"Complicities" VI 199

"Compliments of the Season" V 171–72

"Compline" II 269–70

"Composition in Late Spring" V 190, 205

"Concentration" VI 264

"Concerning Stars, Flowers, Love, Etc." X 328–29

"Concert" VI 173

Concrete Island, The VIII 136

"Condemned, The" VI 248

"Confederation Ode" V 148

Confederation poets I 14, 168 II 7, 8, 9, 11, 12, 13–14, 15, 16–17, 23, 39, 137, 138, 240, 243 V 2, 15 VII 5 IX 3, 92, 97

Confederation Poets series II 144

"Confession" VI 304

"Confessions of a Compulsive Anthologist" IV 241

"Conflict" IV 201

Conflicts of Spring VI 89, 107, 142, 145–48

"Congratulations" X 34

Conlogue, Ray VII 203

Connor, Ralph (Rev. Charles W. Gordon) II 243

Conquistador V 42

Conrad, Joseph III 22, 40, 143 VIII 156, 404 IX 97 X 71, 78, 142

"Conrad Kain" V 42, 57, 58, 65 n.25

"Conspirators, The" II 221

Constable, John I 14

"Constantinople Boots" VIII 148

Contact V 77, 101, 237, 241–42, 243, 269 n.51 VII 254 IX 2, 86, 87 X 24, 191

Contact 1952–54: Being an Index to the Contents of Contact, a Little Magazine Edited by Raymond Souster, Together with Notes on the History and the Background of the Periodical V 243–44

Contact Poetry Readings V 243

Contact Press III 163 V 77, 78, 241, 243, 246 VII 85, 136, 254

Contact Press, 1952–1967: A Note on Its Origins and a Check List of Titles V 243–44

"Contagion" VI 247

Contemporary Canadian Poem Anthology, The VIII 40

"Contemporary Poetry" IV 235, 245

Contemporary Verse III 62, 66 IV 32, 111 n.11 V 240, 241, 244 VI 26, 35, 173, 210 n.5, 222, 224, 279, 280, 290, 293, 299, 300, 301, 302, 312–13 n.33 VII 194, 254 VIII 121

"Contest" VI 65

Continental Trance VIII 278

"CONTINENTAL TRANCE" VIII 335, 337

Continuation I V 78, 92, 120–22, 123

"Convergence of the Twain, The" III 139

"Conversation about Literature, A: An Interview with Margaret Laurence and Irving Layton" V 175

"Conversation of Prayer, The" IX 76 n.64

"Conversation with Margaret Atwood, A" IX 19–20

"Conversation with Margaret Avison, A" VI 25, 37, 46, 48, 56

"Conversations with My Aunt" VI 262

"conversaysyuns in th karibu" VIII 85

Cook, Gregory M. X 204

Cook, Hugh V 246 quoted 246

Cook, John IX 92 quoted 88, 92

Cooley, Dennis VIII 206 quoted 373 X 89–90, 94, 189, 190, 191, 192, 195–96, 197, 199, 206, 215, 218 quoted 9, 10, 113, 127, 179 n.49

Cooperative Commonwealth Federation (CCF) IV 19, 126, 174

Copeland and Day (publishers) II 144

Copithorne, Judith VIII 21, 28, 269

Copp Clark Company I 164

"Copy Writer" V 264

Corbière, Tristan II 242 V 150

Corman, Cid V 207 n.4, 238, 242, 247, 270 n.51 VI 27, 33, 47, 48, 66 n.7 VII 267

"Corn Husking" III 46–48

Corneille, Pierre IV 42

Corners in the Glass VI 89, 107, 135–38, 152

Cornhuskers III 46, 47

"Corpse Song" IX 48

"Corrective Lenses" VI 258

Corrington, J.W. VII 270

Corso, Gregory VII 140

Cortazar, Julio X 78

Corvo, Baron (Frederick Rolfe) VIII 12

Cosmic Chef Glee & Perloo Memorial Society under the Direction of Captain Poetry Presents an Evening of Concrete Courtesy Oberon Cement Works, The VI 33 VIII 62, 265, 293

"Cosmic Religion" V 201

Cosmopolitan II 79

Cotnoir, Louise VIII 203

Coulborn, A.P.R. IV 175

"Coulee Hill" X 72

Count Filippo: or, The Unequal Marriage I 15, 78, 80, 83, 84, 86, 87, 89, 91–92, 98–101

Counterpoint to Sleep VI 279, 280, 281, 282–83, 288–93, 302

"Country Lovers, The" IV 263

"Country North of Belleville, The" VII 8, 136, 161, 167

"Country of the Young, The" VII 164

"Country Snowplow" VII 158

"Country Walk" IV 241

Covenant, The V 147, 198, 199–200

"Covenant, The" V 200

Cow Jumped Over the Moon, The: The Writing and Reading of Poetry V 41

Coward, Barbara III 71

Cowley, Abraham IV 184

Craft Dinner VIII 266, 308, 311

Craft Slices VIII 164, 168, 170

Crafte So Longe to Lerne, The VII 136, 150–52

Crane, Hart IV 235 V 262, 282 VIII 25

Crane, Stephen V 39

Crapsey, Adelaide IV 235

Crashaw, Richard IX 8

Cratylus, The VIII 280

Crawford, A.W. II 145

Crawford, Isabella Valancy I 9, 11, 12, 15, 16, 75, 168 II 8, 9, 13, 21, 135, 170, 200, 201, 202, 243–44, 264, 268 III 24, 65–66 VII 201

Crawley, Alan III 62, 65 quoted 28 V 240, 241, 244 VI 15, 26, 173, 222, 223, 280–81, 300 VIII 121 X 197

"Crazy Riel" X 285, 286, 306, 308, 309

Crazy to Kill VII 194, 197, 208, 234–35

creation X 73, 154

Creative Evolution IV 188, 191, 211

"Creative Hour" VI 64

"Creative Moments in the Culture of the Maritime Provinces" II 198

Creative Writer, The V 39, 51, 52

Creative Writing in Canada IV 239

"Creator Has a Master Plan, The" VIII 155

"Creatures of the Zodiac, The" IX 42

"Credo" V 162, 166, 201–02

"Creek, The" III 174 IV 250, 251

Creeley, Robert V 35, 150, 207 n.4, 238, 242, 247, 254, 255, 256, 258, 270 n.51, 291 VI 27, 33, 94 VII 87, 255, 266, 301 n.31 VIII 8, 121, 123, 124, 139, 189, 192, 194, 369 IX 87 X 198, 232, 260, 284

Creighton, Alan VI quoted 98

Creighton, Donald IX 205

Crémazie, Octave IV 22

"Crepe-Hanger's Carnival" (Layton) V 239

Crêpe-Hanger's Carnival: Selected Poems 1955–58 (Souster) V 264

"Crescent, A" X 328

"Crimes" VII 289, 295, 296

Criminal Intensities of Love as Paradise, The X 73

"Criminal Intensities of Love as Paradise" X 96, 111, 126, 128, 129, 130, 134, 135, 150, 173

"Crisis" VI 111

"Critic of Life, A: Louis Dudek as Man of Letters" V 90

Critically Speaking (CBC) V 155

Criticism: The Silent-Speaking Words X 192, 196, 197–98

"Critics at Large" VII 256

"Critics on Air" VII 256

Croker, John Wilson VII 271

"crooked gods:, the" X 258–60

"Cross" VI 258

Cross-Section: Poems 1940–1980 V 78, 122

"Crow" X 343

Crow Journals, The X 77, 152

"Crow Song" IX 48

"Crowning of Empire" II 33, 65, 66

"Crows, The" IV 243

Crozier, Lorna X 8, 200

Cruikshank, John IX 147 quoted 147

Crusoe: Poems Selected and New X 193, 199, 200, 204, 205

"Cry Ararat" VI 234, 254

Cry Ararat! Poems New and Selected VI 13, 225, 233, 236, 253, 257

"Cry of the Wandering Gull, The" IV 242

"Crystal Cabinet, The" VI 31
Cubism VII 198
"Cucarachas in Paradise" V 57
"Cuckold's Song, The" X 44
Cull, David VIII 192
"Cullen" VI 246, 248
"Cullen Revisited" VI 258–59
Culler, Jonathan X 391 quoted 177
cummings, e.e. III 20, 177 IV 235,
    245 V 104 VI 50, 88, 92 VIII 114,
    134
"Cup of Coffee, A" III 96
"Cup of Life, The" II 162
Curious VIII 126, 131, 135, 145–46,
    160, 174
Curnoe, Greg VII 195
Current Literature II 79
curry, j.w. VIII 30, 281
"Cursed Be Ghouls" IV 75
Curtay, Jean-Paul VIII 60
Cushman, Charlotte I 80
"Cycle No. 22" VIII 288
"Cyclist in Aphelion, The" IX 248,
    49
Cynicism" VII 146

"D.G. Jones: An Interview,
    February, 1978" IX 89–90, 100
Dabrowski, Kazimierz IX 126 n.45
Dagg, Melvin II 247 V quoted 94
Dainty Monsters, The VIII 365,
    367, 371, 375–78, 390 IX 91
Dale, Stephen IX 133, 134, 136
Dale, Thomas Randall I 87, 88, 94,
    101 quoted 88, 94, 101
Dalhousie Review, The II 91 IX 197
    X 88
Dali, Salvador VI 228
Daly, Mary VIII 195, 196
Damnation of Vancouver, The V
    44, 57, 58

"Damside" IX 67
"Dance, The" IX 175
"Dance for One Leg" IX 117
Dance Is One, The IV 174, 189,
    217–18
Dance of Death at London,
    Ontario, The VII 195, 208, 210,
    217, 223–24
Dance of Life, The IV 188
"Dance with a Watermelon" V 180
"Dancer" VIII 101, 106
"Dancing Practice" IX 44, 53, 60,
    73 n.52
Dancing Wu Li Masters, The VIII 66
Daniells, Roy I 30, 95, 173 quoted
    95 II 23, 246 quoted 19, 22, 23,
    248 IV 37, 38 V quoted 29, 36,
    57 VI 281 quoted 35, 284–85 VII
    262, 265 X 192
D'Annunzio, Gabriele V 150
Dante IV 127, 128, 139, 158, 160–
    61 n.11 VI 132, 244
"Daphne Marlatt" VIII 145
"Dark around Light" VIII 134
Dark Huntsman (a Dream), The I
    80, 83, 89, 92, 105–07
"Dark Kingdom" VI 257
"Dark Pines under Water" IX 250,
    254
"Dark Side, The" VI 187 X 377
"Darkinbad and Brightdayler:
    Transmutation Symbolism in the
    Work of Pat Martin Bates" VI
    255
"Darkness, The" VII 178–79
Darkness in the Earth, A VII 82, 90,
    101
Darling, Michael III 171 IV 12, 13,
    16 V 115 VI 66 n.7
Darwin, Charles III 115, 120 VII 80
    IX 94, 198

"Dash for the Border, A" VIII 35
"Dates" VIII 385
"Daughter of Leda" IV 91–92
"Daughter of Zion" VII 107
Daulac: An Historical Tragedy of French Canada in Five Acts II 29, 60–61, 67
Dault, Gary Michael X 390
Davenport, Guy VIII 315
Davey, Frank III 14, 71, 73, 119, 120 quoted 14, 71, 73, 119 IV 34, 47, 58, 58 n.10, 234, 236, 261 V 12, 53, 66 n.44, 86, 91–93, 96, 124, 125, 238, 243, 245, 246–47, 249 quoted 8, 12, 53, 77, 80, 86, 91–92, 93, 243, 249 VI 69 n.37, 104–05 quoted 104–05, 105 VII 12, 16, 32, 34, 49, 57, 198, 200, 206, 209, 270, 271, 272 VIII 23, 30, 33, 50, 91, 116, 120, 121, 123, 162, 168, 192, 205, 276, 277, 312, 369 quoted 9, 14, 34–35, 197–98, 199, 273, 279–80, 289–90, 313, 318, 334 IX 26, 27, 86, 92–93, 137, 195, 234, 237, 238, 239, 261 quoted 26, 93, 195, 234, 237, 239 X 148, 195, 344, 347 quoted 9, 11, 17, 55, 181 n.67, 204–05, 292, 349
"David" V 19, 28, 40, 42, 46, 47, 49–50, 57–58, 66 n.35 X 223, 225–26
David, Jack IV 40 VIII 36–37, 275 quoted 273–74, 307
"David and Abigail" II 168
David and Other Poems V 28, 34, 35, 59
"David McFadden" VIII 145
Davie, Donald II 264
Davies, Barrie II 143, 150 quoted 18, 150

Davies, Robertson I 75, 88 quoted 75, 88 III 5 IV 31, 38, 46, 51 VIII 8 IX 235
Davies, W.H. VII 146
"Dawn, The; the Birds" III 175, 177, 185 n.12
Dawson, David VIII 28, 122, 192
Dawson, Fielding VIII quoted 200
Dawson, Samuel I 82 quoted 82
Day, Margaret IV 176, 202
"Day and Night" III 4, 13, 14, 62, 65, 67, 69, 78, 79, 80–82, 83, 84, 85, 89, 184
Day and Night III 62, 68, 85 VI 32–33
"Day of Atonement: Standing" X 225
"Day of Twelve Princes" IX 231
Dayan, Moshe V 222 n.98
Daybook poems IX 55, 62
"Day-Labourer, The" VI 193
Daymond, Douglas IV 40
"Days of the Unicorns, The" VII 296
Deacon, William Arthur III 26, 117 quoted 117 IV 238, 260
"Deacon and His Daughter, The" I 40, 42–43
"Deacon's Fate, The" I 43–44, 47
"Dead, The" IV 257 V 318
"Dead Poet, The" VII 178
"Dead Rainbow, The" VII 216
"Dead Seal" VII 163
"Deaf-Mute in the Pear Tree" VI 264
Deahl, James VII 29, 35–36, 54, 66–67
"Death" III 178–79 VI 39, 41, 42, 52
"Death by Fire" X 229
"Death by Water" IX 75 n.54
"Death Chant for Mr. Johnson's America" V 258

"Death in America" VI 303
"Death of a Hornet" IX 105, 107
Death of a Ladies' Man (album) X
    23, 31
Death of a Lady's Man X 22, 23,
    25, 30, 32, 43, 45, 47, 50–51
"Death of a Poet" X 221
"Death of a Queen, The" I 36
"Death of a Young Son by
    Drowning" IX 69 n.15
"Death of Dahoum, The" IX 264,
    265
"Death of Don Quixote" X 243
"Death of Harold Ladoo, The" IX
    193, 196, 211–13, 216, 220
"Death of Moishe Lazarovitch" V
    200, 216 n.76
"Death of the Poetess, The" VII 216
"Death of Wolfe" I 191
Death's Jest-Book I 83 VI 29
De Bruyn, J. VI quoted 285
Debussey, Claude VII 198
"Decade of Canadian Poetry, A" II
    146
Decadent poets IX 140
"Decline and Fall" VII 112
"Decree Nisi" VII 152
"Dedication" IV 19–20, 201
"Deed, The" III 129
"Deep Fried Dream" X 383
"Deep Frieze" VIII 33
"Defence of Poetry, A" X 378
Degas, Edgar IX 140
"Déjà Vu" V 306
"Dejection: An Ode" VIII 149 X 43
de la Mare, Walter II 81, 242
    quoted 88 V 39 VI 91
de la Roche, Mazo III 21, 61
"Delayed Mercy" VIII 170
Delayed Mercy and Other Poems
    VIII 169

"Delayed Message" IX 43
"Delicatessen" X 355–56
"Delphi: Commentary" X 76, 96,
    137, 139, 144, 147, 150, 151, 152
Delta IV 239 V 77, 104, 105,
    109–12, 113, 125, 157, 243 VII
    85, 136
Delta Canada V 78
de Man, Paul IX quoted 118
De Mille, A.B. II quoted 87
"Democracy and the Short Story"
    III 22, 24, 25
"Demon of Thursday, The" IX 246
Denham, Paul III 2 V 40
Denison, George Taylor I 122, 146
Dennis, Col. John S. I 125
Dent, W. Redvers (Raymond
    Knister) IV 21
"Departure" IV 190, 211, 213–15
"Departures" IX 265–66
"Depression Ends, The" III 116,
    129, 130–31 VI 192
"Depression Suite" III 78, 82
"Deprivations" VII 176
Deptford trilogy IX 235
"Depth" III 174, 181
Derrida, Jacques VII 268, 273, 283,
    308 n.122 VIII 6, 72, 172, 282,
    314, 326 quoted 53 X 79, 391
Descartes, René IX 202, 205
"Descent through the Carpet, A" IX
    33
"Desert Elm" VIII 126, 131, 148,
    149–50, 152, 153, 165, 167, 172
"Desert Music" X 251
"Desert Stone" V 294
"Desert Words" X 251, 254
Deserted Village I 15
"Design" VI 236
"Design for Mediaeval Tapestry" IV
    146

Desire in Language VIII 195

"Desire under the Elms Motel,
   The" VIII 396

"Desperate sexual admirals" X 49

"Despondency" II 166

"Detail" VII 169

Deutsch, Babette VI 92

"Development" IX 112

*Devil, The: Perceptions of Evil
   from Antiquity to Primitive
   Christianity* X 327

Dewart, Rev. Edward Hartley I
   168, 171–72, 183, 191 quoted
   171–72, 183–84 II 8, 13

Dewdney, Christopher VIII 38

"Dewdrop, The" II 47–48

Dial, The III 163 IV 70, 88, 232, 243

*Dialogue sur la traduction à propos
   du Tombeau des rois* IV 174, 218

"Diamond Sutra, The" IX 122

"Diary of Abraham Segal, Poet" IV
   139, 140, 142, 146, 161 n.14

Dibdin, Charles I 167

Dickens, Charles IV 82 V 39, 109 VI
   278

Dickey, James VII 138

Dickinson, Emily III 64, 65 IV 11,
   78, 80, 246 VI 179, 186, 211
   n.19, 282, 286 quoted 179 VII
   138 VIII 172 X 343

*Dictionary of Literary Biography:
   Canadian Writers* IV 40

Diefenbaker, John IX 191, 192

Dig Up My Heart VII 11–12, 65–66

Digest VI 93

"Digging" IX 47

"Dining at the Savarin" IX 258

"Dinner" IX 60

Direction V 77, 240, 260

"Direction for Canadian Poets" IV
   75, 86, 97–98, 100, 101, 110, 237

Directives of Autumn VI 89, 97,
   108, 142, 148, 150, 150–54

"Dirge" VI 295, 296

"Dirge at a Wake" IX 192

"Dirge for a Penny Whistle" VI 131

"Disasters of the Sun" III 91–92

"Discovery" VI 204 IX 233

"Disguises" X 48, 381   .

"Disintegration in a Dream of
   Love" IX 107

Dismissal, The VII 196, 207, 230

"Dispersed Titles" VI 29, 38, 44,
   45, 51, 56

"Displaced Person" V 198

"Disquisition, The" VI 121

"Dissecting the 'T.B.M.': A Reply to
   S. Laycock's 'Why Be True to
   Life' and a Ruthless Investigation
   of a Certain Mental Viewpoint"
   III 33, 44

"Dissection" VI 292

"Diverse Causes, The" VIII 375, 377

"Divinations" V 297

Divine Comedy, The IV 158

"Divine Image" V 223 n.100

"Divine Madman" V 201

"Divining Rod" VI 303

"Divinity" V 205

Djwa, Sandra I 80, 89, 90, 94, 95,
   102, 173 quoted 80, 89, 94, 95,
   102, 173 II 150, 165 quoted 150
   III 115, 116, 120, 122, 127, 131,
   141, 142, 168 quoted 120, 142,
   168 IV 6, 21, 182, 183, 234, 239,
   240, 246, 247, 276 n.80 VI 36,
   211 n.16 quoted 36, 58, 63 VIII
   quoted 167 IX 107 X 24

Dk/Some Letters of Ezra Pound V
   10, 82–83, 130 n. 74

"Do Seek Their Meat from God" II
   209

"Dobbin" VIII 137

Dobbs, Kildare V 156 quoted 89, 156

Doctorow, E.L. VIII 403

Doctor's Memoirs, A VI 27

Documentaries, The III 63, 65, 74, 79

"Documentary Poem: A Canadian Genre, The" III 63, 66, 135

Doerksen, Daniel W. VI 37–38, 54

"Dog, The" IX 160–61

"Dog and Cat" III 40

"Dog Returned from the Woods, The" VII 104–05

"Dogsong" VII 162

Dollar Woman, The VII 83

"Dome of Heaven, The" VI 258

"Domestic Poem for a Summer Afternoon" VI 261, 262

"Domestic Scene" X 368

Dominion Illustrated, The I 85, 149

Don Juan VI 50, 73–74 n.117

Don Quixote II 140 V 61 IX 252 X 80

"Don Quixote Writes to His Priest" X 243–44

Donaldson, Alan VII 90 X 26

Donne, John I 25, 32, 33 IV 73, 76, 90, 151, 152, 181, 184, 185, 208, 235, 245, 246, 248, 276 n.80 VI 29, 30, 98, 100, 287 VII 94, 138, 202, 262 VIII 151, 152 quoted 83 IX 8, 21, 117 X 30, 40–41, 344 quoted 40

Donnell, David VIII 281

Donnelleys, The VII 15, 196, 203–04, 207, 225–30, 231

"Don't Say Anything" V 297

"don't you think we shud cum bfor yu go" VIII 62

Dooley, D.J. V 36

"Door, The" III 88

Door to Oz VIII 303

"doppelganger:, the" X 262

"doppleganger (2):, the" X 262

"Dorothy Livesay" III 67–68

Dos Passos, John IV 235 V 62

Dostoevsky, Fyodor V 150 VII 294 VIII 377 IX 8 X 16, 190

"Dot" VI 260

"Dot It Down": A Story of Life in the North-West I 125

"Double, The" X 262, 263

Double Dealer, The IV 235

"Double Entendre" VII 279, 287

Double Exposure VII 77, 78, 79, 81, 83, 95–96, 97–98

Double Hook, The VIII 8, 271 IX 235 X 113

Double Persephone VI 211 n.16 IX 18–19, 20, 29–30, 31, 68 n.1

"Double Persephone" IX 29

"Double Surprise, The" I 194

Double Tuning IV 32, 39, 40

"double world:, the" X 263

"Double-Headed Snake, The" X 285, 288, 293, 311, 312

Double-Header: As Is: Lost & Found V 259, 262

"Doubt, The" V 264

Douglas, Charles IX 193

"Doukhobor" X 315

"Dover Beach" II 240, 252 IV 215 IX 63–64, 208

"Dover Beach Revisited" IV 37

Dover Beach Revisited and Other Poems IV 32, 38–39

Down the Long Table V 29, 37, 49, 60, 62–64

Downes, G.V. IV 39, 40

"Downtown Streets" V 304

Dowson, Ernest IV 81, 94 X 17

Doyle, Mike IV 39, 51 V 160 VI 225 VII 143

Dr. Anaconda's Solar Fun Club X 340

Drache, Sharon V 163 quoted 163

Dracula VI 198

"Drag-Irons, The" III 129

Dragišic, Peggy IX 197

Dragland, Stan II 247, 248 VII 198, 203, 207, 209 IX 200, 201, 240, 261 quoted 142–44, 240

"Dramatic Personae" VII 146

"Draughtsman" VI 247

Drawings by Joe Rosenblatt X 340

Dread Voyage, The II 28, 33, 37, 48–50

"Dread Voyage, The" II 35

"Dream" (Page) VI 258

"Dream, A" (Arnold) II 138

Dream Craters X 340, 344, 346, 363–65, 371

"Dream Frost" X 383

"Dream (Green sea water washing over)" X 317

"Dream Man, The" X 316

"Dream of Fair Women, A" II 236

Dream Telescope V 281, 319, 327 n.49

"Dream Telescope" V 281

Dream That Is Dying, A V 258, 261

"Dream (The luxurious trembling sea)" X 317

"Dream Three: The Child" IX 237

"Dream Two: The Beasts" IX 237

Dreaming Backwards X 194, 206, 237–38

"Dreamland" I 142, 143–44

Dreamland and Other Poems I 122, 132, 134, 135, 139–45, 146, 148, 150, 168

"Dreams and the Common Good" VII 291

Dreams Surround Us X 283

Dreiser, Theodore IV 103, 235 V 213 n.62

"Dresden Special, The" V 261

DRIFTING INTO WAR VIII 35, 62

Driftwind VII 194

"Driftwood Logs" VII 150

"Driving" X 327

"Driving a Hard Bargain" VII 125

"Driving Home" V 305

Driving Home: Poems New and Selected V 281, 286, 290, 309, 310, 320

"Driving the Spanish Coast" VII 179

Droppings from Heaven V 147

Drunken Clock, The IX 232

Dryden, John IX 8–9

"Dryness and Scorch of Ahab's Evil Rule" VI 63

Dubliners VI 9

Duchamp, Marcel VIII 298

"Ducharmes of the Baskatonge, The" II 236

Dudek, Louis I 29, 30, 61, 173, 181 quoted 29, 181 II 149 IV 10, 38, 132, 176, 180, 183–84, 236, 239 V 2–3, 4, 5, 6, 7, 9, 10–13, 21, 34, 145, 149, 152, 157, 160, 207 n.4, 210 n.40, 238, 240, 241, 245, 246, 247, 248–49, 252, 254, 269 n.51 quoted 6, 7, 10, 11, 21, 150, 157, 245, 248–49, 252, 265 VI 93, 99, 100, 103, 108, 118, 156 n.4, 223 quoted 99 VII 9, 23, 26, 27, 28, 39, 40–41, 84, 85, 87, 92, 93, 136, 140–41, 198, 202, 208–09, 265, 267, 268, 269, 270, 304 n.71, 304 n.78 VIII 8, 121,

122, 125, 145, 159, 371 quoted 116, 129–30, 12 IX 2, 13, 86, 87, 94–95, 145, 193, 195 quoted 94, 95, 145 X 21, 23, 192 quoted 27, 28

Duer, John King IV 30

Duff, Wilson VII 257, 296

Duffy, Dennis VII 143 IX 195–96

Dugan, Alan V 283–84 quoted 283, 284

Duguay, Raoul VIII 28

Duino Elegies VIII 165, 399–400 IX 205, 222 n.34 X 164

Dumbfounding, The VI 18, 20, 27, 31, 34, 35–36, 39, 49, 55–56, 56–58, 59–60, 60, 64

"Dumbfounding, The" VI 20, 57, 62

Duncan, Chester V 89 quoted 89

Duncan, Robert III 66 IV 261 V 35, 54, 242 VII 255, 267, 276, 301 n.31 VIII 8, 121, 139, 189, 192, 194, 296, 297 X 9, 198, 202, 302

Duncan, Sara Jeannette I 44 II 243, 272 VII 5

"Duncan Campbell Scott" (Johnston) II 12–13

"Duncan Campbell Scott" (Knister) II 246

"Duncan Campbell Scott" (Logan and French) II 245

"Duncan Campbell Scott" (Muddiman) II 245–46

"Duncan Campbell Scott" (Smith) II 246

Duncan Campbell Scott: A Book of Criticism (Dragland) II 247

"Duncan Campbell Scott's 80th Birthday" II 245

Dunciad III 131

Dunkirk III 113, 145–46

Dunn, Margo I 29

"Duplicity of D.C. Scott and the James Bay Treaty, The" II 247

Duras, Marguerite VIII 195

"Dusk on English Bay" I 142 V 28, 46, 49

Dutton, Paul VIII 265, 270, 281 quoted 263

"Dwelling Place" VI 261

Dyck, E.F. X quoted 293

"Dying Lady, A" X 385

Dylan, Bob X 21, 31

Dynasts, The I 92

E.J. Pratt Medal IX 68 n.1

E.J. Pratt on His Life and Poetry III 122

E.J. Pratt Symposium, The III 120, 123, 142

E.J. Pratt: The Evolutionary Vision III 120

E.J. Pratt: The Truant Years 1882–1927 III 122

"Eagle Island" V 59

Eagleton, Terry VII 201–02 VIII 48, quoted 45, 326

Eakins, Rosemary X 27

"Earache the Red" X 122

Earle Birney (Nesbitt) V 59

Earle Birney (Robillard) V 66 n.35

Early, Len II 11–12, 16, 18 quoted 11, 16, 18 VIII 38, 50, 72 quoted 39, 94

"Early Morning in Côte St. Luc" V 184

"Early Morning in Mithymna" V 205

"Early Morning, Kingston to Gananoque" VIII 375

Early New England Gravestone Rubbings VI 214 n.47

Early Poems (Nowlan) VII 84

"Early Spring" IV 246

"Earth" IX 64

"Earth Descending" VII 280–81

"Earth That Falls Away, The" VI 29

Earth-Light: Selected Poetry of Gwendolyn MacEwen IX 12, 232

"Earth's Answer" VI 194

Earth's Enigmas II 195

"Earthworms Eat Earthworms and Learn" X 254

"East Coker" IX 74 n.52

East of the City V 76, 87, 98–99

"East of the City" V 99

"East of the Mountains" X 305

"Easter" VI 32, 54

Easter Egg, The VII 195

"Easter Egg I Got for Passover, The" X 352

"Easter Sketches, Montreal" VI 293–94

"Easter Wings" X 359

Easthope, Anthony VIII 46, 212, quoted 330–31

"Eavesdropping" V 324

"Ebbe and Hattie" VIII 147

"Ecce Homo" VI 236

"Ecclogue 1613, December 26" VIII 152

"Ecological Heroes and Visionary Politics" X 194

"Ecology" VI 261

Eddington, Arthur S. IV 173, 185, 188

Edel, Leon IV 14, 69, 72, 74, 79–80, 124, 130, 175, 183, 184, 231, 234, 235, 239–40, 250, 263, 268 VI 8–9 quoted 10 IX 1

"Eden" IV 211 V 205

"Eden Is a Zoo" IX 41

Edgar, Pelham II 238, 239, 245, 246, 247, 249, 280 n.45 IV 19, 26, 27, 112

Edible Woman, The IX 29, 68 n.1, 236

Edinborough, Arnold V 49 X 27

Edmonton Journal IX 142

Edward VII (King of England) II 29

"Efficiency" IV 198, 199

"Effortless Point, The" VI 59, 67 n.21

"Egg, The" VI 188 VIII 126, 137

"Egg Sonata" X 352–54

"Egg-and-Dart" IV 54–55

Eggleston, Wilfrid II 92 III 27

"Eggplant Poems, The" X 104, 144, 147

Egoff, Sheila VI quoted 285

"Egoist, The" VII 101, 106

"Eight Dollars Will Do It" X 303

Eight More Canadian Poets X 193

"Eighth Letter" VII 223

Einstein, Albert IV 173, 185, 196

Eisenberg, Rochel V 170, 214 n.65

"Election Day" VI 247

"Elegy" X 36

"Elegy for a Grandfather" VII 9, 171; (1956) 149–50; (1974) 174–75; (1983) 174

"Elegy for Marilyn Munroe" V 189–90

"Elegy for Nathan Ralph" V 219 n.87

"Elegy for the Giant Tortoises" IX 38

"Elegy for Wong Toy" X 96, 101

"Elegy Written in a Country Churchyard" I 77 IX 205

"Element" VI 249

"Elephant and the Pansy, The" II 220

"Elephants" IX 152, 153–55 X 298

Elephants, Mothers and Others X
294, 295–98, 304

"Elevator, The" VIII 148

"11/9/75" IX 120

"Eleventh Letter" VII 222, 223

El Greco IX 198

Eliade, Mircea VIII 76

Eliot, George (Mary Ann Evans) II
242

Eliot, T.S. I 32 quoted II 85, 86, 91,
148, 242, 255, 262 III 3, 4, 11,
65, 72, 113, 116 IV 10, 14, 17,
23, 33, 37, 73, 74, 76, 77, 79, 80,
81, 83, 85, 89, 90, 95, 97, 99,
104, 124, 127, 128, 129, 131,
132, 133, 135, 139, 141, 142,
143, 145, 146, 147, 148, 151–52,
159, 160–61 n.11, 161 n.12, 163
n.43, 176, 179, 180, 185, 194,
197, 211, 232, 234, 235, 237,
238, 241, 243, 244, 245, 246,
247, 261, 262, 263, 266, 267,
276 n.80 V 1, 2, 3, 34, 57, 59, 79,
91, 240 VI 29, 30, 34, 48, 53, 55,
67 n.23, 74 n.130, 90, 91, 95, 98,
100, 111, 147, 154, 157 n.17,
162 n.82, 176, 180, 227, 228,
243, 247 quoted 55, 113 VII 138,
200, 259–60, 263, 268 VIII 121,
172, 173 quoted 162, 164, 312
IX 8, 20, 36, 44, 46, 73 n.52, 75
n.55, 87, 192, 198, 205 quoted
74 n.52 X 24, 30, 37, 40, 41, 81,
190, 191, 198, 208, 251, 284,
293, 307, 343, 358, 377, 389
quoted 36, 341, 359

Elizabeth; or, The Exiles of Siberia I
167

Elizabethan sonneteers II 139

Ellenbogen, George VII 140–41

"Ellesmereland I" V 33

Elliot, George P. X 72

ellipse IX 86

Ellis, Havelock IV 188

Ellul, Jacques VI 51, 74 n.124

"Elm Tree and Sun" III 40

Elrod, Suzanne X 22, 23

"em ty" VIII 295

"Embezzler (I): His act (*Luke 16*)"
VI 63

"Embezzler (II): A Classic Case?"
VI 63

"Embezzler (III): '. . . wiser than the
children of light'?" VI 63

"Embezzler (IV): The Wastrel Begins
to Hope" VI 63

"Emblem Drawings for *The
Boatman*" VI 175

"Emergency Ward, The" VIII 52

Emerson, Ralph Waldo I 78 II 15,
30, 77, 79, 83–84, 97, 138, 162,
197, 213, 235, 241 quoted 30 VI
227 VIII 35

Emery, Tony V 131 n.77

"Emmanuel" VI 31, 61, 64

Empedocles VI 297

Emu, Remember! VII 6, 136, 139,
148–50

En México V 3, 10, 77, 83, 89,
113–14, 116, 117, 248, 249

"En Route" II 256 IV 10

Enchanted Echo, The VII 135,
145–46, 147

"Encounter" V 190

"Encounter, the Recognition, The"
VII 99–100

"End, The" VI 205, 207

"End Justifies the Means, The" X
295

Endicott, Norman VI 35

"Endings" VII 115–16, 117

Endres, Robin VII 58
"Ends of the Earth" VIII 397
Endymion II 139
Energy of Slaves, The X 17, 22, 25, 29, 44, 47, 49, 50
Engagements: The Prose of Irving Layton V 161, 211 n.40
Engel, Howard X quoted 86–87
Engel, Marian II 220
Engels, Friedrich V 168
"Engine and the Sea, The" X 289, 312
"Engineer and the Asparagus, The" VI 61
"England" II 33 VII 60
"English Literature from Chaucer to Elizabeth" II 78
English Romantic Writers VIII 24, 72
"Enigma in Ebony" V 44
Enquiry into the Sublime and Beautiful II 160
Enright, Robert VII 145 VIII 206 X 89–90, 94, 113, 127, 179 n.49
Enterprise V 77
"Entomology" X 219
"Envoi" VIII 396 X 244
Epic of Gilgamesh, The VI 200 VIII 279
"Epidaurus" V 54
Epigrams V 78, 84, 122, 126
"Epigrapher, The" III 125
"Epilogue" VI 207 X 263
"Epilogue: A Poetry Manifesto" X 376
"Epipsychidion" II 221
"Epitaph" IV 94
"Epitaph for the Living: A.M. Klein" IV 91
"Epithalamium" IV 73, 88–90
Epithalamium in Time of War VI 87

Epstein, Jacob VI 236
"Equalizer, The" V 219 n.87
"Erie County" X 210
Erigena, John Scotus VI 132
"Eros" X 150
Errata VIII 168, 170–71
"Ersatz" V 253
"Escape" IV 162 n.23
Escape from the Glue Factory: A Memoir of a Paranormal Toronto Childhood in the Late Forties X 340, 375, 376, 380, 382–84
"Eschatology of Spring" VII 250
"Eskimo Graveyard" VII 164–65
Esquire X 22
"Essay on Man" IV 45
Essays on Canadian Writing VIII 38 X 88, 90, 206, 207
Essays on the Constitution: Aspects of Canadian Law and Politics IV 175
"Essentials, The" V 264
"Esta Muy Caliente" VIII 135
"Estevan, 1934" X 10, 254, 255, 256
"estevan, 1934:" X 255, 256, 258
"Estevan, Saskatchewan" X 191, 211, 214, 255
Estevan the Power Centre X 258
"Esther" I 50–52
"Et Meure Paris et Helene" IV 81, 91
"Eternal Recurrence" V 166, 203
Etherege, Sir George I 99
Euripides I 102 V 150 IX 232
Europe (Dudek) V 3, 10, 77, 78, 83, 88, 89, 92, 97, 105–08, 113, 114, 116, 123
Europe and Other Bad News (Layton) V 147, 149, 162–66

"Eurynome" VI 195

"Evangeline" II 254

Evans, Walker VIII 225

"Eve" III 91

"Even beyond Music" II 153

"Even in Reflection" VI 194, 209

Even Your Right Eye VII 254, 263, 269, 281, 305 n.91

Evening Dance of the Grey Flies VI 12, 13, 225, 234, 236, 259, 262, 264

"Evening Dance of the Grey Flies" VI 260, 261

"Evening Trainstation before Departure" IX 66

Events and Signals IV 174, 208–15

Everson, R.G. V 78, 115 VII 28

Evidence VII 136

"Examiner" IV 212–13

"Excelling the Starry Splendour of this Night" VI 117

Excerpts from the Real World X 74, 82, 96, 158, 160, 161, 162–66, 167, 170, 172, 174

"Excessively Quiet Groves, The" V 155

"Exchange" V 319

Exchange of Gifts, An VII 84, 124–26

"Excursion" IV 212

"Execution, The" VII 93, 105

"Exhortation, The" VI 131

Existentialism VII 266, 269–70, 305 n.91

"Ex-Nazi" V 221 n.95

"Exodus" X 37

"Expanded Proverb" IV 45

Experiment 1923–29: Poems by W.W.E. Ross III 163

"Experiments" X 377

"Expiation" II 271, 274, 275

"Exploration: To Therese" VII 105–06

"Expurgated Edition" V 152

Extra Innings: New Poems V 262, 264, 265, 269 n.45

"Extractions, The" VIII 145

"Extra-Political: The Thorned Speaks (While Day Horses Afar)" VI 54

Eye of the Needle, The: Satires, Sorties, Sundries IV 174, 215

"Eyes across Time" V 259

"Ezra Pound" VII 301 n.35

"F.P. Grove: The Finding" X 96, 101, 102

"F.R. Scott and the Modern Poets" V 81, 101

Fable of the Goats and Other Poems, The III 113, 126, 145

Façade VII 216

"Face, The" IX 247

"Factory on a Sunday, A" V 97

"Faculty Party" IX 87, 103

Faerie Queene, The I 120 X 111–12 n.55, 118

Faiers, Christopher VII 29, 66–67 VIII 30

"Failure of Secular Life, The" X 41

"Fainting" VIII 145

"Fair in Town" X 208, 213–14

Fairley, Barker III 21

"Fairy Fountain, The" II 164

"Faith Is a Concrete Object" VI 134

"Faithful Shepherd, The" VI 193, 194

"Falconry" VI 301

"Fall and All: A Sequence" IX 20, 31

"Fall by Fury" V 38

Fall by Fury & Other Makings V
30, 38
"Fall of Snow, The" VI 153
"Fallacy of Literalism and
the Failing of Symbolic
Interpretation, The" V 111–12,
116
"Fallen, Fallen World, The" VI 54,
56
"Falling of the Snow, The" V 253,
269 n.48
"Falling Water" III 9, 176–77, 186
n.12
"Fallout" VI 303
"Falls of the Chaudière, Ottawa,
The" I 190
"Families" VIII 384, 385
"Family" VIII 126 X 381
"Family Portrait" IV 36 V 187
Family Romance, The X 195, 202
"Fantasia" III 82–83
"Fantasia on Christian's Diary" VII
278
"Fantasy in May" III 75
Far Horizons II 115
Far Point, The X 204
"Far West" IV 15, 257–58
"Farm Out the Sydenham Road,
The" V 239, 259
"Farmer Downs Changes His
Opinion of Nature" I 40–41
"Farmer's Daughter Cherry, The" I
40
Farmiloe, Dorothy I 22 quoted 22
"Farre Off" VIII 390
Farrell, Lance VIII 21
Farrugia, Jill VI 267 n.32
"Fat Man, The" X 288, 315, 317
Fat Man, The: Selected Poems X
283
"Father" VI 261

Faulkner, William V 260 VIII 268 X
36, 78
Favorite, The I 22, 34
"Favorites of Pan" II 157, 159
Favourite Game, The X 21, 33, 39,
44, 45, 46
Fawcett, Brian VIII 125, 232
"Fear of Love, The" II 221
*Fearful Symmetry: A Study of
William Blake* VI 175, 181
Fearing, Kenneth V 240, 250
"February Thaw" X 227
Fee, Margery X 191, 193, 194, 195,
197, 200–01, 202, 205
"Feed" III 47
Feeling the Worlds: New Poems III
63, 94
Fencott, P.C. VIII 28
Ferlinghetti, Lawrence VII 53,
140
"Fern Hill" X 39
Ferns, John IV 245, 266
"Ferry Trip" III 88
"Fertile Muck, The" V 180, 190
"Festival without Prayers" VI 242
Festus I 83
Fetherling, Doug VII 138 IX 195,
197 quoted 142
Fiamengo, Marya VII 92 X quoted
346, 347
"Fiat Lux" V 167
Fiction of Contemporary Canada
VIII 126
Fiddlehead, The II 86 III 170–71 IV
238 VI 102, 180, 181, 281, VIII
32, 134 IX 135, 194 X 88
Fiddlehead Books I 9
Fiddlehead Review, The VII 23, 46,
52, 54
"Fiddleheads" VII 177–78
Fiedler, Leslie X 198

*Field Notes 1–8: a continuing poem.
The Collected Poetry of Robert
Kroetsch* X 13, 74, 75, 87, 88,
92, 96, 97, 105, 107–14, 118,
120–23, 126, 128, 129, 130, 135,
140, 147, 149, 155, 157, 173, 174
"Field of Night, The" V 321
Fielding, Henry VIII 153
Fields Osgood (publisher) I 78
15 Canadian Poets IX 233 X 193
Fifteen Winds VII 137, 142
Fifth Business VIII 118
"Fifth Letter" VII 222
"Fights, The" VII 42–43
"Figuring" X 151, 153
"Fiji" X 168
"Filigrane!" I 36
Filippo I 83
"Filled Pen, The" VI 260
"Final Solution, The" V 221 n.95
"Final Spring" VI 111
Finch, Robert III 166 IV 5, 7, 8, 11,
15–17, 199, 232, 254 V 87 VI 9,
91, 92, 156 n.6
"Finches Feeding" VI 12–13, 260
"Finding Amos in Jerusalem" V
317
Findley, Timothy VII 300 n.19 IX
174
"Fingers, The" VIII 144
"Finis the Cenci" IV 209
Finlay, Ian Hamilton X 358
Finnegans Wake IV 158 VIII 268
"Fire and Frost" III 94
"Fire and Ice" IV 181
"Fire and Reason" III 75
"Fire & Water" VIII 290
"Fire of Eros, The" IX 192
Fire on Stone VI 89, 103, 104, 106,
121, 131–35
"Fire Sermon, The" IV 147

"Fire-Crackers" IX 103
Fire-Eaters, The IX 232, 240, 241,
261–62
*fires in th tempul OR th jinx ship nd
othr trips* VIII 32, 61–62, 64, 76
fires in th tempul (art catalogue)
VIII 61
"Fireweed Seeds" IX 161
Fir-Flower Tablets III 181
"First" VI 58
"First and Last Things" VI 200–01,
201
First Book of Kings I 105
*First Day of Spring, The: Stories
and Other Prose* III 22
*First Five Years, The: A Selection
from* The Tamarack Review VI
279
"First Letter" VII 223
"First Part, The" VI 259
First Person in Literature, The V
81, 114–15
"First Political Speech" X 253
"first snow, th" VIII 71, 72–73, 83,
84, 98–99
First Statement I 8 III 118 IV 8, 13,
38, 126, 127, 132, 176 V 2–3,
4–5, 6, 12, 16, 76–77, 79, 80, 81,
84, 87, 145, 152, 170, 214 n.65,
215 n.71, 238, 240, 280, 282 VI
9, 87–88, 223 VII 85, 253, 265
VIII 5, 8 X 24
First Statement press VI 281, 288
"First Thin Ice, The" V 257
"First Time, The" X 303
Fischer, G.K. IV 133, 146
"Fish" III 177, 186 n.12 VI 93
Fisher, Brian X 281
"Fisherman, The" VI 190, 192, 193
"Fishing for Eel Totems" IX 27–28
"Fishwife" VI 303

Fiske, John II 54

FitzGerald, Edward II 83, 112 IV 81

Fitzgerald, F. Scott VIII 404

"Five, The" IV 46–47

"Five Breaks" VI 52, 55

"Five Characters" IV 124, 134, 138

"Five Kine, The" IV 35, 51–52

Five Modern Canadian Poets X 193

"Five Poems for Dolls" IX 54

"Five Poems for Grandmothers" IX 56

"Flashlights and Echoes from the Years of 1914 and 1915" III 127

Flaubert, Gustave II 242 III 25 IV 38

Flecker, James Elroy I 83

"Fleets, The" IV 49

Flemming, Friedrich Ferdinand VI 213 n.42

Fletcher, John I 99

Fleurs du Mal, Les IV 141 X 24, 35

Flight into Darkness VI 87, 98, 100, 104, 111–18, 126, 154

"Flight into Darkness" VI 162 n.81

Flint, F.S. V 1

Flint, G.H. I 79, 85 quoted 79

Flood, John II 247, 275

"Flossie at School" VII 104–05

"Flower, The" II 222 X 304, 316, 317

"Flower Bed, The" VI 261, 262

"Flower of Whitney Pier" V 257

"Flowers" III 180

"Flowers and Gardens of Summer" VII 300 n.14

Flowers for Hitler X 17, 21, 24, 27, 28, 34–35, 37, 38, 40, 41, 42, 43, 44, 46, 48

"FLOWERS / (hours)" VIII 294

"Flowers That I Left in the Ground, The" X 38, 40

"Flute Notes from a Reedy Pond" IX 66, 75 n.57

"Flux" IV 201–02, 211

"Fly, The" VI 31 X 40

"Fly: On Webs" VI 257–58

Flycatcher and Other Stories VIII 146–48, 155

"Flying Fish, The" IV 52

"Flying to Fort Smith" IV 205

Foley, Martha VI 88

"Folk" X 42

"Folk Tale, A: With a Warning to Lovers" VI 290–91

"Folk Tales of the Saints, The" VIII 313–15, 317

"Folkways" V 308

"Following, The" V 317

"Folly of Being Comforted, The" IV 242

"Footnote to the Amnesty Report on Torture" IX 59

"For A" VIII 134

"For a Graduand" IV 45–46

"For Abe Klein: Poet" III 91

"For an Older Poet in Despair with the Times" V 176–77

"For Anne" X 45

"For Doug Jones: The Explanation" X 134

"for ellie" VIII 297

"For Esther" V 53

"For Eve" IX 114

"For Françoise Adnet" IX 109

"For Fyodor" VII 284, 294, 301 n.35

"For G.E.R." VI 248

For Jesus Lunatick VIII 307

"For Judith, Now about 10 Years Old" X 288, 303

"for k, d" VIII 212

"For Mao Tse-Tung: A Meditation on Flies and Kings" V 185, 190

For My Brother Jesus V 147, 195, 198

"For My Brother Jesus" V 198

"For My Friends, Obscurely" X 297

"For My Two Sons, Max and David" V 195–96

"For Nicholas of All the Russias" VII 103

"For Norm in Lieu of an Orgasm" VII 155

"For Oedi-Puss" VII 150

For Openers VIII 37

"For Pegi Nicol" IV 207, 209

"For Play and Entrance: The Contemporary Long Poem" X 83, 100, 103, 127, 138, 167

"For Rita — in Asylum" IX 152, 153

"For 751–0329" V 222 n.97

"For Steve" V 46

For the Back of a Likeness IV 32

"For the Murderous: The Beginning of Time" VI 63

"For the Stinker Who Called Me an Apologist for Nazi Crimes" V 221 n.95

"For Three as Yet Unburied" IV 91

For What Time Slays V 256, 261

"Force That through the Green Fuse, The" VI 282

Ford, Cathy VIII 30

Ford, Ford Madox II 261

"Foreigner" VI 248

"Foreman, The" IV 48

"forest in th shell and water, a" VIII 66–68

"Forest Poem" V 321

"Foreword" (Ross) III 2, 167, 173, 181

"Foreword to the Revised Edition" VI 92, 95–96, 97

Forge VII 254 X 21

"Forgotten Freedom, The" VII 303 n.58

"Formal Garden" IX 29–30

"Forsaken, The" II 250, 254–56, 258

"Forsaken Mermen, The" VI 279

"Fortification, A" IX 37–38

Fortnightly Review VIII 121

Fortune and Men's Eyes VIII 85

"Fortunes" V 287–88, 305–06

40 Women Poets of Canada III 66

Forum II 14, 225 n.10

Foster, William Alexander I 122, 146

Foucault, Michel VI 178, 210 n.11

Foulks, Debbie III 70 quoted 70

"Found Poem" VII 309 n.130

"Found Swahili Serenade/A Jukollage" V 56

"Foundling, A" IX 37

"Fountain, The" IV 35, 59 n.17

Four Ages of Man: The Classical Myths VI 174

"Four Augeries" IX 50

"Four Corners of My World" VI 278, 285

"Four Evasions" IX 50

"Four Feet Between" V 57

"Four Horsemen" VIII 30

Four Quartets VI 147–48 IX 73 n.52, 205

"Four Small Elegies" IX 56

"Four Small Scars" X 302

"Four Swans in Fulford Harbour" VII 264

14 Barrels from Sea to Sea VII 196

Fous de Bassan, Les VI 178

Fox, Gail IX 238 quoted 237–38

Fox, Richard V 106

"Fox Trot" VII 217

Fraggle Rock VIII 266

"Fragment" (Webb) VII 287

"Fragment, A" (Crawford) I 35

"Fragment of a Letter, The" II 253, 259–60

"Fragment of Baroque" X 37

"Fragment of Continuum" V 122

"Frame 5" VIII 300

"Frame 10" VIII 300

Frames of a Story VIII 190, 201, 207–12, 233, 249

France, Anatole IX 253

Francis, Wynne V 13, 75, 84, 90, 91, 160, 163 quoted 13, 14, 15–16, 76, 90

"Francisco Tresguerras" V 45

Franco, Walter VIII 28

Frank, Anne V 197

Frankenstein IX 71 n.46

Frankenstein: The Man Who Became God VII 83

"Frankfurt *Hauptbahnhof*, The" X 96, 130, 137, 147–49, 152, 153, 154, 161, 162

Fraser, G.S. IV 72

Fraser, John IV 73, 90, 97, 185 VII 207

Fraser, Keath VII 93

Frazer, Sir James IX 11, 192 X 36, 144, 145, 147, 377

"Freak" VI 250

Frederick, John T. III 268

"Free Translations" VII 271, 277, 284

"Freedom" II 157, 165

"Free-Fall Lovers" IX 193

French, Donald G. I 86, 191 quoted 86, 191 II 245, 249

French, William X 193

French Individualist Poetry, 1686–1760 IV 31

Freud, Sigmund IV 103 V 197 VI 228, 249 VIII 280 IX 94, 251 quoted 251 X 33

Frey, Cecilia VII 272–73

"Fried Eggs and the Workings of the Right Brain" VI 264–65

"Friends" V 302–03

"Friends as Footnotes" VIII 289, 314, 320–22

Friendship of Art, The II 96, 100

"Frivolities" VII 285, 297

"Frogs, The" II 138, 151, 164 X 343

"From a Dead Poet's Book" V 321

"From a Fake Journal" VIII 160

"From a Hammock" IV 52

"From a Provincial" VI 53

"From Age to Age: Found Poem" VI 63

From Hell to Breakfast V 260, 269 n.44

"From Queenston Heights" 191

"From Stone to Steel" III 126

From the Book of Myths II 87

"From the Bridge: Firth of Forth" V 33

"From the Hazel Bough" V 33

"From 'The Pentagon Papers' " X 249

From There to Here: A Guide to English-Canadian Literature since 1960 VIII 35, 197 X 205, 344

Fromm, Erich V 189, 200, 204 quoted 189, 200, 202, 204–05

Frost, Robert III 11, 29, 30, 76, 114, 181 VI 91 IX 88

"Frost King's Revel, The" I 182, 196

Frost on the Sun IX 1, 2, 86, 89, 92, 99, 100–04, 105, 107, 109, 115, 116, 119, 121

"Fruit Ranch, The" VIII 144
Fry, Roger VII 307 n.112
Frye, Helen IX 191
Frye, Northrop I 14, 16, 28, 29, 30,
    55, 61, 87, 91, 103, 168, 173
    quoted 16, 29, 87, 103, 168 II
    246 quoted 95, 164–65 III 3, 31,
    71, 74, 77, 81, 113, 114, 118,
    119, 120, 123, 130 quoted 3–4,
    71, 74, 81, 114, 118, 130 IV 13,
    14, 38, 128, 180, 182, 186, 215,
    218, 233 V 7, 79, 87, 88, 89, 96,
    118, 119–20, 143, 149, 150, 154,
    155, 156, 160, 209 n.31, 248–49
    quoted 7, 10, 14, 17, 51, 79,
    87–88, 89, 155, 156, 157, 244 VI
    7, 17, 26, 97, 105, 173, 175, 176,
    180, 181, 184, 185, 210 n.4, 280
    quoted 177, 180, 181, 231, 233,
    283, 290 VII 5, 6, 15, 85, 94, 194,
    197, 199, 202, 203, 204, 205,
    211, 214, 216, 218, 219, 225,
    230, 252, 258, 260, 261, 269,
    271, 273, 276, 283, 287, 305
    n.91 VIII 6, 62, 163–64 quoted 5
    IX 2, 4, 86, 90, 94, 116, 139,
    191, 193, 197 quoted 1 X 13, 14,
    26, 197, 198, 200 quoted 8–9,
    36, 94
"Frye Again (But Don't Miss
    Souster)" V 118, 119
"Fulfilment" I 150
Fulford, Robert V quoted 265 IX
    190
"Full Circle" VII 118–19
"Full Moon" VI 237
Fuller, Roy IV 239
"Functional Poetry: A Proposal" V
    104–05
"Funeral" X 297, 298
Fuseli, Henry X 202

"Fuseli: Girl Combing Her Hair,
    Watched by a Young Man" X
    215
Fuseli Poems X 192, 203, 214–23,
    226, 242
"Future of Canadian Literature,
    The" IV 70, 82, 83, 84, 110

Gadd, Maxine VIII 21, 28
Gage (publisher) VI 26
Gagnon, Clarence II 236
"Galilean, The" V 198
Gallagher, W.H. VIII 223
"Gallant Lads in Green, The" I 63
    n.20
"Game, The" VII 223
"Game after Supper" IX 41
"Game of Chess, A" V 170, 215
    n.66
"Game of Snooker, The" VII 64
Ganglia VI 68 n.36 VIII 264, 265
Gangs of the Cosmos VIII 137
Garbage Delight IX 191
"Garden, The" IV 217 VI 295 IX 53
"Garden of Square Roots, The: An
    Autobiography" IX 246–47
"Gardeners, The" V 301
Gardiner, Dwight VIII 232
"Garland of Milne, A" IX 116, 117
Garmaise, Max IV 125
Garneau, Hector de Saint-Denys IX
    207, 209, 210
Garnet, Eldon IX 193
Garrett, Pat VIII 373, 378, 380
Garvin, John I 23, 31, 56, 131–32 II
    90
Gascoyne, David VI 48
Gasparini, Len V 89 quoted 89 IX
    quoted 143 X 390 quoted 346
Gaspé, Phillippe Aubert de II 206
"Gatineau" VI 37, 45

Gautier, Théophile IV 14, 263 VI quoted 11

Gauvreau, Claude VIII 28–29

Gavronsky, Serge VIII quoted 194

"Gawd, the Eumenides!" VII 152–53

Geddes, Gary II 22, 247, 248 IV 71, 73 quoted 71 V 212 n.56 VI 67 n.23 VII 145 IX 142, 177, 233, 234 quoted 9, 10, 93, 142, 195, 233 X 192 quoted 11, 12

"Geelong, Victoria" X 168

Genealogy of Morals, The V 217 n.81

"Genealogy of Morals" VII 101

"Generation" VI 245, 248

"Generation Cometh" IX 244–45

Genet, Jean VIII 25 X 24

Geneve VIII 138, 139–41, 146, 174

"Genius, The" X 47

"Gentle Goddess" VII 26

"Gentle Rain Persists, A" VI 142

"Gents Furnishings" V 183

Geography Match VII 224

Geography of the Imagination, The VIII 315

"Geometaphysics" VI 51

George, Stefan VI 227

George, Vancouver VIII 9, 134, 137, 139, 146, 148

Georgia Straight VII 23 VIII 125, 126

Georgian poets II 86 VI 157 n.17

Georgics V 301

"Georgie and Fenwick" VII 104–05

"Gerald" IX 163

Gerson, Carole II 247

Gervais, C.H. (Marty) V 212 n.56 VII 138 VIII 120

"Gestures Hebraic" IV 125

"Gestures Hebraic and Poems" IV 125, 130

"Getting to Rochdale" IX 201

"Ghazala's Foal" IX 264–65

Ghiselin, Brewster VI 69 n.43

Ghost in the Wheels: Selected Poems V 30, 38

"Ghost Stories" VII 123–24

"Ghost Tantras" VIII 270

"Giant as Outlaw, The" X 368

"Giants" X 366

Gibbs, Jean IX quoted 26

Gibbs, Robert II 92, 222 quoted 82, 222 III 121 VI quoted 31, 35–36 VII 83–84

Gibran, Kahlil X 21

Gibson, Graeme IX 17, 68 n.1

Gibson, Kenneth X 204

Gide, André VIII 25

Gilbert, Gerry VIII 21, 28, 30, 147, 232

Gilbert, Sir William Schwenck V 44

Gilgamesh X 165

"Gilgamesh and Friend" VII 151–52

Gillon, Edmund Vincent, Jr. VI 214 n.47

"Gimli" V 305

Gingell, Susan III 4, 122 quoted 4 IV 8, 11

Ginsberg, Allen IV 261 VII 29, 53, 140, 255, 267–68, 301 n.31 VIII 114, 192 X 9, 24

Giorno, John VIII 28

"Girl and Horse, 1928" IX 41–42

"Girl at the Beach" VIII 134

"Girl at the Corner of Elizabeth and Dundas" V 256

"Girl Sees It!, A" See "In Green Solariums"

"Girl Toy" X 40

"Girl Who Went to Mexico, The"
VII 80

"Girls" V 299

"Gisli, the Chieftain" I 27, 34

"Gist of It, The" V 264

Givens, Imogen Knister III 21, 27,
49 quoted 27

"Glace Bay Cabbies, The" VII 119

Glas VIII 72

Glasgow Commonwealth I 170

Glass Air, The: Selected Poems VI
226, 234–35, 264

"Glass Castle, The" VII 287

"Glass Dog, The" X 34

"Glass House, The" III 64–65, 95

Glass Trumpet, The V 281, 282,
286, 287, 290, 291, 294

Glassco, John IV 6, 234, 235 VII
223 VIII 11

Gnarowski, Michael II 143, 144 III
166 V 85–86, 98, 130 n.60, 243,
246 VI 156 n.4 VII 23, 27, 32, 33,
34, 140

"Go on" VIII 224

Go to Sleep, World V 241, 244,
250, 253, 269 n.48 X 191

"God Bless You" X 316

"God Sour the Milk of the Knack-
ing Wench" VII 101

God, the Invisible King IV 188

"God Who Is Goshawk, The" IX
161

Godard, Barbara VIII 190, quoted
205–06

"*Godfather's Painting*: David
Thauberger" X 267–69

Godfrey, Dave III 14 IX 189, 190,
191, 197 X 264

Gods, The IX 191, 193, 196, 201,
211, 213, 214

"Gods, The" IX 214, 216–18

"Gods Avoid Revealing Themselves,
The" IX 38

Godwin, William I 95

Goethe, Johann Wolfgang von II
140 V 112

Going the Distance V 269 n.45

"going to likely" VIII 84

"Going to Pieces" X 267

Gold, Artie VIII 125

Gold, Joseph II 199–200, 202, 207,
208 quoted 208

"Gold Bug, The" X 218

Goldberg, Strul V 144, 145, 175

"Golden Apples of the Sun, The"
VII 109

Golden Bough, The IV 73, 76, 97
IX 192 X 377

Golden Chalice, The VI 86, 100,
109–10

Golden Dog Press I 80

"Golden Hunger, The" IX 246,
259–60

Golden Treasury, The VI 29

Goldhar, Eleanor VII 208

Golding, William IX 192

Goldman, Emma III 27, 61

Goldsmith, Oliver I 15, 168 II 13

Gone Indian X 73

"Good Angels" III 180

"Good Company, Fine Houses" X
306

"Good Friday" IV 246

Good Soldier Schweik, The V 61

Good Words II 236

Good Words for the Young II 236

Goodman, Paul VII 255, 289, 301
n.33

Goodwin, K.L. IV 181–82

"Goose-Girl, The" VI 201–02

Gose, Eliot VIII 133

"Gothic Fugue" VI 118, 122

"Gothic Landscape" V 155, 172, 192

"Gothic Letter on a Hot Night" IX 46–47

Gotlieb, Phyllis X 28

Gould, Glenn VII 255

Governor General's Award III 62, 113 V 28, 143, 239, 245 VI 27, 35, 89, 156 n.6, 174, 180, 224 IX 24, 68 n.1, 86, 135, 136, 190, 195, 232

"Grab at Proteus, A: Notes on Irving Layton" V 158

Grace Abounding to the Chief of Sinners IX 219

"GRACE OF THE MOMENT, THE" VIII 335, 338

Gradations of Grandeur VI 89, 106, 138–42, 156 n.9, 163 n.94

Graham, Jean II 35 quoted 35

Graham, Ron X quoted 30

"Grain of Rice, A" IV 190, 208, 209–10, 211

Grand Duke of Moscow's Favourite Solo, The IV 32

"Grand Manan Sketches" V 296–97

"Grandfather" VIII 126, 127, 133

Grant, Douglas V 285–86, 319

Grant, George IX 9, 192, 195, 198, 204, 205, 207

Grant, George M. I 146

Grant, Peter IX 189

"Granville Street Bridge" VIII 134

"Grass, The" VIII 127, 135, 137

"Grass Roots" VI 59

Gratiaen, Doris VIII 391

Grave Sirs X 10, 282, 294

"Gravedigger, The" II 108

"Gravedigger's Rhapsody" IV 73, 94–96

Graves, Robert VI 174, 238, 287 VIII quoted 117 X 284

"Graveyard, The" V 194

Gray, Thomas I 77 III 129 IX 205

"Gray Pillar" VII 210, 214–15

"Gray Woods Exploding, The" V 57, 58

"Great Blue Heron" III 9

Great Canadian Sports Stories VIII 126

"Great Feud (A Dream of Pleiocene Armageddon), The" II 219 III 112, 118, 131, 133–34, 136 X 342

"Great Lakes Suite, The" VII 194, 215

"Great Poet of To-Day, Edward Arlington Robinson, Author of 'The Man against the Sky,' A" III 22–23

"Great Winds, The" VI 291

"Greek Fly" V 149

"Green Bird, The" VI 262–63

Green Cloister, The II 237, 238

"Green Man, The: For the Boston Strangler" IX 37

Green Mansions VI 236

Green Pitcher III 2, 12, 14, 61, 67, 94

Green Plain, The X 283, 293

"Green Plain, The" X 283, 325, 329, 330

Green World V 280, 317

"Green World" V 291, 313, 314

"Green World One" V 299

"Green World Two" V 302

Greenbaum X 340

Greenham, Peter VIII 40

Greer, Anne VII 92

Greer, Germaine V 260

Gregory, Lady VII 201

Grierson, Herbert IV 73, 231–32

"Griffin of the Night" VIII 384

Grimm, Brothers VI 201, 278

grOnk VIII 265

"Grosse Lalula" VIII 40

Grosskurth, Phyllis VIII quoted 136

Grosseteste, Robert VI 132

"Ground Swell, The" IV 124

"Groundhog among the Stars: The Poetry of Raymond Souster" V 7, 245

"Groundhogs & Appearances" X 15–16

"Grounds for Translation" IX 99

"Group" III 174

Group of Seven II 13, 17 III 112, 115, 170 IV 179, 182, 192, 193, 195, 196, 214, 235, 250 VII 5

"Group Portrait" III 20, 21

Grove, Frederick Philip I 88 II 9 III 3, 21, 26 V 108 quoted 108 X 5, 78, 102

"Grove beyond the Barley, The" VII 103, 105

Gucci Bag, The V 147, 223 n.102

Guerre, Yes Sir!, La IX 211

Guinness Book of Records VIII 113

Gulliver's Travels I 120

Gustafson, Ralph III 116, 121, 165, 168 quoted 116 IV 8, 32, 38, 233 V 112 quoted 75 VI 7–8, 10, 11–12, 13, 14, 21 n.6, 35 IX quoted 261

Guthrie, Norman II 145, 176 n.52 quoted 176 n.52

Gutteridge, Don VI quoted 103

Gyroscope VII 196, 207, 209, 210, 218, 232–33

H An Excursion VIII 303

H.D. (Hilda Doolittle) III 12, 77, 177 IV 235, 241, 243, 250–51,

277 n.101 V 1, 79, 104 VII 267 VIII 25, 193, 327

"Hace Mucho Calor" VIII 135

"Hackman's Night" III 20

Haggard, H. Rider VII 199, 224

Haiku masters, Japanese VII 263

Hale, Katherine I 23, 30, 31

"Half-Breed Girl, The" II 256

Haliburton, Robert Grant I 11, 122, 134, 135 quoted 11, 134

Haliburton, Thomas Chandler I 122

Halifax Critic I 136

Halifax Daily Reporter I 134

"halifax nova scotia" VIII 29, 85

"Hallowe'en by St Mary's Convent" X 220

"Hamatsa" VIII 137

Hambleton, Ronald V 76, 79 VI 223

Hamburger, Michael V 112

Hamilton, Jamie X quoted 347

Hamilton, Mary IX 89, 100

Hamilton, W.D. I 7, 11, 14, 16 quoted 7, 11–12

Hamlet III 127 IX 252

"Hamlet in Modern Dress" IV 104, 245

"Hammer" X 385

Hammurabi X 165

Hancock, Geoff X 70, 71

Handcuffs VII

Handful of Earth, A VII 177–78

"Handful of Earth, A" VII 178

Hanging In: New Poems V 239, 269 n.45

Hangman Ties the Holly, The VI 279, 283–84, 287, 293–301, 302

"Hans Fingerhut's Frog Lesson" II 164

"Hansel and Gretel" VI 242

Hanson, Sten VIII 28

"Happiness" II 163

"Happy Harvesters, The: A
Cantata" I 189–90, 193
Harari, Josué X quoted 79–80
Harding, Anthony J. VI 107 quoted
107
Hardy, Ann X 192
Hardy, Thomas I 92 II 81, 203, 242
III 3, 9, 113, 114, 115, 139
quoted 139 IV 89 V 39 VI 257 VII
86, 89 IX 20, 66 quoted 77 n.67
Harper's II 27, 144, 193, 209
Harpman, Geoffrey Galt VII 217
Harris, D.W. VIII 270
Harris, John VIII quoted 10
Harris, Lawren II 236 III 27, 32,
115
Harrison, Dick II 175 n.44
Harrison, Keith VI quoted 36
Harrison, Mrs. Francis II 144
quoted 145
"Harry, 1967" X 320, 322
Harsh and Lovely Land: The Major
Canadian Poets and the Making
of a Canadian Tradition II 246
VII 141
Harte, Bret I 40
Harte, W. Blackburn II 29
Hartland Observer, The VII 81
Harvard Monthly, The II 79
"Harvest" (Waddington) V 300–01
"Harvest, The" (D.C. Scott) II 254–
55
Harvey, Gordon IV 89
Harvey, Roderick W. VIII quoted
274
Has and Is IV 32, 33, 40
Hassan I 83
Hatch, Ronald VI 108 quoted 36
VIII quoted 167
Hath Not a Jew . . . IV 22, 23, 126,
131, 153, 161 n.14

Hathaway, R.H. II 89
Haunters of the Silences, The II 200
Hauser, Gwen VIII 30
Hausman, Raoul VIII 37, 40, 41
"have u seen th moovee fortun n
mens eyez or th play iuv seen th"
VIII 85
"Hawk, The" III 11–12, 32,
40–41
Hawkins, William V 151
Haworth, Peter I 90, 92
Hawthorn, Audrey VIII 221
Hawthorne, Nathaniel I 78 III 25,
38, 39 quoted 25 VIII 172
Hay, John I 40
Hayman, Robert I 16
Hayakawa, S.I. IV 84
Hazlitt, William I 82
"He Attempts to Dignify a Quarrel
with His Guests" VII 113–14
"He Couldn't Be Safe (Isaiah
53:5)" VI 62
"He Reproves the Curlew" IV 242
"He Saw Them, at First" V 191
"He Sits Down on the Floor of a
School for the Retarded" VII 124
"He Takes His Leave" VII 115
"He was beautiful when he sat
alone" X 44
"Head against White" IX 50–51
Healy, Jack IX quoted 219
"Heard the Voices Again Last
Night" VII 123
Heart of Darkness VIII 138, 156,
157, 159
Heart of the Ancient Wood, The II
199, 220
"Heart of the Lakes, The" II 30
Heart That Knows, The II 199,
205, 219
"Heat" II 9, 151 III 95

Heavysege, Charles I 7, 8, 9–10, 11, 12, 13, 14, 15, 16, 137, 138, 168 II 8, 9, 13 IV 10

Hébert, Anne IV 174, 218 VI 178–79, 254, 262 VIII 25 IX 20, 104, 106, 110

"Hebraism" X 225

Heenan, J. Michael V 79, 81, 120

Hegel, Georg Wilhelm Friedrich I 27 IX 206

Heidegger, Martin VII 266, 308 n.116 IX 193, 198, 200, 201, 203, 204, 208, 214, 216, 218

Heideman, Margaret V 88 quoted 88

Heidsieck, Bernard VIII 40–41

"Height of Land, The" II 253, 256, 258, 259–61, 265–66, 270, 274 IX 217

Heine, Heinrich V 150 VI 213 n.36

"Heirloom" IV 134

Heisenberg, Werner Karl VIII 59

"Hello Out There" VII 88

Helwig, David VIII 197 IX 195

Hemans, Felicia I 11, 83, 139

Hemingway, Ernest III 20

Henderson, Alice Corbin IV 194, 235, 241

Henderson, Brian VIII quoted 279 X 290 quoted 290, 291, 306

Henley, W.E. II 33, 197, 240

"Henri Rousseau and Friends" VIII 367

Henry V I 146, 147

Henry VI I 147

Henry VIII I 147

Henry James, Man and Author III 19

"Hens" VII 102, 104

"Heraclitos" V 194

Heraclitus I 27 V 11, 183, 190, 195, 201, 205 X 330 quoted 326

Herbert, George I 167 IV 10, 151, 152, 235, 245, 246 VI 15, 31, 65, 68 n.28, 192, 281 VII 262 VIII 6, 23 IX 8 X 30, 359

Herbert, John VIII 85

Here and Now V 143, 152, 162, 170, 171, 175, 215 n.71 VI 48

here & there VIII 241–42

"Here was the Harbour, crowded with white ships" X 49

"Hermit" III 76, 80, 81

"Hero around Me, The" X 324

"Herodotus of Halicarnassus" VII 10

Herrick, Robert I 25, 35, 36, 133, 167 VI 287

Hertz, K.V. VIII 123

Hesiod II 9

"Hesperus: A Legend of the Stars" I 184, 193

Hesperus and Other Poems and Lyrics I 12, 160, 163, 170, 171, 174, 184–93, 195

Hesse, Hermann II 112

"Hialog (Any Number Can Play)" VI 50

"Hiatus" VI 50

"Hibernated Bear" VII 146

Hicklin, Ralph V quoted 55

"Hid Life" VI 61

Hiebert, Eleanor VIII 266

Hiemstra, Mary X 6

Higgins, Dick VIII 28

high green hill, th VIII 63, 89

"High Park, by Grenadier Pond" IX 213–14

"Highest Altitude" IX 67

"Highway, The" III 127

Hildebrand II 58–59, 67

Hill, Beth VII 256

"Hill for Leopardi, A" IV

"Hill Path, The" II 236

Hilmo, Maidie VIII 37

Hindley-Smith, Lea VIII 265

Hindmarch, Gladys VIII 122, 192, 232

Hine, Daryl VI 174, 210 n.5 VII 140–41

Hirano, Keiichi II 247

Hiroshima Poems VII 171

"History" X 364

History of Nothing, The VIII 293

History of Ontario VI 26, 41, 71 n.79, 74 n.122

History of Western Philosophy, A V 216 n.79

Hitchcock, Alfred VIII 367–68

Hitler, Adolf V 31, 183, 188, 221 n.95, 224 n.105 IX 94, 198, 209, 212

Hitleriad, The IV 126, 131, 147, 152–53 X 24

Hiway 401 Rhapsody IX 162

Hjelmslev, Louis VIII 46

"Hockey Players" VII 159

Hoffer, Bill VIII quoted 117

Hoffman, E.T.A. IX 200, quoted 212

Hoffman, Frederick J. IV 200

Hogben, Lancelot IV 276 n.80

Hogg, Bob VIII 192

Hokusai IX 89

"hold on to yr typwritr" VIII 85

Hölderin, Friedrich IX 200 quoted 212

Holism and Evolution III 120

Hollingshead, Greg IX 193

Holman, Hugh IV 42

Holmes, Oliver Wendell I 171 quoted 171 II 27

Holmes, Theodore V 37

Holt, Simma VII 48

"Holy Burlesque, The" IX 258–59

"Holy Sonnets" IV 151, 152

"Homage to Sextus Propertius" IV 264

"Homebrew" VII 104

"Home-Made Beer" VII 158

Homer II 140 III 151 V 151 VI 120 VIII 7, 313 X 147

Honey Drum, The IX 232

"Honolulu" V 44

"Hope" VI 61–62

"Hope for Us" IV 98–99

Hopkins, Gerard Manley II 240 III 11 IV 23, 78, 128, 246, 247 VI 31–32, 34, 40, 68 n.29, 92, 98, 99, 154, 247, 287 VII 202 IX 21, 175, 192 X 191, 373

Horace IV 42 VIII 95

Hornyansky, Michael V quoted 94 VI 101–02 VII 90 X 27

"Horseman of Agawa, The" VII 148, 172–73

Hošek, Chaviva VIII 30 quoted 44

"Hospital" VIII 133

"Hotel" IX 59–60

Houde, Camillien IV 23

"Houdini" X 241–43

"Houdini Eliot" III 65

"Hour of Most Desire, The" II 221

"Hour of the Singer, The" IX 260

House, Vernal VI quoted 98

"House, The" IX 21, 248

"House Guest" VII 157

"House Lights" VI 196–98, 198

House of Anansi Press VII 26 IX 2, 17, 68 n.1, 166, 189, 190, 211, 212, 214

"House of Industry" V 311

House of Intellect, The V 81

"House of Mercury" IX 241

"House of the Whale" IX 262–63

"House on Tenth, The" VIII 155

"Houses" IX 20–21

Housman, A.E. II 81 IV 80 VII 138

Hovey, Henrietta II 80

Hovey, Richard II 79, 80, 83, 89, 97, 112, 115, 206 quoted 83

"How Can Words" VI 312 n.33

"How Deacon Fry Bought a 'Duchess' " I 40, 42

How Hug a Stone VIII 240–45

"How I Joined the Seal Herd" X 88, 96, 99, 105, 114, 115–16, 120, 128, 129, 142, 150, 166, 168, 174

"How I Spent the Year Listening to the Ten O'Clock News" V 297

"How One Winter Came in the Lake Region" II 38

Howe, Joseph I 15, 168, 194–95

Howells, William Dean II 29, 144, 242, 276

Howl VIII 120, 127 X 24

Howith, Harry V 151

Huckleberry Finn V 62

Hudibras III 3

Hudson, William Henry VI 236

Hudson's Bay Company I 122, 123, 124, 126

Hugh and Ion I 23, 24, 25, 27, 56, 57

Hughes, Kenneth I 30

Hughes, Ted VI 301 X 343

Hulme, T.E. III 6, 7 V 1 VI 227 VII 200–01 VIII 11

"Human Fly, The" VI 88

"Hummingbird" VII 62

Hundred Proof Earth VII 25, 27, 35

"Hunger" V 251–52

Hunt, Holman II 236

Hunt, Peter III 121, 142, 143 quoted 142–43 V 253

"Hunt, The" IV 57

Hunter, Rose (publisher) I 128

"Hunter's Moon" VI 153–54, 163 n.94

"Husband" (Bowering) VIII 135

"Husband, The" (Livesay) III 88

"Husbands" V 318

Husserl, Edmund VIII 59, 373

"Hut in the Global Village, A" VII 223, 226

Hutcheon, Linda VI quoted 71 n.73 VIII quoted 47–48, 374 IX quoted 95

Hutchinson, Sybil VII 215

Huxley, Aldous IV 80, 103 X 257

Huxley, T.H. III 115, 120

Huysmans, Georges X 17

"Hyacinth for Edith, A" IV 34, 246–47

Hyman, Mac V 36

Hymn Book VI 174, 213 n.42

"Hymn to the Lightning" I 176–77

"Hymn to the Republic" V 221 n.94

Hynes, Samuel VI quoted 90

Hyperion I 140

"I.T.A.N.U.T.S." VIII 305

I Am a Hotel X 23

"I am no longer at my best practising" X 45

"I Am So Tired" VI 295, 296

"I Am Tired of Your Politics" IX 13, 138, 158–59, 172

"I am too loud when you are gone" X 51

"I Can Call Nothing Love" VII 287

"I Couldn't Have My Cake and Eat It" VI 25, 27, 55

"I Daniel" VII 250, 259, 272, 283, 284, 297–98, 310 n.153
"I dress in black" X 45
"I Fled the Night" IX 106, 107
"I Get High on Butterflies" X 354
"I Guess a Poem" VII 169
"I have no talent left" X 45
"I, Icarus" VII 107–08, 123
"I Knew the Seasons Ere I Knew the Hours" VII 113
"I Know Not What to Do, Love" VI 293
"I Know the Dark and Hovering Moth" V 180
"I Laugh to See the Year In" I 40
"I Long to Hold Some Lady" X 40
"I Met You" X 46
I Might Not Tell Everybody This VII 122–24
"I saw no way, the Heavens were stitched" VII 210
"I See No Hand" VII 147–48
"I Shout Love" VII 29, 34, 52–53, 54
I Shout Love and On Shaving Off His Beard (1963) VII 54
I Shout Love and Other Poems VII 25, 35, 52; (1987) 54
"I Talk to You" X 46
I, The Parade VII 197, 207–08, 231
"I Think It Was Wednesday" VII 161
"I threw open the shutters" X 44
"I Was Born a Boy, and a Maiden, a Plant . . ." VI 298
"i was just cummin" VIII 89
"I Was Witch, or Skilled Magician" VI 302
"I Will Arise and Go Now" VII 44
"I Wonder How Many People in This City" X 46

"I wonder if my brother will ever read this" X 49
"I wore a medal of the Virgin" X 49
"I Would I Were" I 194
Ian of the Orcades; or, The Armourer of Girnigoe II 29, 61
Ibsen, Henrik II 85, 97 V 81, 213 n.62 VII 202
Ice Age III 63, 66, 72, 74, 89, 91
"Ice Age" III 93
Ice Cod Bell or Stone: A Collection of New Poems V 3, 29, 33, 37
"Ice Storm" IX 161
"Iceberg, The" II 20–21, 198, 216, 222–24 IV 10
Iceberg at Godhaven III 116
"Ice-Floes, The" III 124–25
"Ichthycide" X 357
"Iconic Landscape" IX 29
"Iconoclasts, The" VI 45
"Icons" V 305
"Ideas" VII 255
Ideas (CBC) V 114
"Identifier Effect, The" VII 199, 216
"Identity" VI 43, 53
Idiot Joy, An X 192, 198, 200, 204, 207, 220, 232–43, 250, 251
"If" IX 157
"If Birds Are Silent" III 9, 175–76, 177, 185 n.12
"If I could cut out hate" VI 312 n.33
"If I Could Stop the Clock" VI 312 n.33
"If I Travel Alone" IX 148–49
"If It Were Spring" X 57 n.67
"If you should die" VI 303
"If You Were Here" V 33
Il Freddo Verde Elemento V 143
"Iliad for His Summer Sweetheart, An" IV 263, 264

Iliazd VIII 40

Illustrated American, The II 191

I'm a Stranger Here Myself VII 83,
92–93, 115–18

"I'm stiff with sleep . . ." VI 312
n.33

I'm Your Man X 23, 31, 51

"image pool" VIII 84

Images: 1923–74 VII 214 n.47

"Images of Angels" VI 251–52

Imaginary Conversations II 242

Imaginary Hand VIII 129, 172–73

Imagists IV 176, 181, 193, 194,
196, 197 V 1, 2, 4, 6, 7, 10, 79,
82, 93, 96, 97, 98, 101, 124 VI
243 IX 3, 88

Imago VIII 125, 135

"Immigrant, An" III 65

"IMPERFECTION: a Prophecy" VIII
335

Imprecations VII 197, 208, 233–34

"Impressions of a Lay Reader" VI
41, 49, 67 n.19, 72 n.90

Impromptus VI 89, 108

*Improved Binoculars, The: Selected
Poems* V 13, 156, 207 n.4

"Improvisation" V 96–97

"Improvisation on an Old Theme"
III 80

Impulse VI 68 n.36

"In a Corridor at Court" V 310–11,
312

"In a Summer Pool" II 209

"In a Wood Clearing" IV 236

"In Apple Time" II 101

"In Autumn" II 33

"In Cathedrals, Concert Halls" VI
151

In Cold Hell, in Thicket V 103

In Divers Tones II 205, 206, 210

"In Eporphyrial Harness" VI 40

"In Green Solariums" ("A Girl Sees
It!") III 65, 77, 78, 79, 87

"In His Bandages, the Poet" X 384

"In Holyrood" II 61, 64

"In Iffley Churchyard" VI 110

"In June and Gentle Oven" VI 294

"In Less Time Than It Takes to Tell
It" VII 113

In Love and Anger VII 22, 31, 38–
41

In Memoriam IX 205

"In Memoriam A.H.H." II 159

"In Memory of Thomas D'Arcy
McGee" I 142

"In Memory of William A. Foster"
I 150

"In Mid-Atlantic" VII 148

"In My Dream Telescope" V 320

"In My 57th Year" X 267

"In November" II 9

"In Search of America" IX 99

"In Search of Canada: Dennis Lee's
Ironic Vision" IX 98, 99

In Search of Innocence VIII 19

In Search of Owen Roblin VII
174–75

"in th desert in nevada we wer
inside our frends littul hous n"
VIII 86–89

"In That Cellar" VI 201, 202–03,
206

In the American Grain X 292

"In the Beginning" VIII 135–36

"In the Caves of My City" X 215

"In the Country Churchyard" II 251

"In the Darkness of Cities" VII 176

In the Flesh VIII 136, 146

"In the Foothills" VII 173

"In the Forest" X 305

In the Midst of My Fever V 156,
207 n.4

In the Month of Hungry Ghosts VIII 237, 242

In the Morning of Time II 192, 199, 219

"In the Night Watches" II 222

"In the Park" V 299

"In the Pine Groves" II 164

"IN THE PLUNKETT HOTEL" VIII 335, 337

"In the Rain, Sowing Oats" III 32

In the Skin of a Lion VIII 370, 371, 387, 393, 400–05

"In the Study" II 30

"In the Valley of Wenkchemna" VI 129

In the Village of Viger II 237

"In the Wilderness" VII 160

"In the Wilds" II 160

"In the Yukon" VI 129–30

"In This Place" VII 261

"In This Round Place" VII 216, 217

"in ths forest" VIII 78

"In Time" VI 60

"In Truth" VI 49

"Inarticulate, The" VI 244

"Incendiary, The" III 93

"INCHOATE ROAD" VIII 335

"Incident Observed While Picking Up the Mail" VII 118

Incredible Murder of Cardinal Tosca, The VII 83

"Independence" X 48

Independent, The II 27, 79

"Indian Place-Names" II 253

"Indian Summer" II 42 VIII 135, 137

"Indian Tent Rings" IX 175–76

"Indictment" VII 148

"Infinito, L' " IV 216

"Influence of Spenser on Yeats, The" [diss.] VII 200, 221–22

Innis, Harold VII 225 IX 198

"Innocence" I 144–45

"Innocent Man" III 20, 21, 40

"Innuit" VII 163

"Inquest, The" VII 146

"Inside the Mill" VII 177

"Inside the Tulip" VIII 127, 135

"Inspiration of Song, The" I 35–36, 50

"Instance of Lobelia and Maple Examined, The" VI 153

"instructions:" X 263

"INTERLUDE: Double Vision" VIII 323–24

"Interruption" VII 169

"Interval" V 321

"Interview with a Tourist" IX 42

"Interview with Dennis Lee, An" IX 222 n.39

"Interview with Dorothy Livesay, An" (Barber) III 72

"Interview with Dorothy Livesay, An" (Beardsley and Sullivan) III 72

Interview with Gwendolyn MacEwen (Bartley) IX 231, 234

"Interview with Gwendolyn MacEwen" (*Poetry Canada Review*) IX 262, 263, 264

"Interview with Gwendolyn MacEwen" (Smith) IX 11, 266

"Interview with Irving Layton, An" V 224 n.105

"Interview with Louis Dudek, An" (Darling) V 82, 115–16

"Interview with Louis Dudek, An" (Nause and Heenan) V 6, 79–80, 81, 120–21

Interview with Louis Dudek (Stromberg-Stein) V 76

"Interview with Margaret Atwood, An" (Hammond) IX 20

"Interview with Margaret Atwood,
An" (Struthers) IX 19
Interview with Miriam Waddington
V 286
"Interview with P.K. Page"
(Enright) VI 221
"Interview with P.K. Page, An"
(Keeler) VI 222, 224
"Interview" with Patrick Lane IX
133, 134, 136–37
"Interview with Ralph Gustafson"
VI 94, 109
"Intimates and Strangers" VII 112
"Intimations" II 43, 70 n.33
"Into My Green World: The Poetry
of Miriam Waddington" V 289
"Into the Morning" V 299
"Into the Tonquin Valley" VI
123–26
"Intractable between Them Grows
. . ." VI 250, 251
"Intra-Political: An Exercise in
Political Astronomy" VI 29, 31,
43, 50, 51, 52, 53–54, 64
Introduction to Canadian Short
Stories III 21, 25
Introduction to Collected Poems by
Isabella Valancy Crawford
(Reaney) VII 201
Introduction to I've Tasted My
Blood (Purdy) VII 22, 30, 40, 41,
51
Introduction to The Penguin Book
of Canadian Verse VI 8, 93, 94,
157 n.17
Introduction to The Terror of the
Snows IX 123
"Introvert" V 47, 48
"Invasion Spring" VI 312 n.33
"Invert" IV 215
"Investigator" V 309, 311

"Invisible Line, The" X 383
"Invocation" (Purdy) VII 148
"Invocation to the Lakes" II 30,
32–33
"Invocations" (Macpherson) VI 205
"Inward Angel, The" VI 186, 194
Ionesco, Eugene VII 266
Iphigenia I 102
"Iraklion" VII 170
Irigaray, Luce VIII 203
Iron VIII 125, 126
Iron Door, The: An Ode III 112,
119, 120, 129–30
"Ironist" X 222
"Iroquois at the Stake, The" I 150
"Irrealistic Verses" III 180
"Irritable Reaching" VIII 170
Irvine, Lorna IX 29
Irving Layton V 158, 211 n.43
"Irving Layton, Pseudo-Prophet —
a Reappraisal" V 160
"Is" IV 207
Is. (periodical) VI 68 n.36
". . . Is Our Distress" VII 282–83,
286, 287
Isabella Valancy Crawford (Hale) I
23
"Isabella Valancy Crawford"
(Reaney) I 9, 29
Isaiah V 13, 150, 153, 179, 186, 195
Ishtar X 164, 165–66
Island VIII 190
"Island, The" VI 186 VII 42
Island Means Minago, The VII 25,
26, 60–63
"Island with Trees" III 177, 178,
185 n.12
"Isolationist" VI 247
Isou, Isidore VIII 23, 40
"Israelis" V 196
"Issue" III 180

It Needs to Be Said V 86, 100
"It Was the Light" VI 142
"Italian Primitive" VI 296
"Itch, The" X 358
"Items of Chaos" VI 295, 296
"It's true, philosophies . . ." III 77
Itter, Carole VIII 232
"ium in my nu apartment hiding
    from no wun 7 blocks" VIII 84
"I've Come to Say Au'voir" VI 313
    n.33
I've Tasted My Blood VII 11, 24,
    39, 51–52, 137 IX 236
"I've Tasted My Blood" VII 1, 37
"Ivory Steeple, The" VII 216
Ixion's Wheel VI 89, 100, 101–02,
    131, 159 n.45, 163 n.87

"J.S. Bach" X 298
"Jack and the Beanstalk" X 366
"Jack Pine, The" III 168
"Jack, to the Nova Scotians" I
    194–95
"Jacket Too Big" VIII 170
Jackpine Sonnets VII 25, 63–65
Jackson, A.Y. III 27, 115, 116, 168
Jacob, Max III 180
Jacob Faithful I 120
Jacobs, Maria V 289, 290, 291
    quoted 290, 291, 296
"Jael's Part" VI 32
Jakobson, Roman VII 302 n.44
James, Esther VII 206
James, Henry II 242, 272, 276 III
    23, 25, 143 VIII 159, 193 X 71
James, William VI 27
James Bain and Son (publisher) I 23
Jandl, Ernst VIII 40, 269, 304
"Janitor Working on Threshold" VI
    60
"January" VII 220

"Japanese Flowers, Autumn Vistas"
    V 283, 284
"Jardin de la Chapelle Expiatoire"
    IV 37
Jardine Memorial Prize III 61
Jarrell, Randall IV 131
Jarry, Alfred VIII 11, 268
Jaspers, Karl VII 217
Jawbreakers VII 23, 30, 33, 46–51
Jaynes, Julian VIII 77 IX 57 X 260
"Jealousy" X 348
Jean, Duc de Berry IX 89, 108
Jeans, James IV 185
Jeffers, Robinson V 39 VII 139
Jeffrey, David L. VI 71 n.76
"Jelly Bean Man, The" VII 118
Jelly Belly IX 191
Jennings, Elizabeth VI 182
Jephthah's Daughter I 80, 82, 83,
    84, 85, 86, 87, 89, 92, 102–04,
    107
"Jeshua" V 186, 198
Jesuit Relations III 113, 142
"Jeu, Le" (Baudelaire) IV 145
"Jeu, Le" (Saint-Denys-Garneau)
    VII 223
"Jewellery" IX 260
Jewett, Pauline VII 256
Jewinski, Ed VII 11–12
Jewish Dialog X 341
"Jewish Main Street" V 173
Jewish Publication Society IV 126
"Jewish Rabbi, A" V 172–73,
    174–75, 215 n.71
Jewish Standard, The IV 69, 131
Jezebel: A Poem in Three Cantos I
    8, 80, 89, 90, 92, 104–05 II 8
jinx ship nd othr trips, the VIII 41
"Joe Derry" III 65, 78
"Joe Harris" V 31, 38, 39, 63
John, W. David V 161

John Creighton and John Duff
(printing firm) I 160
"John Donne" IX 103
"John Marin" IX 92, 100, 101,
109, 122
John Sutherland: Essays,
Controversies and Poems V 280,
281, 285
"John Sutherland 1919–1956" V
259
Johnson, B.S. VIII 306
Johnson, Bryan VII 207
Johnson, James I 29
Johnson, Lionel X 17
Johnson, Lyndon B. V 221 n.94
Johnson, Pauline II 29 III 114
Johnson, Samuel IV 184–85 VII 86,
89 VIII 145 IX quoted 9
Johnston, George VI 229
Johnston, Gordon II 12, 13 quoted
8, 12, 21–22 VI 36, 72 n.85
quoted 43 IX 27
"Joints, The" VIII 144
Joliat, Eugène IV 31
"Jonah — Chamber Cantata for
Chorus, Four Soloists, and
Instruments" VI 174
Jonas, George VII 181
"Jonathan, O Jonathan" VI 50, 53
Jones, D.G. II 150, 246 quoted 248
III 71, 116, 119 quoted 119 IV
182, 183, 184 V 110, 112, 290,
292 quoted 290, 291–92 VI 106,
229 quoted 101 VII 6, 85, 94,
140–41, 144, 199 VIII quoted 367
IX 1, 2–5, 9, 12, 20, 196–97, 235
quoted 1, 4–5 X 132 quoted 286,
287
Jones, Lawrence M. VI quoted 25
Jong, Erica IX 20, 22
Jonson, Ben I 16, 25, 35, 36

"Journal" (Marlatt) VIII 216
Journal (Nichol) VIII 266, 307,
310–12
Journal of Canadian Fiction III 22
Journals of Susanna Moodie, The
VI 178 VII 60, 61 IX 40–41, 69
n.15, 73 n.49, 73 n.50 X 24,
181
"Journey" IV 215, 246, 247 VIII
234, 236
"Journey of the Magi" VI 30
"Journey to the Clinic" V 308
"Journey to the Sea" VII 179
JOURNEYING & the returns VIII
11, 265, 272, 289
"Joy of Conquest" X 214
"Joy Ride, The" IV 107
Joyce, James II 166 III 20 IV 11, 14,
23, 126, 128, 129, 130, 158, 159
V 1, 3, 39, 50–51, 62, 91, 115,
260 VI 9, 104, 179, 181 VII 202,
254, 302 n.46 VIII 268, 319 IX
193 X 78, 190, 333 n.28
"Joy's City" I 26
Jubilate Agno VIII 279
Judaean, The IV 124
"Judgement: Helwig the
Underrated, Souster the
Overrated" V 246
"Julian Huxley, Robert Graves and
the Mythologies" V 111
Julian the Magician IX 231, 232,
237, 243
"July" IX 165–66
"July 15" VII 107
"July First 1867" I 8, 194, 198
"July Man" VI 57, 62
"June" IX 165–66
Jung, Carl Gustav VI 176, 228 VII
284, 309 n.135 IX 11, 94, 96, 97,
198, 236, 242, 250, 253

"Just About Forty Degrees Off
  Course" X 310
"Justice" IV 197–98 VI 204
Juvenal VIII 95

Kafka, Franz V 150 VI 292 VIII 25
  X 190, 355
"Kahoutek" VI 56
Kamboureli, Smaro VIII 281 X 73,
  83, 124, 206, 261 quoted 117,
  122, 130
Kamouraska VI 178
"Kamsack" X 311
"Kanata" I 150
Kane, Sean IX 200
Kant, Immanuel VIII 373 X 290
Kareda, Urjo VII 207
"Karl Marx" V 183
"Karloff Poem" VI 206
"Katherine Mansfield" III 24
Kavanaugh, Patrick VII 86
Kearns, Lionel IV 261 V 86 VI 96
  VII 269 VIII 28, 30, 122, 192, 288,
  369 quoted 141, 272 IX 194
Keats, John I 11, 133, 136, 139,
  140–41, 167, 187 II 13, 17, 18,
  30, 41, 138–40, 142, 159, 168,
  173 n.15, 197, 239, 258 quoted
  18 III 11, 21, 46, 64, 114 IV 10,
  20, 72, 85, 91, 94, 128, 131, 153,
  176 VI 31, 47, 90, 94, 287 VII 86,
  89, 201–02, 220, 271 VIII 149 IX
  20, 53, 75 n.56, 192 quoted 111
  X 36, 284
"Keepers" IV 60 n.40
"Keewaydin Poems" V 113–14
"Keine Lazarovitch 1870–1959" V
  178–79
Keith, W.J. II 14, 198, 199, 200,
  222, 223, 260 quoted 14, 20 VII
  62, 201–02, 217 X quoted 292–93

Keitner, Wendy VI 104, 105–06,
  109, 155 n.2, 156 n.7, 160 n.55,
  162 n.81
Kelley, Thomas VII 226
"Kelligrew's Soiree, The" III 131
Kennedy, Leo II 148 quoted 148 III
  2, 10, 21, 26, 27, 46, 116 quoted
  26–27, 46 IV 11, 12, 17–18, 32,
  78, 124, 131, 175, 180, 199, 232,
  234, 236, 237, 238 VI 9, 91, 92,
  223 VII 28 VIII 121 IX 192
Kenner, Hugh V 150 quoted 150
Kent, David A. VI 66 n.12
Kenyon Review VI 27, 35
Kepler, Johannes VI 45
Kermode, Frank VI 184
Kern, Bliem VIII 40
Kerouac, Jack V 51 VIII 25, 33, 114,
  151, 162 X 24
Kerrisdale Elegies VIII 160, 165–67,
  169, 174 X 164
Kertes, Joseph X quoted 30, 58 n.84
Kertzer, J.M. VI 38, 67 n.23 quoted
  68 n.25 IX 197 X quoted 87–88,
  206
Keyes, Mary IX 194 quoted 194
"Keynote" IX 103
Khlebnikov, Velemir (Victor) VIII
  23, 60
"Kids and Crossovers" VII 196
Killdeer, The VII 15, 195, 206, 224
"KILLER WHALE" VIII 83
"Kim, at half an inch" VIII 384
Kinch, Martin X 267
Kindred of the Wild, The II 200,
  223
King, Bishop VI 287
King, Carlyle X 191
King, Mary Perry II 80, 89
King, William Lyon Mackenzie II
  28 IV 20, 198

King of Egypt, King of Dreams IX 232

"King of the Jews" V 198

King Whistle! VII 197, 208, 230–31

Kingdom of Absence IX 189, 193, 194, 201–04

"Kingdom of Absence" IX 190, 202

Kingston British Whig, The I 160, 169, 195

Kingston Commercial Advertiser I 169

Kingston Daily News I 161, 169, 195

Kipling, Rudyard I 8, 91 II 8, 29, 33–34, 197, 239–40, 243 quoted 34 IV 72

Kirby, William I 168, 200 n.2

"Kispiox Indian Village" VII 153

"Kiss, A" IV 162 n.23

"Kissing Bug" VI 211 n.16

Kissing Goldfish of Siam, The X 340, 345, 375, 384–88

"Kite Is a Victim, A" X 41

"Kites, The" IV 37

Kiyooka, Roy VIII 125, 232, 240 X 132, 133, 281 quoted 70

Klee, Paul VII 198, 225 IX 89

Klein, A.M. III 83, 150, 151, 166 IV 5, 8, 11, 13, 18, 21, 22–24, 32, 38, 69, 72, 78, 110, 176, 180, 199, 202, 207, 232, 238 V 79, 91, 152, 153, 169–71, 172, 173, 174, 175–77, 214 n.64, 216 n.75, 281, 282, 287, 310–11, 314, 315 quoted 150, 152, 171, 315 VI 10, 42, 91, 92, 93, 107, 186, 208, 223, 229, 253, 255 VII 85, 138, 304 n.70 IX 19, 204 X 24, 29

Klein Symposium IV 123, 132–33

Klinck, Carl F. I 88, 89 II 37 quoted 37 III 121 IV 40

Knight, Charles I 120

Knight, W.F. Jackson VI 205, 213 n.39 quoted 201, 214 n.46

Knightley, Philip IX 265

Knister, Raymond II 34, 36–37, 243, 246 quoted 36–37 III 1, 2, 6, 9–12, 13, 14, 64, 116, 167, 170 IV 70, 103, 235, 237 V 34 VI 87 See also Dent, W. Redvers

"Knitter's Prayer" VI 259

Koch, Vivienne VI quoted 98

Koestler, Arthur IV 202–03 IX 199

Kogawa, Joy III 85

KonfessIons of an ElizAbeThan Fan Dancer VIII 265, 286

"konkreet vizual" VIII 62

"Kookaburra's Song, The" VII 119

Kootenay Highlander, The V 28

Koran I 25

Kostelanetz, Richard VIII quoted 267–68

Kovaly, Hedy V 197

Kreisel, Henry X 192

Kristeva, Julia VIII 59, 203, 277 quoted 54–55, 57, 195, 196 X 79, 176

Kroetsch, Paul X 70

Kroetsch, Robert V 91 VII 29, 141–42 VIII 30, 195, 204, 206, 366, 370 quoted 275–76 IX 175, 234, 235 X 8, 13–15, 69–186, 200, 285 interviewed 70, 71, 73, 75, 77, 81, 90, 94–95, 96, 97–98, 116, 117, 136, 154

"Kropotkin" VII 293–94, 301 n.35

Kropotkin, Peter, Prince VII 16–17, 255, 289, 292–93, 301 n.33

"Kropotkin Poems, The" VII 16, 289, 291–94, 299 n.3, 301 n.35, 306 n.100

Kubose, Gyomay M. VIII quoted 56

Kuropatwa, Joy III 10 quoted 10

LSD Leacock, The X 339, 345, 350–56

Laakso, Lila III 121

Laakso, Raymond III 121

"Laboratory" III 164–65, 182

Labour and the Angel II 237, 252

"Labour and the Angel" II 267–69

"Labrie's Wife" II 271

Labyrinths of Voice: Conversations with Robert Kroetsch X 70, 75, 76–77, 79, 83, 84, 85, 86, 92–94, 96, 97–98, 100, 124, 125, 155, 174

Lacan, Jacques VII 268, 273, 283 VIII 172, 280 X 162, 181 n.73

Lachance, Bernard VIII 30

Laconics III 163, 166, 169, 170, 171, 172, 174, 177, 181, 183, 184 V 2

Ladies and Gentlemen . . . Mr. Leonard Cohen X 23

"Ladies and Gentlemen, Stompin' Tom Connors!" VII 88–89

Ladoo, Harold IX 211–12

"Lady" IX 203

Lady Chatterley's Lover IV 174, 206

"Lady Lazarus" IX 72 n.47

"Lady of Shalott, The" I 187–88

Laforgue, Jules II 242 IV 10, 33 VI 227

Laing, R.D. VII 255, 256, 301 n.33 VIII 373

Lake, The III 62

"Lake" IV 33

"Lake Harvest" III 29

"Lake Isle of Innisfree, The" IV 242

Lake Lyrics and Other Poems II 28, 30, 48

"Lake of Death, The" IX 240, 259, 260

"Lake of Dreams, The" IX 240, 259–60

"Lake Ontario" VII 212

"Lake Song" VI 291, 292

"Lakeshore" IV 19, 20–21, 179, 181, 183, 209, 211

Lamb, Charles I 82

"Lambton November" IV 33

"Lambton Riding Woods" V 8–9, 257–58

"Lament" (Webb) VII 263

"Lament, A" (Avison) VI 29, 65

"Lament for Robert Kennedy" VII 170–71

"Lament for the Dorsets" VII 166, 173

Lampman, Archibald I 169 II 7, 8, 9, 11, 12, 15, 16, 17–19, 22, 23, 18, 29, 38, 81, 82, 91, 195, 200, 201, 202, 216, 224, 236, 237, 238, 239, 240, 241, 243–44, 263, 266, 267 quoted 16 III 1, 3, 9, 23, 24, 29, 64, 76, 172, 184 IV 7, 10, 20, 70, 82, 85, 86, 97, 109, 177, 178, 234 V 77, 84, 149 VI 29, 45, 145, 146, 148, 177, 227, 228 quoted 145 VII 28 IX 3, 88, 92 X 284, 343

"Lampman Poems, The" IX 86, 117–18, 121

Lampman Symposium, The II 143, 151

Lampman's Kate: Late Love Poems of Archibald Lampman, 1887–1897 II 143, 146

Lampman's Sonnets 1884–1889 II 143

"Land of Pallas, The" II 142, 168

"Land Where He Dwells In, The" V 321

"Landlady" VI 247

Landor, Walter Savage I 136 II 242

"Landscape of John Sutherland, A" V 314–15

"Landscape of Love" VI 242

Landscape with Rain VI 89, 106, 107, 142–45, 148

Lane, M. Travis VIII 205

Lane, Patrick V 151 VI 10, 229 VII 6 VIII 168 IX 1, 2, 11, 12–13 quoted 12, 13

Lane, Red VII 29 VIII 114, 118–19, 134, 161, 162, 169 quoted 132 IX 133, 135, 137, 148

"Language as I Used to Believe in It" V 323

Lanman, Charles I 75, 76, 79, 81, 85

Lanthier, Philip IX quoted 146

Lao-tse V 189 X 133

Lapointe, Jeanne IV 218

Lapointe, Paul-Marie IX 85–86, 123

"Lapis Lazuli" VI 101

"Lapwing You Are. Lapwing He — A Note on Icarus in Myth and Poetry" X 212

"Largest Life, The" II 158

"Largest Life, III, The" II 163

"Lass in Wonderland, A" IV 206

"Last Barrier, The" II 200, 208, 210

Last Barrier and Other Stories, The II 199, 200

"Last Bison, The" I 134, 149–50

"Last Child" II 153

"Last Climb, The" III 95

"Last Day" IX 65–66, 75 n.57

"last daze uv th hous" VIII 84

"Last Experiment of Dr. Brugge, The" VI 86

"Last Poem" IX 63–64, 65, 67

"Last Rites" IV 185, 209, 211, 215

"Last Waltz, The" VII 108–09

"Late August" IX 53–54, 75 n.56, 75 n.57

"Late Movies with Skyler" VIII 392

"Late Night" IX 59

"Later in Belleville: Career" IX 69 n.15

Latham, Alan IV 175

Latham, George IV 124

Lauder, Scott VII 93

"Laughing Corn" III 47

Laughing Rooster, The V 210 n.31, 231 n.62

Laurence, Margaret III 14 VIII 25, 92, 114, 162 IX 88 X 5, 78, 161, 311

"Laurentian Shield" IV 19, 21, 179, 182, 188, 191, 203–06, 208, 209

Laurier, Sir Wilfrid II 28

"Law I Love Is Major Mover, The" VIII 296, 297

Lawrence, D.H. II 98 III 11, 69, 81, 95 IV 174, 176, 192 V 81, 150, 179–80, 216 n.79, 219 n.87 VI 29, 30 VII 9, 80, 87, 89, 107, 139 VIII 193 IX 165, 197 X 343, 371–72

Lawrence, T.E. IX 12, 262, 263, 264, 265

"Lay of the Last Mariner" VII 146

Layers 1–13 VIII 135

Layton, Betty VII 265

Layton, Irving II quoted 149 IV 13, 36, 123, 124, 131, 132, 139, 176, 236, 262, 271 n.13 V 2–3, 4, 5, 12–16, 19, 39, 76, 77, 79, 81, 82, 84–85, 87, 89, 93, 94–95, 122, 124, 125, 238, 240, 241, 242 quoted 14, 15, 84–85, 239 VI 33,

48, 87, 92, 93, 105, 107, 128
quoted 48 VII 7, 9, 10, 13, 24, 27,
28, 38, 84, 85, 86, 87, 90, 136,
139, 140, 141, 265, 268, 289 VIII
7, 8, 121, 122, 123, 159 IX 19,
85, 87, 91, 97, 138, 139, 147 X
24, 24, 27, 28, 29, 192, 197, 284,
343
"Layton Now and Then: Our
Critical Assumptions" V 85
"Layton on the Carpet" V 85, 95,
157
Lazarovitch, Keine V 144, 145,
163, 164, 175, 177–78, 179
Lazarovitch, Moishe V 144, 163,
167, 174–75, 177, 179, 200, 216
n.76
"Lazarus" II 51–53, 54, 67
Leacock, Stephen II 243, 272 IV
124 IX 120
leaf leaf/s VIII 190, 201, 212–15
League for Social Reconstruction,
The IV 174
League of Canadian Poets III 64 V
238 VI 89, 225 IX 2
"Leather Jacket" VI 258
Leaven of Malice I 75, 88
"Leaves" II 253
"Leaving Greensleeves" X 42
Leavis, F.R. IV 92 VII 201–02, 259
LEBANON VOICES VIII 32
Lecker, Robert IV 40 VI 38, 286 VIII
200–01 X 85, 94, 100, 110
quoted 89, 90, 92, 95, 103, 106,
114, 116, 126
"Leda" IV 91
"Leda and the Swan" VI 143, 306
VII 259, 264 X 40, 211
"Leda in Stratford, Ont." VI 303,
305
Ledger, The X 13, 14, 73

"Ledger, The" X 80, 96, 104, 106,
109–10, 112, 113, 148, 150, 157
Lee, Alvin VII 199, 204–05,
208–09, 218
Lee, Dennis III 116 V 86, 91 VII 11,
137, 142 VIII 8, 15, 30, 31,
33–34, 369 quoted 374 IX 1, 2,
8–10, 12, 17, 20, 98, 233
Lee, H.D.C. II quoted 88
"Lee Side in a Gale" VII 61
"Left Hand and Hiroshima, The"
IX 246, 249
"Left Hand Exercise, The" VII 250
"Legacies" IX 151
*Legacy of Government Spending,
The* VIII 92
Le Galliene, Richard II 80
"Legend" VI 118–19, 120, 121, 123
"Legend of Chileeli, The" I 149
LeGuin, Ursula VII 273
Leland, Doris III 69
Le Moyne, Jean IX 210
Lenin, V.I. III 65, 79–80 quoted 65,
79
Lennon, John X 31
"Lens" VI 287, 298
Leonard Cohen VIII 365–66
Leone, Sergio VIII 368
Leopardi, Giacomo IV 216, 217
Le Pan, Douglas IX 20
Leprohon, Rosanna I 81
Leslie, Frank I 22
Lessing, Doris VI 228, 264
"Lesson" (F.R. Scott) IV 209
"Lesson, The" (D.C. Scott) II 252,
256
"Let me swallow it whole and be
strong" X 325
"Let Us Assert Affirmatives" VI 134
Let Us Compare Mythologies X 16,
21, 24, 26, 27, 35–37, 39, 43

Let Us Now Praise Famous Men
VIII 225

"Letter" X 37

Letter, Charles Heavysege to
Charles Lanman, 12 Oct. 1860 I
75, 76–77

Letter, Charles Heavysege to
Charles Lanman, 2 Oct. 1865 I
75, 76, 79, 81

Letter, Charles Mair to *The Globe*
(Toronto), n.d. I 124–25

Letter, Charles Sangster to David
Gibson, 24 Nov. 1875 I 161

Letter, Charles Sangster to W.D.
Lighthall, 8 July 1888 I 162

Letter, Charles Sangster to W.D.
Lighthall, 18 July 1888 I 184

Letter, Charles Sangster to W.D.
Lighthall, 15 Nov. 1888 I 161–63

Letter, Charles Sangster to W.D.
Lighthall, 12 Mar. 1889 I 163

Letter, Charles Sangster to W.D.
Lighthall, 14 July 1891 I 163–64

Letter, Charles Sangster to William
Kirby, 30 Apr. 1886 I 168

Letter, D.G. Jones to E.D. Blodgett,
13 June 1982 IX 85, 88

Letter, E.J. Pratt to Dorothy Livesay,
5 Dec. 1935 III 4

Letter, Earle Birney to E.K. Brown,
30 May 1941 V 34

Letter, Earle Birney to Lois Wilson,
24 Jan. 1956 V 49

Letter in *First Statement* (Layton) V
152

Letter in *The Canadian Forum*
(Layton) V 152–53

Letter, Irving Layton to Wynne
Francis, 12 June 1967 V 222 n.98

Letter, Irving Layton to Wynne
Francis, Summer 1967 V 195

"Letter on Poetry and Belief, A" IX
97, 123

Letter, Patrick Lane to George
Woodcock, n.d. IX 133

Letter, Raymond Knister to
Elizabeth Frankfurth, 19 Nov.
1925 III 20

Letter, Raymond Knister to Myrtle
Knister, 11 May 1928 III 27

Letter, Raymond Souster to Cid
Corman, 15 Aug. 1954 V
246–47

Letter, Raymond Souster to Cid
Corman, 8 Aug. 1976 V 269 n.44

Letter, Raymond Souster to Louis
Dudek, 23 June 1951 V 77

Letter, Raymond Souster to Robert
Creeley, 27 Mar. 1954 V 270
n.51

Letter, Raymond Souster to Robert
Creeley, 12 June 1954 V 247–48,
249, 255

Letter, Raymond Souster to Robert
Creeley, 30 Oct. 1954 V 270 n.53

Letter, Raymond Souster to Robert
Creeley, n.d. [22 Nov. 1954] V
255

"Letter to a Conceivable Great-
Grandson" V 33

"Letter to a Cuzco Priest" V 52–53

"Letter to a Friend's Wife" X 73

"Letter to Be Opened Later" X 236

"Letter to Larry Sealy, 1962, A" X
306

"Letter to My Children" VI 16,
286, 297, 302

"Letter to My Children: Postscript"
VI 286, 302

"Letter to My Redheaded Son" VII
22

"Letter to My Sister, A" VII 101

Letter, W.W.E. Ross to Ralph
  Gustafson, 14 May 1943 III 168
"Letters" IX 55
"Letters & Other Worlds" VIII 385,
  386
"Letters from a Rainy Season" VIII
  291–92
Letters from Geeksville VIII 118
Letters from the Savage Mind IX
  135, 142, 147, 148–53, 161, 166
Letters Home VIII 11, 265, 272
"Letters in Canada 1951: Poetry" II
  246
"Letters in Canada 1955: Poetry" V
  88
"Letters to Margaret Atwood" VII
  256
"Letters to Salonika" X 137, 138,
  140
Levenson, Christopher VI 106
  quoted 106 X 205
Lever, Bernice III 72
Levertov, Denise VI 27, 33 VII 255,
  266, 301 n.31 VIII 172, 192 X 9
Levi, Primo X quoted 46
"Leviathan in a Pool" VI 258
Levin, Harry II quoted 159
Levinson Prize VI 174
Levi-Strauss, Claude X 175
Lewalski, Barbara Kiefer VI 191,
  192 quoted 191
Lewes, George Henry II 161, 175
  n.48
Lewis, Cecil Day (Nicholas Blake) II
  17 III 4, 65 IV 6, 177 V 31 VI 228
Lewis, David IV 124, 126, 175 V
  169
Lewis, Jane X 72
Lewis, Sinclair IV 235
Lewis, Wyndham V 1 VIII 23 IX 9,
  222 n.50

Lewisohn, Ludwig IV 22, 125,
  131
LIBERATING SKIES VIII 63
Liberté IX 190
Lies X 238, 289, 290, 292, 294,
  317, 318–25
Life VI 93
"Life and Letters" II 28
"Life and Times" VII 100
Life in the Clearings X 181
"Life Notes" X 340, 376
Life Sentence X 194, 200, 254,
  264–69
"Light" VIII 391
"Light (I)" VI 58
Lighthall, William Douw I 85, 161,
  162, 163, 164, 165, 168, 172,
  174, 175, 184 quoted 85, 172 II
  195, 225 n.5, 236
"Like a Canadian" X 311
"Like a Mother Demented" V 190,
  191, 194
"Like a River" X 290
"Like an Eddy" V 55
"Like an Old Proud King in a
  Parable" III 76 IV 34, 236,
  252–53, 268
"Like Mother, Like Daughter" III
  129
"Lilies at Mount St. Helens" VI 153
"Lily Bed, The" I 56–57 II 244
Linden, Marjorie III 121
Linder, Norma West IX quoted 145,
  146
Lindsay, Vachel VI 29, 91 VII 138
Line VIII 281 X 206
"Line and Form" V 102–03
"Line Telling" VIII 305
"Lines for a Peace" V 32
"Lines from My Grandfather's
  Journal" X 38, 46

"Lines in Memory of Edmund
Morris" II 253, 258, 259–60,
264, 266
"Lions" III 180
Lions in the Way: A Discursive
History of the Oslers VI 15, 16,
278, 279, 285, 306–10
Lipari, Joseph X quoted 87
Li Po X 140
Lippincott (publishers) II 190
Listen to the Wind VII 196, 202,
206–07, 224
"Listen, the sea" X 239–40
"Listening" VI 49 VII 163
"Listening to the Radio: For
Michael Ondaatje" X 132
"listnr, th" VIII 85
Literary Garland, The I 160
Literary History of Canada IV 12,
17, 40, 80, 180–81, 182 VIII 35 X
8, 205–06
"Literary Studies in English" V 288
Literary Theory: An Introduction
VIII 45
Literature and Revolution V 31
Literature and the Press: A History
of Printing, Printed Media, and
Their Relation to Literature V
78, 82, 92, 105, 108–09, 118
Little Anthology of Canadian Poets,
A IV 32 VI 87
"Little Bat at Last Broken" V 263
"Little Blue Eyes and Golden Hair"
II 35
"Little Gidding" X 307
"Little Girls" VI 245–46
"Little Men Slip into Death" VI
295, 298
"Little Milliner, The" II 270
"Little Night Journey" IX 107,
114

"Little Pome for Yur Fingertips, A"
VIII 286
"Little Prairie Pictures" V 297
"Little Stranger at Rideau Hall,
The" I 194
"Little Wren, The" I 140
"Live Bait" VIII 384
Live Songs X 22, 31, 42
Livesay, Dorothy I 21, 30, 56 III 1,
2, 4, 6, 10, 12–15, 21, 22, 24, 26,
27, 28, 29, 33, 135, 150, 151,
184 quoted 2, 13, 28, 33 IV 12,
13, 78, 236, 238 V 2, 34, 90, 94,
100, 112, 240 quoted 90, 100 VI
32, 46, 92, 107 quoted 37, 282
VII 24, 28, 32–33, 55, 67, 255,
265 VIII 31 quoted 32 IX 91, 93,
137, 138 quoted 91. See also
Katherine Bligh
"Living" VIII 230
Lloyd, Charles I 83
"Loading, The" III 39
"Loading Boxcars" IX 161
"Local Grains of Sand" VII 200
Local Pride, A V 257, 260
Locke, John IX 205–06
"Locksley Hall" I 190
"Locus Solus" VIII 128, 133
Logan, J.D. I 86, 191 quoted 86,
191 II 245, 249 quoted 90
"Logos" V 181
London, Jack III 115 VII 79, 80
London Free Press, The I 21 IX 142
London Mercury, The III 115
"London Night" V 322
London Observer, The VI 222
London Times, The II 87
"Lone Bather" III 83
"Lonely Land, The" III 168 IV 12,
92, 234, 235, 239, 242–43, 250,
250–52, 277 n.101 VI 8, 93

"Lonely Lovers" VI 41
"Long Continual Argument with
    Myself, A" X 310, 324
"Long Line of Baby Caterpillars,
    A" VII 287
Long Poem Anthology, The VIII
    366
"Long Weekend of Louis Riel,
    The" VIII 309
Longfellow, Henry Wadsworth I 25,
    44, 57, 61, 65, n.56, 78, 167,
    172, 178 II 13, 37, 197, 254
Longinus VIII 42 quoted 43, 44
"Looking at Painting" V 283
"Looking for Ebbe" VIII 147
"Looking for Nancy" VII 103, 105,
    106, 107
"Looking for Strawberries in June"
    V 322
"Loon" III 9
Loosely Tied Hands: An
    Experiment in Punk X 340,
    371-73, 376
"Lorca" III 82
Lorca, Federico García VI 228
"Lord's Plan, The" VI 262
Lorne Pierce Medal II 81, 192, 238
    III 62, 113 V 29, 37
lost angel mining company VIII 83
"Lost and Found" I 190, 193, 199
Lost & Found: Uncollected Poems
    V
"Lost Books and Dead Letters" VI
    195, 207
"Lost Gentleman, The" III 25, 39,
    44
"Lost in the Badlands" VII 180
"Lost Leader, The" V 45
"Lost Soul, A" VI 198-99
Lothian, John X 191
"Louis Dudek" VIII 145

Louis Dudek & Raymond Souster
    V 91-93, 243, 264, 247
Louis Dudek: Texts & Essays V 78,
    91, 123, 124
"Louis Dudek Writes" V 100
"Louisbourg Fortress
    Reconstructed" VII 165
"Love" X 350
love: a book of remembrances VIII
    266, 299-300, 302, 305, 325
Love Affair VIII 303
"Love at Roblin Lake" VII 165
Love in a Burning Building VII 171
"Love in the Valley" II 258
"Love Letter" X 301
"Love Poem" (Waddington) V 319
"Love Poem [For we can live now,
    love . . .]" (Page) VI 247
"Love Poem [Remembering you and
    reviewing . . .]" (Page) VI 249
"Love Poems" VIII 325
"Love Song of J. Alfred Prufrock,
    The" IV 73, 139, 141, 142, 145,
    146, 247, 268
"Love, Stay for Me" I 32-33
Love the Conquering Worm V 216
    n.76
"Love, the Little Cavalier" I 194
Love Where the Nights Are Long
    VIII 134
"love yr hair on th pillow foldid in
    dreems" VIII 68-70
Lovell, John I 160
"Lovely the Country of Peacocks"
    VIII 376
Lovely Treachery of Words, The:
    Essays Selected and New X 73,
    85
"Lover Who Knows, A" V 319
"Lovers" V 17, 317, 318
"Lovers in the Park" VII 147

"Love's Morning Lark" I 183
"Love's New Era" I 183
"Loving She Stood Apart" IX 152
"Low Tide on Grand Pré" II 22, 31–32, 91, 96, 101–02, 118–19
Low Tide on Grand Pré: A Book of Lyrics II 79, 80, 86–87, 90
Lowell, Amy III 181 IV 30 VI 91
Lowell, James Russell II 81
Lowell, Robert VI 101, 233 VIII 207
Lowey, Mark X 190–91
Lowry, Malcolm III 65 V 29, 40 VII 145 VIII 370 IX 193
Lowther, Pat VI 229 IX 140
Lucas, Alec II 199, 200 VII 90–91
"Lucifus Enamoured" IV 104, 108
"Luck of a Canuck, The" V 148
Lucretius IX 216
"Lullaby" VI 292
"Lumumba Arrested" VII 49–51
Lundy's Lane and Other Poems II 238
Lure of the Wild, The II 199
"Lycidas" IX 205
Lye, John VII 144
Lynch, Faye V 215 n.66
Lynn, Helen II 143, 171 n.1
"Lynn Valley: Depression" X 303, 307
"Lyric, A" II 32
"Lyric Craft of Miriam Waddington, The" V 289, 306–07
"Lyric to the Isles" I 181
Lyrical Ballads VIII 150
Lyrics of Earth (1896) II 143
Lyrics of Earth: Sonnets and Ballads (1925) II 143
Lyrics Unromantic VI 87, 97

"Ma Belle Canadienne" II 78

Macbeth, Madge II 245
Macbeth I 77, 83, 167 III 131 X 224
MacCallum, Hugh III 171 VI quoted 35–36, 101, 284 IX 194 quoted 24–25, 194–95
"Macchu Picchu" IX 164–65
Macdonald, Goodridge VI quoted 282
MacDonald, J.E.H. III 115, 168
Macdonald, Sir John A. I 26, 105, 161, 198 quoted 105 II 236 VI 307 IX 205
Macdonald, R. St. J. IV 183
MacDonald, Wilson III 21, 27 IV 177, 236, 241
MacEwen, Gwendolyn V 243 VI 96–97, 229 VIII 31 IX 1, 2, 10–12, 13, 20 quoted 10–11 X 8
"MacEwen's Muse" IX 11, 239
MacFarlane, David VI quoted 107 X quoted 346
MacFarlane, Roderick I 130
Machar, Agnes Maule II quoted 144
Macherey, Pierre VII 268
"Machinery" III 184
"Mack" III 45
MacKay, Charles I 171
MacKay, L.A. II 34, 37, 123 n.43 quoted 37, 91, 111 V quoted 36–37
MacKendrick, Louis III 121, 123 X 88
Mackenzie, William Lyon I 159 VI 307 IX 205, 207
MacKinnon, Brian X 91 quoted 70, 75, 97, 136
Macklem, Michael V 261
MacLaren, I.S. IV 252–53
Maclean's IV 186 VI 224 X 25, 72
MacLeish, Archibald IV 254 V 42, 315

MacLennan, Hugh V 39 VII 304 n.70 X 78, 94

MacLow, Jackson VIII 28

Maclure, Millar VI quoted 233

MacMaster, R.D. X 203

MacMechan, Archibald I 198 quoted 198 II quoted 90

Macmillan (publisher) VI 222, 293

MacMurchy, Archibald I 198 quoted 198

MacNeice, Louis II 17 III 65 IV 6 VI 90, 111, 154 X 190

Macpherson, Jay III 63, 131 IV 34 V 112 VI 7, 10, 14, 16–18, 229, 280 VII 15, 195, 200, 201, 203, 205, 206, 207, 218, 237 n.43, 258 IX 17, 19, 20, 69 n.8, 191, 193, 233 X 8

Macri, Francis M. VI 267 n.32

"Macumba: Brazil" VI 261

"Mad Boy's Song" IV 87

"Mad Gardener to the Sea" VII 287

"Mad Mother, The" IX 31–32, 35

"Madman Smart" X 242

"Madness of Our Polity, The" X 233

Maeterlinck, Maurice VII 202

Magazine Digest V 280

Maggs, W. Randall III 114–15

Magic Animals: Selected Poems Old and New IX 12, 232, 241, 245, 261–62

Magic House and Other Poems, The II 237

Magritte, René V 314

Maimonides V 197

Mair, Charles I 8, 9, 10, 11, 12, 13, 15, 16, 81, 170, 168 II 7, 8, 13 IV 22

"Make a Wish" VIII 230

Make This Your Canada: A Review of C.C.F. History and Policy IV 175

Makers of Canada series II 238

"Making" VII 287

"Making Literature Hum" IV 84

Making of Personality, The II 85, 96

"Making Poems" V 99

"Malachi" V 166

Malahat Review, The VI 234, 264 IX 136, 144 X 341

"Malcolm's Katie" I 24, 25, 27, 29, 40, 57–59, 65 n.56 II 201 III 66

"Malediction, The" V 222 n.97

Mallarmé, Stéphane IV 10, 14, 33, 139, 263 VI 226 VIII 6, 55, 282

Malle, Louis VIII 368

Mallinson, Jean VI 234, 267 n.30 quoted 234 VII 271 IX 6–7, 8, 69 n.8, 71 n.43, 144, 145 quoted 5, 6, 7, 143

"Mammorial Stunzas for Aimee Simple McFarcin" V 51

"Man and Nature" II 157

Man and Superman III 123

"Man and the Machine, The" III 129

"Man and Wife" V 219 n.87

Man in Yellow Boots, The VIII 135, 137

"Man Who Dreamed of Faeryland, The" IV 242

"Man with a Hole in His Throat, The" IX 57

"Man with One Small Hand" VI 250

man with seven toes, the VIII 365, 384

"Mandan Massacre" VIII 21

Mandel, Eli IV 239, 240 V 149, 150, 151, 157, 158, 159, 160,

175, 211 n.43, 213 n.60 quoted
158, 159 VI 68 n.29, 97, 185
quoted 35, 42 VII 15, 16, 24, 28,
85, 90, 91, 92, 95, 104, 112, 137,
195, 200, 201, 206, 265, 299
n.11 VIII 25, 205, 277 IX 20, 28,
87, 92, 197, 234 quoted 92, 237,
238 X 8, 9–10, 25, 27, 81, 132,
189–277, 343, 346 quoted 74,
84, 96, 168, 175, 177 n.21, 189,
190, 191, 193, 199, 202–03, 212,
250–51, 254, 264, 345
Mandelshtam, Nadezhda V 197
"Manifesto" IV 29
Manitoba Arts Council awards IX
136
Manitoba Arts Review IV 237
"Manitoba Childe Roland" III 47
Mann, Thomas V 150 X 190,
197
"Manner of Suicide" X 237
"Manny" X 383
"Man's Future" II 159
Mansbridge, Francis VI 65–66 n.2,
66 n.8 quoted 34
Mansfield, Katherine III 64, 65,
95
Mantegna, Andrea VI 45
"Many as Two" VI 56
Mao Tse-Tung V 185
"Maple Leaf Forever, The" VII
210–11
"Mappemounde" V 33, 41
"Maps" VII 210
"March" I 35 VI 61
"March, April, June" VI 282, 302
"March Morning" VI 59
"Marché Municipale" V 194
Marchessault, Jovette VIII 195
Marconi, Guglielmo III 128, 135,
140

"Margaret Avison: The
Dumbfoundling [sic]" VI 25, 27,
29–30
"Margot" I 39
*Marguerite; or, The Isle of Demons,
and Other Poems* I 81
"Marian at the Pentecostal
Meeting" VII 101
"Mariline" I 187–89, 193
Marin, John IX 89, 100, 116
"Marina" X 236
"Marine Conjecture" VI 120
"Marine Life" VII 252
Maritain, Jacques V quoted 160
Marlatt, Daphne IV 236 V 86, 91
VII 273 VIII 5, 13, 14, 281, 369
quoted 190, 192–94, 195, 196,
190, 193–94, 196, 208–49 X 81,
84, 148
Marlowe, Christopher IV 128, 139
VI 213 n.40
Márquez, Gabriel García VIII 370,
374 IX 236, 252 X 78
Marquis, Thomas Gutherie I 85,
191, 198 quoted 86, 191, 198
Marriage of Heaven and Hell, The I
50 II 214
"Marring of Malyn, The" II 111
Marriot, Anne III 62, 65, 66 V 34,
280 VI 222
"Marrying the Hangman" IX 57
"Marsh, Hawk" IX 57–58
Marshall, John II quoted 87, 145–46
Marshall, Tom II 22, 92, 246, 248
quoted 86 III 70 quoted 70 IV
234 V 255, 298, 299, 309 quoted
10, 18, 255, 298, 309 VI 67 n.23,
96, 234 quoted 37, 160 n.56 VII
56, 141, 144, 276
"Marsyas" II 100
Martin, George I 79, 81, 85

Martin, M.H. V 35

Martin, Mary I 30

"Martinigram" IV 207

Marty, Sid VI 10 IX 140, 175

Martyrology, The V 262 VIII 7, 12, 72, 265, 266, 271, 273, 274, 275, 276, 277, 278, 279, 280, 281, 282, 283, 285, 291, 297, 298, 302, 303, 305, 306, 312–39 X 84, 131

"Martyrology of Saint And, The" VIII 315

Marvell, Andrew I 25 IV 73, 181, 216, 217, 263 VI 15, 218, 287, 295 VII 262, 263–64, 280 IX 53

"Marvellous Work, The" II 215

"Marvell's Garden" VII 264, 280, 287

Marx, Karl II 15, 268 III 80, 81 IV 17, 75 V 3, 81, 150, 154, 168, 172, 179, 183, 184, 186, 197, 214 n.64, 217 n.82, 246–47 VI 249 X 148, 151

"Mary" V 197

Mary Midnight X 202

"Mary Midnight" X 226–27, 228

"Mary Midnight's Prologue" X 226–27

Masefield, John II 109, 242 III 114, 115 V 240, 250

"Maschil of Abraham: A Prayer When He Was in the Cave" IV 149–52

Mask in Place, The VIII 161, 162, 163, 164

"Masqueraders" VI 258

Masses [Toronto] III 61, 77, 78

"Master of the Isles, The" II 109

Master-Works of Canadian Authors I 132

Mathers, Kay IV 44

Mathews, Robin I 30 II 15 IV 239 VI quoted 99 VII 56, 269 VIII 371 quoted 161–62 IX 216

Matisse, Henri IX 89

Matrix IX 146

"Matrona: Dorothy Livesay" [interview] III 72, 88–89

Matthews, John I 133, 151 n.1 II 247 IV 132

Maugham, W. Somerset IX 203

Maupassant, Guy de III 24

Mauve VIII 249

Maximus Poems, The V 103, 247, 258, 262

May, James Boyer V quoted 131 n.78 VII 268–69

"May Queen, The" I 140

Mayne, Seymour III 66 IV 132–33 V 86, 151, 161 quoted 151 VIII 123, 168 IX 135, 137, 140

"Mayor's Papers, The" X 230, 231

Mays, John Bentley VII 16, 270–71, 307 n.101 VIII quoted 199

"Maze, The" VI 260, 261

McCabe and Mrs. Miller X 22, 45

McCaffery, Steve VIII 30, 41, 57, 265, 275, 281 quoted 28–29, 37–38, 270, 280

McCarthy, Brian X 203 quoted 28

McCarthy, Bryan V 151 VII 28, 47, 55

McCarthy, Cavan VIII 264

McCarthy, Dermot VI 8, 12

McClelland, Jack V 207 n.4

McClelland and Stewart VI 28

McClung, Nellie X 6

McClure, Michael VIII 29, 270

McColm, Sheila VI quoted 36

McCombs, Judith IX 28, 73 n.50, 74 n.53

McCourt, Edward X 191, 257

McDougall, Robert II 247
McDougall, William I 123, 125, 126
"McEacheren" I 194
McFadden, David IV 236 VIII 123, 125, 264
McGee, Thomas D'Arcy I 81, 142
McGill Daily, The IV 124, 231, 241 V 76, 80, 95, 213 n.63, 214 n.65
McGill Daily Literary Supplement, The III 166 IV 193, 231
McGill Fortnightly Review, The III 2, 166 IV 5, 11, 13, 17, 69, 70, 72, 74, 75, 81, 82, 91, 103, 104, 108, 124, 174, 175, 177, 184, 185, 193, 218, 231, 234, 235, 237, 241, 243, 246 V 2 VI 9 VII 253 VIII 5 IX 1
McGill movement III 166
McGill poets III 167 V 4, 79
McGilliad, The (McGill Univ.) IV 70, 75, 82–83, 124–25 V 213 n.63
McKay, Don VIII 272 X 92
McKillop, A.B. II quoted 39
McKim, David VIII quoted 155
McKinnon, Barry VIII 121
McLachlan, Alexander I 15
McLaren, Floris Clark III 62, 65
McLeod, Dan VIII 192
McLuhan, Marshall V 91, 118–19 VII 194, 211, 218, 225 VIII 44, 275 quoted 45
McMullen, Lorraine II 143, 202, 207 quoted 207–08 IV 78–79, 91, 96
McNally, Paul VI quoted 36 IX quoted 196
McRobbie, Kenneth V 238
"Meadow Spring, The" II 43–44, 48
"Meander" VII 147
"Measure, The" IX 174
Measure, The IV 235 IX 138,

146–47, 170–72, 174
"Measure of the Sentence, The" VIII 221
"Meatgrinder, The" VIII 133
MEDICINE MY MOUTH'S ON FIRE VIII 60, 62, 63, 64, 70, 78, 89
"Meditation on Tom Thomson" X 96, 102
"Meditation Tanks, The" X 382
Meditation xvii VIII 83
"Medusa" IX 72 n.47
"Meeting Together of Poles and Latitudes (In Prospect)" VI 29, 39, 45
Melnyk, George IX quoted 142
Melody Maker X 21
Melville, Herman III 25, 131, 138
"Memoir" (Brown) II 246
"Memoirs and Reminiscences" (Mair) I 120, 125
"Memoirs of a Mad Cook" IX 258
Memoirs of a Survivor VI 264
"Memory No Servant" V 52
"Memory Room" VIII 246
Mencken, H.L. III 19 quoted 19 IV 69, 193, 235
"Menelaus and Helen" VII 180–81
Menorah Journal, The IV 124, 125
Merchant of Venice, The VI 142
Meredith, George II 242, 258, 272, 276 VI 291
Mermaids and Ikons: A Greek Summer IX 232
Merrett, Robert James VI 71 n.76 quoted 107
Merritt, John VII 256
Merton, Thomas VI quoted 243
"Message" (Page) VI 260
"Message, The" (Purdy) VII 146
"Message to the Youth of Canada, A" I 131

Message to Winnipeg, A VII 205–06, 217–18

"Messages" VII 282, 287

"messenger among barking dogs" VIII 61, 62

Metal and the Flower, The VI 224, 233, 236, 250–51

"Metal and the Flower, The" VI 250

"Metallic Anatomy, The" IX 247

Metamorphoses X 80

"Metamorphosis" IV 264, 265–66

Metaphysical poets I 32, 33 V 282, 286, 319–20 VI 34, 281 IX 192

"Metaphysical Poets, The" IV 76, 243–44

Metcalf, John X 283

Metcalfe, Ben VII 256

Methuen (publishers) II 237

"Metrics" VII 163

Meyer, Bruce VII 29, 145 X 202, 262

Mezei, Kathy VIII 190

Michael Ondaatje: World, Image, Imagination VIII 373

"Micro-Metro" VI 52

Micros, Marianne VII 142

"Middle Distance" VII 296–97

Middlebro', T.G. IX 9 quoted 9

Middlemarch VII 297

Middlemiss, Mrs. (daughter of Charles Heavysege) I quoted 79, 103

Midland, The III 10, 19, 20

"Midnight dinner at the *Vesta Lunch*" VIII 396

"Midnight Landscape, A" II 156, 164

"Midnight *Schochet* and the Pond, The" X 386

"Midsummer Christmas" VI 59

"Midwinter Night's Dream" II 30

"Migrating Dialogue, A" X 41, 47, 48

"Migration: C.P.R." IV 209

"Mike" VII 43

Miki, Roy VIII 205, 281 quoted 277–78 X 206

"Mildewed Maple, The" V 149

"Mile Zero" X 76, 83, 113, 134, 154, 155, 157

Milhaud, Darius VII 198

Mill, John Stuart IX quoted 198–99

Millais, Sir John Everett II 236

Millay, Edna St. Vincent IV 11, 74, 80, 83–84, 85, 90, 91, 100, 105, 109 VI 91

Miller, Henry IX 141

Miller, J. Hillis II 47 quoted 47

Miller, Muriel II 97 quoted 90–91

Miller, Orlo VII 226

Miller, Orton and Mulligan (printers) I 160

Miller, Peter V 238 VIII 132

Milne, David IX 4, 89, 116–17

Milosz, Czeslaw V 150

Milton, John I 77, 82, 83, 88, 94, 96, 101, 107, 133, 139, 140, 167, 184, 187 quoted 96 II 154 III 131, 169 IV 124, 148, 150, 153 VI 29 VII 201–02, 262 VIII 361 IX 205

"Milton and the Pastoral Tradition" VI 173

"Minago" VII 60

"Mind Process Re a Faucet" VII 153–54

"Mind Reader, The" VII 287

Minden, Robert VIII 190, 225

"Mineral" VI 250

"Minerve, La" V 205

"Minotaur Poems" X 208, 210, 211, 214

Minovitch, Miriam X 208, 210, 211, 214
"Minstrel, The" II 153
Mintz, Helen III 71
Miracle at Indian River VII 83
"Miracles" VI 263
"Mirage" (Carman) II 107
"Mirage, The" (MacEwen) IX 263–64
"Miriam Waddington's New Talent" V 312
"Mirror for Lovers, A" IV 91
Mirror on the Floor, A VIII 7, 135, 136–37, 146, 147
"Mirrored Man, The" VI 31, 32, 52, 56
Miscellaneous Man VII 82
"Miser's Grace" VI 295, 296
Missing Book of Cucumbers, The X 104, 165
"Missipowistic" I 150
"Mist Green Oats" III 19
Mister Never V 281, 319, 320
"Misuses of Information, The: A Rib-Roasting of Some Recent Canadian Critics" V 118–19
Mitchell, Beverley III 70, 78 quoted 70
Mitchell, Ken X 8
Mitchell, W.O. X 5, 78
Mitre, The IV 176 VI 86
"Mob and the Elite, The" V 81
Moby Dick III 131, 132, 138 VII 219
Modern American Poetry: A Critical Anthology II 88 IV 74, 87, 91
"Modern Canadian Poetry" X 194
Modern Canadian Verse: In English and French IV 234, 236, 260
"Modern Love" VI 291
"Modern Parable, A" VII 146
"Modern Poetry" IX 190

"Modern Politician, The" II 18
"Modern School of Poetry in England, The" II 139–40, 142, 161
Modernist poets, Canadian II 10–12
"Modest Locke" X 242
Moers, Ellen IX 22, 71 n.46
"Moloch" I 25
Moment IV 59 n.25 VII 23, 136 IX 231
Moment Is All, The: Selected Poems, 1944–83 VI 89, 163 n.87
"Moment Is Not Only Itself, The" VI 138, 146
"Moments Musicaux" IV 50
"Moments When I'm Feeling Poems" III 29, 30, 42–43
"Monarch II" IX 176
"Monarch IV" IX 176–77
"Monition" II 216
"Monk, The" II 164, 168
Monkman, Leslie IV 40
Monotones VIII 266
Monroe, Harriet III 26 IV 92, 194, 235, 241
"Mont Rolland" V 155
Montagnes, Ann IX 194
Montcalm de Saint-Véran, Marquis Louis Joseph de I 178
Monthly (Univ. of New Brunswick) II 77
"Montreal" IV 134
"Montreal, 1964" X 40
Montreal Daily Transcript I 79
Montreal Gazette V 78, 114, 162
Montreal Group I 28
Montreal Herald, The IV 70
Montreal Literary Club I 81
Montreal Star, The IV 69 V 244
Montreal Witness I 79, 80, 85

Montrealer X 72

Moodie, Susanna I 21, 86, 168 II
136 III 85, 135 V 148 IX 88 X
180–81

"Moon down Elphinstone" V 38,
56, 57

"Moon in All Her Phases, The" X
241

"Moon Landing, The" VII 112

"Moon Shadow" VIII 135

Moore, Henry IX 207, 208

Moore, Marianne III 169, 172, 177,
182 quoted 169 IV 235 VII 263

Moore, Mavor VII 206

Moore, Thomas I 167, 191

"Mordent for a Melody" VI 40, 51,
53

Mordred II 57–58, 67

*Mordred and Hildebrand: A Book
of Tragedies* II 28, 48, 57–59

More Poems for People VII 24,
55–60

"More Poems for People" VII 34

Morenz, Howie X 132

Morgan, Henry J. I 122, 184

Morgenstern, Christian VIII 40

Moritz, Albert VI quoted 36, 106 X
284, 294, 298, 323 quoted 8,
298

Morning II 29, 67

Morning and It's Summer VII 135

"Morning at the Window" VI 111

"Morning Bus" VI 58–59, 65

"Morning in Summer" I 182–83,
197

"Morning Like the Morning When
Amos Awoke, A" V 317

"Morning, Noon and Night" VI 246

"Morning on Cooper Street" V 297

"Morpheus" X 381

Morris, Alexander IV 217

Morris, Edmund II 236, 238, 239

Morris, William II 13, 142, 239 IX 8

"Morrison, Sweeney, and Mr.
Standersdt" IV 104

Morte d'Arthur I 83, 120

Moscovitch, Henry V 151

"Moses Talked to Jupiter" V 180

"Mosherville Road, The" VII 109

Moss, John VI 106

"Motel Pool" VI 261

"Moth, The" VI 222

"Mother" (Rosenblatt) X 378, 379

"Mother, The" (Campbell) II
54–56, 57, 67

"Mother, The" (Livesay) III 87–88

"Mother Nature's Helpers" X 360,
363

"Mother Nature's Proletarians" X
359

"Mothers" II 226 n.15

Mothersill, Sue II 143

Moths in the Iron Curtain VII 178

"Motor, The: A Fragment" III 31,
38

"Mount Royal" IV 216

"Mountain Lions in Stanley Park"
VII 161–62

Mountain Oysters IX 156, 159–61,
167

"Mountain Oysters" IX 160, 165

Mouré, Erin VIII quoted 247, 248

"Mouth to Mouth Heat" X 385

Movies VIII 303

Moving in Alone X 286, 287,
298–306, 307, 325

"Mowing, The" II 20

Moyles, Gordon III 122

Mozart, Wolfgang Amadeus IV 200
VII 198

"Mr. Wilson, the World" IX 112

"Mrs. Polinov" V 221 n.97

Muddiman, Bernard II 36, 245–46
  quoted 36
Mukherjee, Bharati VIII 370
Mulhallen, Karen IX 196
Mullins, S.G. VI 99, 100, 101
  quoted 100
*Munchmeyer and Prospero on the
  Island* VIII 173
Mundwiler, Leslie VIII 373 quoted
  374
Munro, Alice X 311
Munton, Ann VIII 205, 277, 281
  quoted 278 IX 200–01 X 13
"Murals for a House of God" IV
  138
Murnau, Friedrich VI 198
Murphy, Ed VIII 92
Murray, George I 84 quoted 84
Murray, Louisa I 85
Murtha, Thomas III 21, 26
"Musée des Beaux Arts" VIII 139 X
  213
Musgrave, Susan VIII 30
"Mushrooms" IX 65, 67–68
"Music Crept by Us, The" X 37
"Music on a Tombstone" VII 161
"Music Teachers, The" V 313–14
"Musing with Mothertongue" VIII
  195–96, 203, 244–45
"Muskoka Elegiac" IX 201–02
"Mutability" II 200, 208
"My Amoeba Is Unaware" IV 209
"My Canada" VII 261–62
"My Daddy Drowned" X 296, 304
"My Death" IV 264, 265
"My Father" V 174–75, 215 n.71
"My Grandfather Talking — 30
  Years Ago" VII 160
"My Grandfather's Country" VII
  167
"My Lessons in the Jail" V 313

"My Life in Art" X 43
"My Lost Youth" IV 247, 253, 268
"My Love Eats an Apple" VI 131
"My New Found Land" III 67
"My Philosophy of Poetry" VII 27
"My Shrine by Numbers" X 382
"My Sister's Sleep" IV 247
My Star Predominant III 11, 21
"My Teacher" II 95–96
"My Travels" V 305
Mystère de la parole VI 179
Mysterious Naked Man, The VII 83,
  92–93, 109–12
"Mysterious Naked Man, The" VII
  110–11
"Mystical" X 356
"Mystics Like Miners" VI 251–52
"Myth" III 181
"Myth, Frye and Canadian
  Writers" IX 106
"Mythos" VI 113–17, 118, 119,
  162 n.81
Myths and Mythmakers II 54
"Myths in Some Nineteenth-
  Century Ontario Newspapers"
  VII 226

NMFG VIII 125
Nabokov, Vladimir X 78
Nail Polish V 197, 215 n.65
Naipaul, V.S. VIII 370
Naked Poems VII 17, 255, 263,
  264–65, 266, 267, 270, 276, 288,
  289–91, 292, 297, 306 n.100,
  308 n.116–17, 310 n.153 X 325
"Nameless One, A" VI 113–17,
  118, 119, 162 n.81
Names and Nicknames VII 195,
  206–07, 214, 224
Namjoshi, Suniti V quoted 161 VI
  182, 184–85, 234 quoted 184

"Nance" III 45
Nannucci, Maurizio VIII 40
Narcissistic Narrative: The
  Metafictional Paradox VIII 47
"Narcissus, or the Pastoral of
  Solitude: Some Conventions of
  Nineteenth-Century Romance"
  VI 173, 208
"Narcissus: Some Uncertain
  Reflections" VI 175
"Narcissus: Some Uncertain
  Reflections; or, From 'Lycidas' to
  Donovan's Brain" VI 175
"Narrative Poem" X 251, 254
National Dream, The: The Great
  Railway, 1871–1881 III 150
National Film Board V 281 VI 224,
  236
National Magazine I 14, 169
National Magazine Awards VI 264
"Nation's Welcome, A" I 194
"Nativity" (Roberts) II 226 n.15
"Nativity, The" (Layton) V 163
"Natural History of Elephants,
  The" X 343
"Nature" II 30, 213 IX 198–99
"Nature Be Damned" VI 301, 302
Nature of the Physical World, The
  IV 188
Nause, John V 79, 81, 120
"Nayarít" V 54–55
Near False Creek Mouth: New
  Poems V 242
"Necropsy of Love" VII 8, 159
"Needy" VI 62
"Neighbor, The" VI 262
"Neighbours?" VI 62
"Nell" III 30
Nelligan, Emile II 14
Nepomuceno, José Augusto VIII 28
Neruda, Pablo VII 116, 138 IX 141

Nerval, Gérard de VII 266
Nesbitt, Bruce II 143, 151
Net Work: Selected Writing VIII 241
"Network, The" IV 44
Neuman, Shirley VIII 281 X 74, 85,
  86, 92–93 quoted 91, 127, 134,
  140, 147, 151, 153
"Neverness, or, The One Ship
  Beached on One Far Distant
  Shore" VI 32, 46, 52
New, William H. III 149 quoted
  149 VI 37, 68 n.29 quoted 43 IX
  quoted 94
New: American and Canadian
  Poetry IX 134
New American Poetry 1945–1960,
  The VIII 122, 192
"New Breed, The" V 196
New Country IV 5
New Criterion, The III 27
New Directions IV 126 IV 126 VI
  87, 92
New Dominion Monthly I 80, 105
New England Magazine, The II 27
New Frontier III 62 IV 17, 71, 97,
  101, 236, 237 VI 9
New Frontiers VII 22, 38
"new incens" VIII 89
New Masses IV 235
"New Names" IV 195
New Outlook, The IV 237
New Oxford Book of Canadian
  Verse in English, The III 3 IV 261
"New Paths" IV 193
New Poems (Livesay) III 63
New Poems (Roberts) II 198
New Poetry, The IV 194, 235, 241
New Provinces: Poems of Several
  Authors III 3, 116, 166 IV 5, 10,
  11, 17, 32, 36, 40, 51–52, 70, 71,
  125, 127, 130, 139, 141, 145,

174, 176, 177, 199–200, 232, 253–54 VI 9–10, 91, 157 n.17
New Republic, The IV 235
"New Roads of Peace" V 112
"New Sensibility, The" V 193–94
"New Shoes o' Protection, The" I 40, 43
New Signatures IV 5, 6–8, 177 VI 9
New Skin for the Old Ceremony X 22, 31, 42
"New Tables" V 180, 205
New Verse IV 5, 236 VI 9, 21 n.6
"New Voices in Revolt: 'Other Canadians' the Latest Work of Left Wing Versesmiths" V 244
New Wave Canada: The New Explosion in Canadian Poetry V 267 n.16 VIII 189, 264
"New Wave in Canadian Poetry" VI 95
New Word, The II 264
New World Lyrics and Ballads II 238
"New World Northern: Of Poetry and Identity" VI 109, 149
New Writers' Series VI 288
New Writing IV 5 VI 9
"New Year's Day" V 302
"New Year's Poem" VI 45, 54 IX 215
New Yorker IV 107
Newbolt, Henry II 8, 35
NeWest Review X 88
Newfeld, Frank IX 191 X 26
"Newfoundland" III 123–24 VII 33
Newfoundland Verse III 2, 112, 117, 123, 127
Newlove, John III 66, 116 V 86 VI 96 VII 138 VIII 30, 31, 116, 125; 162 IX 2, 20, 137, 139, 140, 175, 235 X 7, 8, 10–12, 281–336

quoted 282, 284, 285, 294, 298, 299, 314, 317, 323
Newlove, Mary Constant X 281
Newlove, Thomas Harold X 281
"News" VIII 135
News from Nowhere II 142
"News of the Phoenix" IV 236, 253, 255, 258, 268
News of the Phoenix and Other Poems IV 232, 233, 237 VI 284
"News Report at Ameliasburg" VII 158
"Newsboy" V 155
Newton, Sir Isaac IV 211 IX 202
Newton, Norman I 47, 90, 91, 173 quoted 90, 91, 173 II 8 quoted 10, 21
Nexus V 19
Ni Tsan IX 89, 90
"Ni Tsan" IX 89–90
"Niagara" I 194
"Niagara Falls" VII 215–16
Nichol, bp V 29, 34, 53, 54, 86, 91 quoted 53–54 VI 33 VII 52, 195, 208, 255, 302 n.42 VIII 5, 7, 8, 10–12, 13, 15, 19, 21, 22, 25, 28, 29, 30, 31, 32, 33, 35, 37, 38, 40, 72, 125, 162, 163, 173, 195, 366, 369 quoted 41–42, 264, 265, 268–70, 282–87, 289–306, 308–40 X 81, 84, 131, 148, 343, 359, 388 quoted 181 n.67
Nicholas Knock and Other People IX 191
Nicol, Pegi IV 207
Niechoda, Irene VIII 281
Nietzsche, Friedrich IV 149, 151 V 15, 81, 150, 160, 179–80, 183–84, 185, 186, 190, 194, 195, 196, 198, 199, 200, 201, 202, 203, 204, 205, 209 n.31, 215

n.68, 216 n.79, 217 n.81, 218
n.82, 222 n.97 quoted 180, 217
n.81 VI 189 VII 266, 268 IX 13,
134, 155, 218 X 197, 200–01
"Night" II 155–56
"Night and Day" (Porter) III 79
"Night and Morn" I 142
"Night before Morning, The" VIII
133
"Night Burial in the Forest" II 250,
253, 258, 262
"Night Edition" VI 51
"Night Hawk Fell with a Sound
Like a Shudder, A" VII 101
"Night Hymns on Lake Nipigon" II
250, 258–59, 272, 274
"Night of Voices" V 294–95
"Night on Gull Lake" IX 233
"Night on Skid Row" V 313
"Night Scene" III 7
"Night Song for a Woman" VII 158
Night the Dog Smiled, The X 283,
298, 325–31
"Night Walk" III 31
Night-Blooming Cereus VII 195,
219
"Nightmare at Dawn" VII 146
"Nine Arcana of the Kings, The" IX
240, 260–61
"Nine Bean-Rows on the Moon"
VII 170
Nine Poems of Farewell III 89
Nineteen Poems VI 174
"Ninth Letter" VII 223
Nixon, Richard VI 63
"No Body" V 33
"No Flowers" VI 242, 247
No Longer Two People IX 136,
169–70
"No Music in the Nightingale: An
Ironic Comedy" VI 88

No Other Country VII 136
No Pain Like This Body IX 211
"No Second Spring" VII 179
No Time for Sergeants V 36
"No Use Saying to Whom" X 300
"No Wild Dog" V 190
"No. 68 Rue Alfred de Musset" II
271, 272
Nobel Prize for Literature V 143
NOBODY OWNS TH EARTH VIII 15,
33, 34
"Noctambule" IV 253, 258, 265,
268
"Nocturnal" V 239
"Nocturne in C Minor" VI 110
"Nocturne of Consecration, A" II
221
"Nocturne: Prague 1968" VI 89
"Noël" VI 303
Noel-Bentley, Peter V quoted 42–43
Noman IX 232
"Nominalist" V 165
"Non linear" VII 289–91
"Noon Hour" VI 244
Noonan, James VII 207
Norland Echoes and Other Strains
and Lyrics I 163, 174, 193, 194
Norris, Frank III 115, 149
"North" III 170
"north aint easy to grow food in,
th" VIII 89
"North and South" V 192
North British Review, The I 78, 84
North of Intention VIII 38
North of Summer VII 162–65, 171
"North Wind's Tale, The" I 141
Northern birds in colour VIII 44
Northern Review III 116, 118 IV 8,
38, 176, 180, 202, 203 V 5,
76–77, 240, 241, 282 VI 9,
87–88, 156 n.6, 223, 231, 281,

294, 300 VII 194, 254 X 191

Northern Review prize VI 88

"Northern Rune, A" I 194

"Northern Vigil, A" II 104–05, 106, 107

"Northern Water Thrush" IX 102

"Northrop Frye's Untenable Position" V 119

Norwood, Robert I 132

Nosferatu VI 198

"Nostalgia" IV 36

"Not Abstract Harmonies But" IX 214–16

"Not in Time" VIII 41

"Not Moving" X 297

"Not the Sweet Cicely of Gerardes Herball (i.e., Oriental Myrrh, Not English Myrrh)" VI 42–43, 44, 54

"Not What the Siren Sang / But What the Frag Ment" VIII 287–88

"Notations of Love, The" III 92

"Note on Metrics, A" V 103–05

"Note on Poetic Style, A" III 181

"Note on Reading *The Martyrology* Book v, A" VIII 332

"Note on the Text" X 376

"Notes and Acknowledgements" VI 175, 196, 200, 205, 212–13 n.35, 213 n.42

"Notes from and among the Wars" X 322, 324, 325, 329

"Notes from the Underground" X 215

Notes from the Warsaw Ghetto V 287

"Notes from Various Pasts" IX 36

"Notes on Robert Burton's 'Anatomy of Melancholy' " VI 281, 301–02

Notes on the Mammals and Birds of Northern Canada I 130

"Notes toward a Poem That Can Never Be Written" IX 62–63

"Nothing Is to Be Said" X 200

Novalis VIII 280

"November" VII 220–21

"November 23" VI 53

"November Walk near False Creek Mouth" V 19, 20, 33 VI 10

"Now at the Ocean's Verge" VI 121, 122–23

Now Is the Place V 153–54, 172, 179, 209 n.26

Now Is Time V 28, 32, 35, 40

"Now That I'm Older" V 184

Nowlan, Alden V 86, 112, 151, 243, 283, 284 VII 6, 12–14, 43 IX 139, 233, 235 X 8 quoted 203

Nowlan, Michael O. VI quoted 107

Noyes, Alfred II 242 III 115 IV 30

Nude Descending a Staircase VIII 298

"Nurse, The" VI 193

"Nurse Miller" I 63 n.20

"Nurselog, The" VII 179–80

"Nursery Rhyme" VI 303

"Nursing Home" VI 258

Nyland, Agnes III 120, 142

Ó Broin, Pádraig VIII 123

"O Canada" V 148

O Earth Return VI 174

"O Jerusalem" V 197

"O Troy's Down: Helen's Song" VIII 378

"Oarsman of St. John, The" I 194

"Obituaries: Three for Five" IV 91

"Objective Correlative: Poor Child" VI 173

"October Light" X 99

"October Stars" III 31

Octopus, The: A Story of California III 149

"Ode" (Heavysege) I 80

"Ode" (Sangster) I 194

"Ode for the Keats Centenary" II 253, 258

"Ode: Intimations of Immortality from Recollections of Early Childhood" VI 30

"Ode on a Grecian Urn" X 36

"Ode: On the Death of William Butler Yeats" I 140

"Ode: The Eumenides" IV 246–47, 256–57, 268

"Ode to a Nightingale" II 41

"Ode to a Wornout Electric Stove in the Snow" VII 175

"Ode to Autumn" IX 53

"Ode to Drowsihood" II 217

"Ode to the Hills, An" II 165

"Ode to the Nineteenth Century" II 50–51

"Ode to the West Wind" I 141 II 38

"Ode to Thunder Cape" II 30

"Odes" (Patmore) II 240

"Odour of Chrysanthemums" VI 29

"Odysseus" IX 107

Odyssey, The I 107, 120 III 138 IX 48 X 80, 138

Oeuvres complètes (Béranger) I 37

"Of Castles in Spain" IV 161, n.14

"Of Daumiers a Portfolio" IV 153, 161 n.14

"Of Eros, in Shiny Degree" IX 213–14

"Of Mourners" III 83, 86

"Of One Dead" IV 94

"Of Some of the Silences" VI 144

"Offices" VI 244, 245

"Offshore Breeze" VII 61

O'Flaherty, Patrick III 121

O'Grady, Standish I 15, 168

O'Hagan, Howard VIII 173, 370 IX 235

O'Hara, Frank IV 261

O'Huigan, Sean VIII 28

"Old Adam" VI 249

"Old Age of the Teddy Bear" VI 199, 203

"Old Alex" VII 160

"Old and New Canons of Poetical Criticism" II 175 n.49

"Old Bottles" VIII 164–65

"Old Chair Song" V 301

"Old Enchanter, The" VI 194

"Old Girl Friend, The" VII 159–60

"Old Man" (Page) VI 249

"Old Man, An" (Kennedy) IV 104

"Old Man, The" (Newlove) X 311

"Old Man Stories" X 96, 97

"Old Memory" IV 242

Old Mother IX 135, 146, 163–64, 173, 174–78

"Old Olives at Bordighera" II 267

"Old Song" IV 179, 195–96, 206, 214 VI 93

"Old Spense" I 40, 41

"Old Spookses' Pass" I 29, 31

Old Spookses' Pass, Malcolm's Katie and Other Poems I 23, 30, 31, 40, 54, 56

Old Testament I 102, 103, 176

"Old Woman" VII 279

"Old Women of Toronto" V 314

"old years poem" VIII 298

"Old . . . Young . . ." VI 44

"Oldest Song, The" IV 81

"Oldster" V 45

Oliver, Michael IV 175 VII 6, 13–14 VIII quoted 141–42

Olsen, Tillie VI 211 n.19
Olson, Charles III 66 IV 236, 261 V
 35, 54, 91, 103, 150, 207 n.4,
 237, 238, 242, 243, 247, 249,
 250, 252, 254, 255, 258, 270
 n.51 quoted 239, 259 VI 27, 33,
 47, 94 VII 29, 53, 255, 266, 301
 n.31, 304 n.78 VIII 8, 121, 123,
 123, 135, 139, 189, 192, 193,
 194–95, 271, 369 quoted 207,
 228 IX 87 X 9, 82, 198–99, 232,
 251, 358
"Olympia Kaput" V 191
"On?" VI 48, 62
"On a Bench in a Park" VI 295
"On a Diary" V 35
"On a Picture of Your House" IX
 112
"On a Text Heard in the Street" I
 63 n.20
"On an Exhibition of Polish
 Tapestries" VI 260
"On Being an Alberta Writer" X
 172, 174–75
"On Being Romantic" VII 171
On Canadian Poetry II 246 III 117
 IV 77, 131
"On Cartagena de Indias" V 20
"On Christmas Eve" II 43, 45,
 46–47, 48
"On First Looking into Stalin's
 Coffin" V 184
"On Going to the Wars" V 59
"On Hearing of the Death of Dr.
 William Carlos Williams" VII 107
"On Her Long Bed of Night" X 296
"On Her Twenty-Sixth Birthday" V
 59
"On Knowing Nothing" IV 264–65
"On Looking into Henry Moore"
 III 88, 91

"On Love" II 160
"On National Poetry" III 167
"On Not Being Banned by the
 Nazis" VII 58
"On Poetry" V 99
On Poetry and Poets: Selected
 Essays of A.J.M. Smith IV 262
"On Poetry and Poets: The Letters
 of W.W.E. Ross to A.J.M.
 Smith" III 164, 165, 171, 172,
 173, 174, 177, 178
"On Reading Aloud" III 42, 46
"On Realizing He Has Written
 Some Bad Poems" VII 178
"On Saint Urbain Street" VII 48–49
"On Saying Good-Bye to My Room
 in Chancellor Day Hall" IV
 217–18
"On Seeing the Statuettes of Ezekiel
 and Jeremiah in the Church of
 Notre Dame" V 182–83
On Shaving Off His Beard VII 52
"On Shaving Off His Beard" VII
 29, 53
On Target V 250, 259, 260, 269
 n.44
"On the Assassination of President
 Kennedy" V 189
"On the Barrens" VII 119
On the Bearpaw Sea VII 174
"On the Cessation of the Oracles"
 III 172
"On the Death of a Young Poet" VI
 295, 296
"On the Death of Gandhi" IV 209,
 211, 212
"On the Decipherment of 'Linear
 B'" VII 152, 157; (1968) 157
"On the Elevated Railway at 110th
 Street" II 216
"On the Ledge" II 30

"On the Line" VII 267, 275, 276–77

"On the Murder of Salvador Allende" X 267

"On the Naming of Streets" V 192

"On the Paucity of Canadian Poetry" V 246

"On the Proposed Air Pact Outlawing the Bombing of Cities" V 214 n.64

"On the Quay with My Mother's Ghost" V 177

"On the Renewal of Bombing in VietNam December, 1972" X 250

"On the Sickness of My Love" X 44

"On the 25th Anniversary of the Liberation of Auschwitz" X 245–48, 254

"On the 24th of May" IX 101–02, 121

"On the Upper Deck" II 221

"On the Way to the Mission" II 256, 257–58

"On the Yukon Run" VI 129

"On This Sea-Floor" VI 131

"On W.W.E. Ross" III 168, 170

"On Yoho Pass" VI 128–29

"Once High upon a Hill" V 40–41

"once i workd in a mental hospital" VIII 89

"Once Upon a Great Holiday" VI 284, 294

Ondaatje, Michael V 34, 86 VII 302 n.42 VIII 5, 12–14, 31, 131, 173, 195, 238, 265, 272, 309 quoted 362–64, 366–68, 371, 375–405 IX 25, 91, 190, 219, 222 n.50, 233, 235 quoted 25 X 24, 27–28, 32, 41, 81, 84, 132, 133, 224 quoted 25, 26, 27, 33, 43

"One Day" X 314

"One Ex-Sandlotter to Another" V 263

"One Gun and Providence" IV 105–06

One Hundred Years of Solitude VIII 374 IX 252

"One Last Try at a Final Solution" V 194

"One Modern Poet" III 47

"One More Garden" IX 59

"one night I burned the house I loved" X 49

"One of the Nights I Didn't Kill Myself" X 48

"One Rural Winter" VII 158, 161

"One Sort of Poet" IV 15

One Step Forward, Two Steps Back III 79

"One Thing" (Newlove) X 325

"One Thing, The" (Knister) III 19, 38

One-Man Masque VII 195, 205–06, 222, 224

Onley, Gloria IX 28–29, 74 n.53

"Only Child" VI 248

"Onondaga Madonna, The" II 256

Ontario Arts Council awards IX 136

open is broken VIII 206

Open Letter V 78, 91, 123 VIII 6, 126, 197, 265–66 IX 190 X 73, 85, 158

"Open Letter to Louis Dudek, An" V 85, 210 n.40

"Open, my heart, thy ruddy valves" I 107

Opening Doors: Vancouver's East End VIII 14, 190

"Operations, The" VIII 144

Opinion IV 125

"Opium and Hitler" X 35

"Optional" VI 43

Optophonetic Dawn, The VIII 41

"Or Alternately" X 321, 322

"Or Consider Lilacs" VI 143–45

". . . Or Hold Your Peace" VI 313
n.33

Orange, John VI 11, 12, 13, 234
VIII quoted 160

"Orchids" VI 292

"Order" X 41, 48

Order of Canada V 143 VI 225

"Ordinary People in the Last Days"
VI 173

"Oread" IV 250

"Organist, The" II 153

Origin V 207 n.4, 238, 242, 254,
269 n.51 VI 27

Origin of Consciousness and the
Breakdown of the Bicameral
Mind, The VIII 77

"Orion" II 205, 217

Orion and Other Poems II 16, 137,
138, 190, 197, 205 IV 91

O'Riordan, Brian VII 145 X 202,
262

"Orphan Girl, The" I 160

"Orphanage, The" VII 216

"Orpheus" X 211, 305

"Orpheus and Eurydice" X 229

"Orphic Songs" V 316

Orwell, George (Eric Blair) I 91
quoted 91 III 5, 45 V 9 IX 158

Osborne, Harold VIII 304

Oscar Blumenthal Prize VI 223

"Osip Mandelshtam (1891–1940)"
V 197

Ostenso, Martha X 5

"Other" III 88

"Other Beginnings and Starts" V
163–64, 166

Other Canadians: An Anthology of
the New Poetry in Canada
1940–1946 IV 238 V 5, 242, 244

Other Side of the Room, The VIII
11, 266, 295–98

"Other Side of the Street, The" III
102 n.81

"Other Underground, The" IX 259

"Ottawa — Before Dawn" II 236,
266

Ottawa Citizen V 280

Ottawa Evening Journal, The II 28

Ottawa Little Theatre II 238

"Ottawa October 70" X 244–45

"Ottawa River — Winter" VII 254

"Otter's Creek" X 16, 317

"Où sont les jeunes?" V 101

"Oughtiness Ousted" VI 31, 65

"Our Lady of the Miraculous Tin
Ikon" X 34

Our Lives VIII 200, 201, 220,
229–32

Our Norland I 164

"Our Norland" I 194

"Our Own Far North" I 94

"Our Working Day May Be
Menaced" VI 50

"Ours" VI 260

Out of Place X 189, 193, 201, 206,
208, 254–64, 265

"Out of Pompeii" II 54, 56–57

"Out of the Pulver and the Polished
Lens" IV 23, 127, 139, 145,
146–47

"Outcasts" VI 247

Out-Posts VIII 36, 264, 268, 283,
293–94, 297, 298, 335

"Outrider, The" III 28, 62, 67, 78,
80

"Over the Garden Wall" VIII
375–76

"Over the Slow Rivers" IX 178

"Over the Water" III 164
"Over-Soul, The" II 213
"Overture" IV 200
Overture: Poems IV 174, 201 VII
  253
"Overwhelming Green, The" VI
  136–38
Ovid X 80
Ovum VIII 28
Owen, Don X 23
Owen, Ivon VI quoted 279–80
Owen, Robert Dale I 25
Owen, Wilfred II 241–42 IV 72 VI
  228, 291
"Owen Sound" VIII 30
Ower, John I 29, 31 quoted 31 II 38
  quoted 38 X 205
"Owl" (Nichol) VIII 288
Owl, The (Heavysege) I 80, 106
"Owl Song" IX 48
"Owning Everything" X 4, 46
Oxford Book of American Verse,
  The (1927) II 81
Oxford Book of Canadian Verse,
  The (1913) II 29 IV 9, 260–61
Oxford Book of Canadian Verse,
  The: In English and French
  (1960) VI 231, 301
Oxford Book of English Verse, The
  IV 74, 81
Oxford Companion to Canadian
  Literature IV 17, 23 VIII 30, 39
Oxford Poetry VI 86
Oxford University Press VI 174,
  212–13 n.35, 226

P.K. Page: Poems Selected and New
  VI 225, 233, 236, 257
PM Magazine VII 254
"Pace" VI 40, 57, 60
Pacey, Desmond I 29, 30, 61, 88,
  133–34, 151 n.1, 152 n.6, 173,
  191 quoted 29, 88, 134, 173, 191
  II 91–92, 93, 150, 197–98, 246
  quoted 91–92, 150–51, 197–98
  III 63, 68, 69, 83, 119, 122, 142,
  170, 171 quoted 68 IV 80, 152,
  180, 181, 238–39, 267, 276 n.80
  V 89 quoted 59, 89, 241, 309 VI
  quoted 100–01, 102, 233, 281,
  284, 285 VII 92, 269 X 24, 26,
  27, 197 quoted 203
Pacey, Peter VII 93
Pachter, Charles IX 17, 68 n.1
"Pachucan Miners" V 41, 47–48
"Pacific" III 7, 167–68, 182
"Pacific Door" V 19
"Pagans" X 37
Page, P.K. III 2, 13, 14, 65 IV 8, 38,
  163 n.43, 176, 202, 233, 236,
  262 V 2 VI 7, 10, 11, 12–14, 16,
  178 VII 140, 258, 265, 302 n.42
  VIII 131 IX 19, 20 X 8
"Page One" III 75, 87, 97
"Paging Mr. Superman" V 180
"Painted Harlot, A" X 375
"Pair, The" IV 35
Palgrave, Francis Turner VII 29–30
"Palladia and Others" VI 193, 199,
  204
Pancheco, Manuel VIII 169
"Pang Cantata, A" VII 277
"Panorama" VI 247
"Paper Bag, A" IX 54
" 'Paperback Revolution,' The —
  Has it Guillotined Poetry?" V 110
"Parachutist" VI 251
"Paraclete" V 184
Paradise Lost I 94, 101, 140 III 131,
  133 IV 148, 151 VI 29
Paradise Regained VIII 361
"Paranoid" VI 250

"Parasite, A" V 152

Parasites of Heaven X 21, 28–29, 38, 41, 44, 45, 48–49

Parker, Brian VII 202

Parker, Gerald VII 202, 207, 226

Parker, Sir Gilbert II 243

Parkin, Sir George II 77, 78, 84–85, 189

"Parque de Montjuich" V 222 n.97

"Part Two: Magic Animals, 1972–1974" IX 232, 245–46

Parti pris des choses, Le VIII 189

"Partial Argument" VI 136

Particular Accidents: Selected Poems VIII 133, 137, 159

"Parting, The" I 194

"Party, The" III 97 VI 50

Pascal, Blaise IX 203, 210

pass th food releas th spirit book VIII 15, 41, 62

"Passer-By" IV 192

Passing into Storm IX 162

"Pastoral" VI 299–300 IX 30

Pataphysical Hardware Co., The VIII 268

Patchen, Kenneth V 150, 154, 240 VI 48

Paterson V 262, 265 X 81

"Patience" VII 287

Patmore, Coventry I 78, 84, 86, 171 quoted 78, 84 II 240, 252–53, 258 VII 282

"Patterns of Recent Canadian Poetry" V 85

Patterson, E. Palmer II 247

Patterson, Evangeline VI 33

Paul, Saint IX 218

Pausanias X 104, 144, 145, 147

Paz, Octavio VII 138

"Peace" I 63 n.20 II 163

"Peaceable Kingdom, The" VII 172

"Peaches, Peaches" III 22

Peacock, Thomas Love V 112

"Pear Tree" III 91

Pearson, Alan VII 270

Pearson, Ian IX quoted 196

Peek VI 93

Penfield, Wilder IX 199

Penguin (publishers) VI 8, 87, 92

Penguin Book of Canadian Verse, The VI 34, 88, 90

Pentland, Barbara III 62

Percival, W.P. II quoted 78

"Percy Lawson" VII 160

"Perdu, The" II 218

"Perfect Colours of Flowers, The" X 330, 331

"Perfect Essay, The" VII 232

"Perfectability of Man, The" VII 122

"Performance" VII 273, 274, 283, 285

periodics VIII 190

Periods of the Moon V 192

"Perishing Bird, The" IX 110

Perkins, David VIII quoted 24, 73

Perkyns, Richard VII 203, 207, 208–09

Perloff, Marjorie VIII quoted 267, 271

"Permanence" II 267

"Permanent Tourist Comes Home, The" X 328

Perry, Sam VIII 31

Perse, St. John VIII 193

Persky, Stan VIII 125, 126

"Person" VI 52, 58

". . . Person, or, A Hymn on and to the Holy Ghost" VI 49

Personal Fictions: Stories by Munro, Wiebe, Thomas, and Blaise VIII 366

"Personal Landscape" VI 242, 247
"Personal Poetry of Miriam
    Waddington, The" V 289
"Perspective" VI 45, 51
Perth County Conspiracy, The VII
    26
"Pessimist, The" I 24, 59
Peter, John IV 38–39
"Peter Hoskin Goes Home" IV
    108
"petroglyphs at st. victor:" X 257,
    260
Petrone, Penny I 30 quoted 30
Pettigrew, Damien VI 94, 109
Pettigrew, Harriet (daughter of
    Charles Heavysege) I quoted
    76
Phaedrus VIII 77
Phases of Love, The III 63, 94
"Philistine, The" VII 289
Phillips, Andy VIII 307
Phillips, Susan Mary X 282
"philosophical investigations:
    ontological argument No. 1" X
    372
"Philosophy of Composition" II 82
"Phobos" IX 257
Phoenix, The X 21
"Phone Call from Mexico" VI 260
"Photograph" VI 247
"Photograph My Mother Keeps,
    The" X 295
"Photos of a Salt Mine" VI 250
Phrases from Orpheus IX 4, 86, 87,
    91, 93, 103, 110–15, 116, 120
"Phrases from Orpheus" IX 93,
    111, 112–15
"Piazza San Marco" V 191
Picasso, Pablo V 150 IX 89 quoted
    170
Pickthall, Marjorie II 242 III 114

"Picture" III 176, 186 n.12
"Pictures by Colville" IX 115, 119
"Pictures from a Long Lost World"
    V 251, 259, 262, 269 n.45
"Pictures in an Institution" X 234,
    236, 263
"Pied Piper of Edmonton, The" III
    92
Pierce, Lorne I 86, 181, 196, 200
    n.2 quoted 86, 161, 181, 196 II
    quoted 77, 90, 121 n.1 III 115 IV
    163 n.43, 232 V 207 n.4, 241 VII
    44, 45 X 197
Pierre II 238
"Piety" V 167
"Pig Glass (1973–78)" VIII 390
"Pig Song" IX 47–48
"Pigeon, The" VI
"Pig-Girl" IX 30–31, 38, 47
Pilgrim's Progress, The I 120
Piling Blood VII 180–81
Pindar III 129
"Pines, The" I 141
"Pining" VII 287
"Pink Ballad" III 77
"Piper of Arll, The" II 237, 242,
    247, 250, 254 VI 253
Pipes of Pan, The IV 177
"Pipes of Pan, The" II 210–11
Pipes of Pan series II 87, 95, 115
Pirandello, Luigi VII 254, 266
Pisan Cantos VI 128
Pitt, David G. III 122
"Place, A: Fragments" IX 36
"Place for 'P,' A" IX 110
"Place of Fire" VII 175
Place of Meeting (Beckwith) IX
    189, 209
Place of Meeting: Poems
    1958–1960 (Souster) V 257
Place to Die, A VIII 164

"Places of Memory" IX 111
"Plains of Abraham, The" I 191
Plainsongs III 63, 69, 74, 89
Planes VI 225
Plantos, Ted VII 29
Plaskett, Joe VII 266, 302 n.40
Plath, Sylvia VIII 207 IX 21, 22, 40, 44, 66, 72 n.47, 75 n.57 quoted 72 n.47, 75 n.57
Plato VIII 74, 77, 195, 213, 280
"Play-box" VII 210
Playboy X 22
"Playing" VI 205
Playing the Jesus Game VII 83, 94
Plaza, Julio VIII 28
"Plaza Mayor" X 250
"Pleased" X 378
Plekhanov, Georgy IV 98–99
"Plot against Proteus" IV 14
"Plowman, The" III 29, 36–39
"Plowman's Song" III 10, 35–36, 38
"Plum Tree, The" VII 214, 215
Plumly, Stanley IX 76 n.59 quoted 75 n.56
"Plunging Into" III 185 n.12
plutonium missing VIII 89
"Plymouth Valiant Song, The" VII 120
pnomes jukollages & other stunzas V 29
Poe, Edgar Allan I 61, 88, 106, 139, 140, 141, 167 II 13, 37, 82, 89, 104, 148, 155 III 24, 25, 73 VI 279 VIII 151 IX 19
"Poem" (Birney) V 46, 47
"Poem" (MacEwen) IX 248
"Poem as Person as Place as Words" X 266
"Poem for a Friend" X 294
"Poem for a Pupil" V 314
"Poem for King Dracula" X 367

"Poem for Living" IV 191, 206
"Poem for One of the Annettes" VII 155, 157
"Poem (for the Heroes)" V 260
"Poem for the Next Century" V 184–85
"Poem in Five Parts" VIII 286
"Poem in Three Parts" VI 297
"Poem Like a Stone, Like a General" X 267
"Poem of Albert Johnson" X 96, 101, 102
"Poem of Anxiety" VI 293
"Poem on the Astronauts in Apollo XIII's Near-Disaster" VI 56
"Poem to My Mother, A" VII 104–05
"Poem with Fat Cats in the Background" VII 47–48
Poems (Auden) IV 177
Poems (Finch) IV 8, 29, 32, 33, 37 VI 156 n.6
Poems (Gustafson) VI 87
"Poems" (1932, Klein) IV 125
"Poems" (1934, Klein) IV 125
Poems (Klein) IV 126, 131–32, 147–52, 153 V 171
Poems for All the Annettes VII 136, 140; (1962) 153–57; (1968) 157–58; (1973) 158 VIII 139
Poems for People III 62, 68, 85 VII 55
Poems from Atlantis V 78, 94, 122–23
"Poems in Braille" IX 246, 248
Poems New and Selected (Lane) IX 135, 145–46, 157, 166–68, 169
Poems of Al Purdy, The VII 137
Poems of Archibald Lampman, The (1900) II 143, 145, 156, 171 n.1, 243; (1974) 171 n.1

Poems of Bliss Carman, The (1976)
II 124 n.50

"Poems of Dublin" VII 264

*Poems of Duncan Campbell Scott,
The* II 246, 254

Poems of Earle Birney, The V 29, 40

"Poems of Failure" VII 249, 256,
277–78, 289, 293

Poems of French Canada IV 174,
218

*Poems of Loyalty by British and
Canadian Authors* II 29

Poems of Today IV 176

Poems of Wilfred Campbell, The II
28, 59

*Poems Twice Told: The Boatman
and Welcoming Disaster* VI 174,
175, 185–86, 212–13 n.35, 213
n.39, 214 n.47

Poesiaem G VIII 28

Poésie/Poetry '64 IX 20, 21, 31 X
282, 286

Poesie Sonore Internationale VIII
34

"Poet" (Webb) VII 280, 287

"Poet, The" (Emerson) II 138

"Poet, The" (Lampman) II 153

"Poet and the Publisher, The" VII
255

"Poet as Philosopher" V 90

"Poet at Sinai" V 194

"Poet in Exile, A" VI 110

"Poet on Poet" IV 41

"Poetic Interpretation" II 152, 167

"Poetic Muse in Canada, The" III
24, 33–34, 48–49

"Poetic Principle, The" III 73

"Poetic Process" (Mandel) X 222

"Poetic Process, The" V 207 n.4

"Poetic Vocation, The" V 89

Poetical Tragedies II 29, 59–61

"Poetics against the Angel of
Death" VII 17, 264

"Poetry" (F.R. Scott) IV 209

Poetry [Chicago] III 10, 169, 180 IV
77, 101, 124, 201, 237, 238 V 88
VI 26, 35, 174, 223 IX 68 n.1

Poetry 62 VII 82

*Poetry and Canada: A Guide to
Reading* VI 112–13, 116, 117–18

"Poetry and Progress" II 241

Poetry and the Body VIII 282

*Poetry and the Colonized Mind:
Tish* VIII 120

"Poetry as a Moral Procedure" VI
163 n.92

Poetry as Discourse VIII 330

Poetry Canada Review IX 262

"Poetry Chronicle" V 89 VI 29, 30,
33, 43, 48

"poetry dusint have to be" VIII 77

*Poetry Hotel: Selected Poems
1963–1985* X 340, 375–76

"Poetry of Archibald Lampman,
The" III 23, 24, 26

"Poetry of Byron, The" II 140, 167

"Poetry of Duncan Campbell Scott,
The" II 246

Poetry of Life, The II 83–84, 85,
88, 96–99

"Poetry of Nature, The" II 207,
225 n.10

"Poetry of Reason, The" V 124

Poetry of Robert Bridges, The IV
244

"Poetry of the Forties, The" V 79,
124

Poetry Year Book: 1928–29 VI 86

Poets '56 IX 86

"Poets and Muses" VI 207

"Poets and Statues" V 286, 306–07

"Poets in Canada" VI 29, 39

"Poet's Mother, The" X 154, 155, 156, 165

"Poets of a Golden Age?" IV 10

"Poets of Revolt . . . or Reaction?" V 98

Poets of the Confederation II 7

Poets of the Late Sixties VIII 19

"Poet's Possession, A" II 266

"Poet's Song, The" II 152

"Poet's-Eye View, A" VI 291

Points on the Grid VIII 132–34, 135, 137

"Poison Pen Points" IV 102

"Poisons" III 32, 39

"Polemics" V 324

Pole-Vaulter, The V 197

"Political Intelligence" IV 258

"Political Meeting" IV 23–24

Pollock, Zailig IV 23 VI 38 VII 34, 53, 65

Polson, James V 161

"Polyphony, Enacting a Meditation" IX 191

"pome in praise of all quebec bombers, a" VIII 62

"Pomegranate, The" V 101

Pomeroy, Elsie M. II 197

Pomes for Yoshi VIII 39

Ponge, Francis VIII 189, 193, 194

"Pool, The" X 318

"Poor Child" VI 190, 192, 193

"Poor Innocent" IV 253, 268

Pope, Alexander I 167 II 84 III 131, 139 IV 45, 46, 47, 51, 153 V 285, 286 VIII 151

"Pope's Pennies, The" VIII 170

Popper, Karl VI 228, 258

"Popular Geography" V 297, 305

Porphyrius, Publilius Optatian VIII 23

"Portage, The" IX 233

Porter, Cole III 79

Porter, John VIII 371

"Portion of Your Breath" IV 105–06, 109

"Portrait" V 300

"Portrait in Six Sonnets, A" II 163

"Portrait of a Lady" IV 73, 247

"Portrait of a Pseudo-Socialist" V 214 n.64

"Portrait of Ann" X 268

"Portrait of Anne Hébert" IX 104–05, 110, 117

"Portrait of Marina" VI 233, 250

"Portrait of Ned" VI 93, 94

Portrait of the Artist as a Young Man, A IV 108, 158 VII 108

"Portrait of the City Hall" X 39

"Portrait of the Poet as Landscape" IV 24, 129, 130, 146, 147, 159 V 315 VI 186, 208

"Portrait: Old Woman" V 297, 314

"Portraits" VII 251, 281, 289, 294–95

"Portraits of a Minyan" IV 138, 146

"Portraits of the Landscape as Poet: Canadian Nature as Aesthetic Symbol in Three Confederation Writers" II 38

"Poseur" X 380

"Post Script" VII (1956) 149; (1962) 156; (1965) 160; (1968) 157

"Postcard" IX 59

"postcard between" VIII 298

"Postcards from China" X 96, 137, 141, 150, 151, 159

Pound, Ezra II 12, 85, 242, 248, 261, 262 III 3, 4, 11, 12, 24, 66, 73, 113, 116, 171, 177, 178, 181 quoted 4, 67–68 IV 11, 14, 37, 92, 124, 129, 133, 161 n.12, 180,

235, 236, 241, 243, 261, 264,
267, 268 V 1, 6, 10, 39, 80,
82–84, 88, 90, 91, 94, 99, 101,
104, 105, 115, 120, 121, 130
n.75, 150, 207 n.4, 241, 242,
250, 254 quoted 82, 84, 97, 130
n.74 VI 91, 93, 94, 95, 104, 132,
133, 138, 140, 150, 154, 227,
229 quoted 128, 132, 133, 163
n.93 VII 87, 107, 138, 200, 267,
268, 294, 304 n.78 VIII 8, 115,
121, 125, 135, 192, 203, 214,
268, 271, 331 IX 2–3, 20, 85,
87, 88, 91, 93, 175, 189 X 140,
284
"Pour, pour" VIII 227
"Pouring, The" V 257
"Powassan's Drum" II 256 IX 217
Powell, S. Morgan V quoted 244
Power Politics VI 189 IX 5, 7, 22,
30, 40, 44–46, 48–49, 55, 60, 61,
62, 74 n.53, 74 n.54, 76 n.57
"Prairie" X 7
"Prairie as Hawk, Cock, Belly,
Lover" X 266
"Prairie Counterpoint" V 46–47
"Prairie Poems" IX 176
Prato, Edward IX 145
Pratt, E.J. I 12, 28, 138, 187 II 9,
20, 111, 171, 219, 244 III 1, 2–5,
6, 10, 11, 13, 14, 66, 67, 73, 166,
168 quoted 4, 67–68 IV 5, 6, 7,
10, 17, 18, 32, 76–77, 79, 90,
110, 131, 134, 175, 177, 179,
199, 232, 233, 234, 254 V 10, 35,
39, 56, 58, 84, 251 VI 8, 9, 26,
91, 93–94, 105, 177, 192, 280 VII
33, 201 IX 19, 88, 97, 190, 191,
192, 201, 202 X 342, 343, 368
quoted 389 n.5
Pratt, Mildred Claire III 112, 121

Pratt, Viola Whitney III 112, 152
n.1
Pratt's Romantic Mythology: The
Witches' Brew VI 177, 184
"Prayer" IV 243
"Prayer for Messiah" X 37, 39
"Prayer for My Daughter" VIII 149
"Prayer for Sunset" X 37
"Precious Speck of Life, The" II
200
Precosky, Don III 6, 30, 46 quoted
6, 30, 46 VI quoted 108 VIII 120,
152
"Predator, The" V 190
"Prediction without Crystal" VI 245
"preface:" X 261, 263
"Preface: I Never Felt Such Love"
VIII 146
Preliminary Report, A VIII 303
"Prelude" (Avison) VI 32, 48, 53,
56, 59
"Prelude" (Livesay) III 96–97
"Prelude" (Mansfield) III 65
"Prelude, The" (Wordsworth) II 69
n.32
"Preludes" (Eliot) VI 30, 111
"Preludium" III 87
"Premonition" VII 146
"Preoccupation of a Puppet" IV
104–05, 108
"Preparation" VI 258
"Pre-Raphaelites" II 9, 13, 14, 82,
142, 194–95, 262
"Presence, The" V 164
"Presentation" VI 250
President's Medal (Univ. of Western
Ontario) V 239 VI 174 IX 86
Pressed on Sand VII 136, 139,
147–48
"Pressure of the Night, The" VI 298
Preview IV 8, 13, 126, 127, 174,

176, 184, 202 V 2, 16, 80, 240,
282 VI 9, 87–88, 223, 224, 229,
230, 231, 232, 262, 267 n.34 VII
253, 265 VIII 5
Price of Gold, The V 281, 297,
300–01, 303
"Price of Gold, The" V 303
"Pride, The" X 12, 284, 285, 286,
289, 292, 293, 309, 311
Priest, Robert VII 29
"Priest in the Family, A" IV 107
"Priest Says Goodbye, The" X 48
"Priests 1957" X 46, 57 n.70
Princess, The IV 258
Prism VIII 122 X 21
Prism International III 63 IX 136
Pristine Forest, A X 108
Pritchard, James B. VI 200
"Private Property" VII 167
Prix, David VI 86
"Prize Cat, The" III 126 X 343
"Probable Systems" VIII 305
"Problem, The" IV 185–86
"Problem of Space, A" IX 89, 100,
115
Procedures for Underground IX 26,
30, 41–44, 69 n.15
"Professional Jew" V 222 n.97
"Professor as Bridegroom, The" X
219
Progressive Arts Club III 62
"Progressive Insanities of a
Pioneer" IX 40, 73 n.48, 208
"Projected Visit" X 99
Projective Verse V 242 VI 47
"Prolegomenon at Midnight" VI
118, 120
"Prologue to a Poetry Reading:
Address to the Audience" IV
268–69
"Prologue to Summer" VI 111–12

"Prologue to Tecumseh" I 141–42,
145
"Prometheus — 1" III 172
Prometheus Unbound I 95
"Proof Reader" V 183
*Prophecy of Merlin and Other
Poems, The* I 81
"Prophet of the New World" III
85–86, 90
"Prophetess, The" III 90
"Propositions" VII 283, 295–96
"Prospector" IX 152, 153
Protective Footwear VIII 155, 164
Proteus X 174
"Prothalamium" IV 73, 88, 247–49,
253, 265
Proust, Marcel V 115
"Provincial" V 3–4, 304
Prufrock and Other Observations
IV 276 n.80
"Ps. 19" VI 56
"Ps. 80:1 — 'Thou that dwellest
between the cherubim, shine
forth!'" VI 32, 62
"Psalm of Abraham, When He
Hearkened to a Voice, and There
Was None, A" IV 147–49
"Psalm 24" X 234–35
"Psychology, Evolution and Sex" V
110
"Psychology of Literature, The" V
120, 248–49
"pull tord th north, th" VIII 62
"Pulvis et Umbra" II 104
"Pumpkin: A Love Poem" X 100,
102, 129, 173
"punk snake poem (for several
eunuch voices)" X 371
"Puppet of the Wolf, The" IX 58
Purdy, Al II 13, 244, 168 III 116 IV
38, 59 n.25, 179, 209 V 19, 37,

39, 86, 89, 93, 112, 151, 294, 297 quoted 40, 89, 150–51, 293 VI 10, 37, 89 quoted 233 VII 6, 7–11, 13, 16, 22, 22–23, 23, 27, 28, 30, 34, 38, 41, 65, 85, 92, 195 VIII 7, 30, 31, 32, 114, 121, 127, 131, 133, 134–35, 138–39, 147, 160, 168 quoted 134 IX 2, 20, 91, 134, 137, 138, 139, 140, 175, 190, 194, 231, 235 quoted 142, 194 X 7–8, 282, 284–85, 339 quoted 27, 289

Purdy, James V 51

Purdy-Woodcock Letters, The VII 137

"Puritan, The" VI 292

"Purposes of Fiction" III 40

Pushkin, Alexander Sergeevich V 279

"Putting On and Taking Off" V 323

"Putting On the Storms" IX 114

Quarles, Francis VI quoted 191, 212 n.32

"Quarrel, The" VII 153

Quarry VIII 41 IX 135, 195 X 204, 286

"quebec bombers" VIII 36

"Québec May" V 44

Quebec States Her Case: Speeches and Articles from Quebec in the Years of Unrest IV 175

"Queen City, The" V 258

"Queen Street Serenade" V 244

Queen's Quarterly II 36, 89, 145 IV 70, 239 VI 88 IX 196 X 21, 88

Queen's Silver Jubilee Medal III 64

Quest for Corvo, The: An Experiment in Biography VIII 12

Quest for Ouzo, The VII 169–71, 171–72

"Question as an Instrument of Torture, The" VII 256, 308 n.116

"Question of Questions, A" VII 256, 276, 284

"Question of Winter, The" VI 11, 163 n.94

"Quiet" V 322

"Quiet Haven" IV 241

"Quiet Normal Life, A" IX 69 n.3

"Quiet Snow" III 31

Quill & Quire IX 143, 147, 196

"Quinté" I 194

"Quotations" X 322, 323, 325, 329

"Rabbi, The" V 163

Rabelais, François IV 82 V 36, 61, 150

Rabkin, Eric S. IX 251, 252 quoted 251, 253

"Race, The" II 33

Rachel: A Sea Story of Newfoundland in Verse III 111, 123

Racoons, The VIII 266

Radcliffe Medal (Radcliffe College) IX 68 n.1

Rader, Ralph IX 73 n.49

"Radio in the Ivory Tower (1937–Sept. 1939), The" III 128–29

"Radio Jazz" VIII 127, 133

Radisson Society I 132

Rag & Bone Shop V 29, 38

Ragtime VIII 403–04

"Rain" IV 30 IX 66–67

Rain-Check V 259, 262

"Railroad Station" III 183, 184

"Ramble on What in the World Why" VI 145

Ramus, Peter VIII 280

Rand, Theodore H. I 75

Rans, Dr. G. III 51 n.34

Ransom, John Crowe IV 235 VI 27

Rape of the Lock III 139

"Rapid, The" I 191, 93

"Rapunzel" X 230

Rashley, R.E. I 29, 61 quoted 29 IV 80

Rasky, Harry X 23

Rat Jelly VIII 384–87, 390

"Rat Song" IX 48

"Raven, The" I 106 VI 279

Ravitch, Melech V 170

Raw Edges, The: Voices from Our Time III 89, 93

Ray, Wayne VII 66–67

Raymond, W.O. VI quoted 91, 157 n.15

"Raymond Knister: A Memoir" (Livesay) III 13, 24, 28, 64

Raymond Knister: Poems, Stories and Essays III 22

"Raymond Souster's Letters to Charles Olson" V 237, 242, 249, 268 n.41, 270 n.51

Read, Herbert III quoted 27 IX 8

Read, Robert IX 193

Read Canadian: A Book about Canadian Books IX 190

Read the Way He Writes: A Festschrift for bpNichol VIII 278, 281

Reade, John I 77, 79, 81, 85, 168, quoted 77, 79

"Reader" VI 189

Reader's Digest, The IV 71

"Reading, The" I 194

"Reading Room: Periodicals" X 249

"Reading *Savage Fields*" IX 191, 197

"Real Values, The" V 187

"Reality" II 269 III 75, 76

Reaney, James I 9, 29, 30, 91 quoted 91 III 9, 10, 27, 28, 31, 33, 48, 49, 148 quoted 31, 33,

48, 149 V 15, 93 VI 174, 175, 181, 182, 183–84, 185, 280 quoted 35, 183, 184 VII 207 VIII 114, 272 IX 19, 20, 22, 91, 135, 193, 201, 233 quoted 87, 91 X 8, 192, 202 quoted 203

"Reason I Write, The" X 45

"Rebel, The" I 160

"Recall, The" II 34

Recent Songs X 23, 31

"Recluse, The" II 152

"Reconsiderations" VIII 148

"Red and the Green, The" VI 294–95

Red Carpet for the Sun, A V 146, 157, 174, 177, 186, 187, 208 n.4, 216 n.76, 219 n.87

"Red Cross Corps, The" I 63 n.20

Red Fox II 218–19

Red Heart, The III 28 VII 15, 12, 15–16, 90

"Red Moujhik, The" V 194

"Red Sash, The" V 256

"Red Shirt, A" IX 55, 58

"Red Wheelbarrow" VIII 159 X 16

"Red Wool Shirt, The" VII 119

"redecorate now" VIII 61

"Rededication" X 36

Redekop, Ernest VI 30–31, 37, 39, 53, 67 n.23, 68 n.26, 70 n.61, 71 n.76 quoted 59

Reed, Henry IX 21

"Refining Fire: The Meaning and Use of Poetry" IV 262

"Reflection" VI 236

"Reflection in a Train Window" VI 251

"Reflections" X 194

"Reflections of Uncle Nathan" X 378

"Refuge at Eight" VII 101

Refus Global VIII 29

Regina Manifesto IV 174

Reid, Jamie VIII 122, 192

Reid, Robert X 281–82, 294

Reigo, Ants VII 144

"Reingemacht" V 166

"Rejected Preface to *New
Provinces*" IV 34

"Rejoice in the Lamb: The Offering
of Christopher Smart" VII 256

"Rejoinder" IX 216

"Relations between Literature and
the Press, The" V 76

"Released Flow" VI 59

"Remains of an Indian Village" VII
156–57; (1968) 156–57

"Remarks Decoded from Outer
Space" V 40

"Remarks for the Part of Death" V
40

"Remember the Wood" VI 242

"Remember, Woman" IX 213–14

"Remembering Christopher Smart"
X 324

"Remnant, The" V 197

"Renascence" IV 91

Renoir, Pierre Auguste V 300

"Rent Collection" VII 61

"Reply" V 110–11

"Reply to August" III 31

"Report on the Poetry Readings" VI
175

"Republic, The" VIII 376–77

"Request" IX 104

"Requiem for A.M. Klein" V 216
n.75

"Research" VI 64

*Research Compendium, The:
Reviews and Abstracts of
Graduate Research, 1942–1962*
VI 41, 67 n.19

"Resignation, The" VI 263

"Resolution and Independence" VIII
149

"Resources, Certain Earths" X 306

"Resurrection of Arp" IV 236, 258

"Reticent Phrase, The" IV 42–43

"Retina" VI 187, 189, 193, 194

"Return" (F.R. Scott) IV 206

"Return, The" (Finch) IV 56

"Return, The" (MacEwen) IX 254,
255–56

"return:, the" (Mandel) X 256, 257,
260, 261, 263

"Returning with an Annual
Passion" V 171–72

"Reunion" VIII 155

"Revelation" II 115

"Revenant, The" IX 62

"Reverie" II 253

Revolt of Tartarus, The: A Poem I
7, 77, 78, 81, 83, 92, 101–02

*Revolution in European Poetry,
1660–1900* V 81

"Rewards for Ambitious Trees" VII
216

"Rewards of Poetry, The" II 95

Rexroth, Kenneth V 1, 10, 51 X 9

"Rhapsody on a Windy Night" VI
111

"Rhine Boat Trip" V 191–92

Rhodenizer, V.B. II quoted 90

"Rhyme" VI 303

*Rhymes and Reasons: Nine
Canadian Poets Discuss Their
Work* IX 10–11, 231–32

"Rhythm and Sound in Contemporary Canadian Poetry" III 2,
63, 66, 73

"Ricardo and the Flower" VIII 148

Rich, Adrienne VIII 195, 196 IX 20,
21, 22, 69 n.12

"Rich Boy's Birthday through a Window" VI 40

Richards, David Adams VII 89

Richards, I.A. V 110 VIII 46 IX 75 n.55

Richardson, Dorothy III 64

Richardson, John I 168 VII 197

Richardson, Keith VIII 120 quoted 124

Richardson, Samuel I 99

Richler, Mordecai IV 124 VIII 162

Richter, J.P. VIII 280

Ricou, Laurence V 282, 289, 291, 292, 298–99, 308–09 quoted 283, 291, 298 VII 144, 272–73 X 132

"Riddle, A" VII 215

"Ride Off Any Horizon" X 285, 286, 293, 308–09

"Riding and Waves" VI 41

Riel, Louis I 26, 124, 126, 145 III 86 V 148 VIII 309

Riffaterre, Michael X 33–34, 41

"Riffs" IX 214

Rig Veda I 25

"Right Hand Fights the Left, The" IX 57

Right Hand Left Hand III 13, 27, 63, 65, 67, 71, 74, 84, 93, 94, 96

"Rigor Viris" VI 52

Riley, James Whitcomb I 40, 61

"Rilke" VII 263, 306 n.100

Rilke, Rainer Maria III 28 VI 227, 228, 233, 243, 256 VII 200, 254, 263, 266, 289, 304 n.62, 304 n.63 VIII 165–67, 399–400 IX 200, 201, 205, 207, 222 n.34 X 164–65

Rimbaud, Arthur IV 233 VI 226 VIII 193

"Rime of Our Time" VIII 135

"Rime of the Ancient Mariner" VIII 159

"Ring, The" V 166, 201

Ringelblum, Emmanuel V 287

Ringrose, Christopher Xerxes VI 102–03, 104 quoted 102–03

Rings VIII 14, 197, 201, 205, 215–20, 221, 240, 241

Rising Fire, The IX 232, 234, 236, 237, 239, 241, 244, 255, 256

Rising Village, The I 15

"Rite of Spring" IV 73, 95

"Rites of Manhood, The" VII 118

Rittenhouse, Jessie B. II quoted 88

"Ritual, The" III 139

"Ritual Cut, The" V 187

"River, The: North of Guelph" IX 1, 4–5, 105–06, 110

Rivers among Rocks VI 88, 98–99, 100, 104, 118–22, 123, 126, 158 n.31

Rizzardi, Alfredo X 341

"Road, The" VI 51

"Road by the Lake, The" VI 152

"Road to Newfoundland, The" VII 166–67

"Road to Nijmegan, The" V 20, 33, 40

"Road to Thebes, The" VII 213

Rob Roy I 120

Robb, Wallace H. I 164, 198 quoted 164–65, 198

Robert Kroetsch: Essays X 71, 72, 76–77, 78, 80, 81–82, 83, 85, 90, 100, 101, 102, 103, 104, 110, 111, 114, 121, 123, 125, 127, 135, 138, 167, 173, 174

Roberts, Sir Charles G.D. I 10, 12, 132, 136, 142, 146, 167, 168 quoted 136–37 II 7, 8, 9, 14, 16, 19–21, 22, 23, 29, 31, 38, 77, 79,

81, 82, 83, 107, 135, 137, 139, 144, 238, 240, 243 quoted 14, 77, 104, 111, 137, 152 III 1, 9, 21, 23, 224, 64, 113, 172 IV 7, 10, 20, 32, 82, 91, 177, 178, 179, 196, 234 V 1, 35 VII 28, 47, 49, 55, 90, 201 IX 9, 88, 205

Roberts, George Goodridge II 188, 189, 204–06, 208, 212

Roberts, Lloyd II 205 quoted 121 n.5, 205–06

Roberts, Michael IV 72

Robillard, Richard V 66 n.35

"Robin" IX 101

Robinson, David VII 256

Robinson, Edwin Arlington III 22

Robinson Crusoe I 120, 167

"Robinson Treaties, The" IV 217

"Roblin Mills (Circa 1842)" VII 167; aka "Roblin's Mills (2)" 172

"Roblin's Mills" VII 161

"Rochel" V 215 n.65

"Rock Bottom" VIII 396–97

"Rocking Chair, The" IV 154–58

Rocking Chair and Other Poems, The IV 23, 126, 128, 129, 130, 132, 135, 153–58, 159, 163 n.43

"Rocks" III 167, 186 n.12

"Rocky Bay" III 8–9, 177, 186 n.12

Rocky Mountain Foot VIII 135, 137

Rocky Mountain Poems VI 10, 88, 99, 100, 104, 105, 123–29, 155, 163 n.87

"Rodeo" VII 175

Roethke, Theodore V 282 X 29

"Roger Bontemps" (Béranger) I 37–39

"Roger Bontemps" (Crawford) I 36–39

Rogers, Robert II 92

Rogers, Samuel I 11

"Rogers Pass" X 305

Rolle, Richard VI 29, 59

"Rolling-Pin, The" I 24, 27, 59–61

"Rolling Stream" III 177, 186 n.12

"Roman Jew to Ovid, A" V 181

"Roman Rose-Seller, The" I 52–54

"Romance" IV 81

"Romantic" VI 250

Romantic poets II 29–30, 82–84, 137, 139–42 VI 30–31, 47, 52, 227 IX 54

Romeo and Juliet VI 29

Rooke, Constance VI 234, 252 quoted 267 n.34

"Room, A" X 328

"Room for Sleep, A" VI 303

Room of One's Own III 67, 72 VIII 190

"Roominghouse, Winter" IX 39

Roosevelt and the Antinoe, The III 112, 117, 135–39

"Roots" VII 114

Rose and the Puritan, The VII 82, 90, 101

"Rose off a Nation's Thanks, The" I 24, 63 n.20

"rose th night nd th green flowr" VIII 78–81

Rosen, Allan VIII 22

Rosenberg, Harold IV 77, 80, 96, 97, 101 V 300

Rosenberg, Suzanne V 213 n.62, 213 n.63

Rosenblatt, Joe IV 38, 59–60 n.25 VI quoted 103 VII 24, 52 VIII 28, 168, 264 X 8, 15–16, 339–95 quoted 341, 342, 389 n.7

Rosenthal, M.L. IV 235, 239–40, 264 V 157 quoted 54

Roskolenko, Harry V 154 quoted 154

Ross, Catherine I 29, 31 quoted 31
VII 208–09, 232
Ross, Gary IX 25 quoted 25
Ross, George A. III 29, 30 quoted 30
Ross, Malcolm II 7, 81, 92 quoted
7, 90, 91, 121 n.6 IV 180 X 197
quoted 94
Ross, Sinclair IX 1 X 5, 78
Ross, W.W.E. III 1, 2, 5–9, 12, 14,
32 IV 11, 20 V 112 VI 11, 93 X 11
Rossetti, Christina VI 286
Rossetti, Dante Gabriel II 13, 189,
197, 236, 239, 258 IV 81, 247
Rossetti, William Michael II 13
"Rosy Dreams" I 194
Rotella, Mimmo VIII 40
Rothenberg, Jerome VIII 28
"Rotorua" X 168
Rotstein, Abraham IX 190
Rouge et Noir (Trinity College,
Toronto) II 135
Roughing It in the Bush X 181
"Round Trip" VI 248
Rousseau, Douanier VII 277
Rousseau, Henri VI 14
Rousseau, Jean-Jacques II 194
"Row of Horse Stalls, A" III 32, 44,
45
Royal Society of Canada I 85, 149,
165 II 28, 81, 136, 190, 192, 238
V 29, 78 IX 86
Royce, Josiah II 15, 78, 84–85, 97,
99, 100–01, 213
Rubaiyat of Omar Khayyam, The
IV 81
Ruddick, Bruce IV 176, 202
Rugging and the Moving Times,
The: Poems New and Uncol-
lected V 30, 38
Rumi, Jalal al-din VI 228, 249, 256
quoted 257

"Runners, The" VII 180
"Running" VII 177
"Running and Dwelling: Homage to
Al Purdy" IX 190
Running in the Family VIII 13, 361,
362–64, 368, 372, 374, 387,
391–93
Ruppenthal, Steve VIII 28
Rushdie, Salman VIII 370
Ruskin, John VII 211 IX 207
Russell, Bertrand V 216 n.79
Russell, Jane X 386
Russell, Jeffery Burton X 329
quoted 327
"Rust on an Anchor" VII 287
Ryerson Press III 112, 115, 164 V
207 n.4, 280–81 VI 224

Saannes Publications VI 17, 174
Sabatier, Roland VIII 60
"Sacrament by the Water" V 205
Sacred Wood, The II 86
Sad Phoenician, The X 73, 87, 116
"Sad Phoenician, The" X 83, 96,
105, 114, 116–18, 120–22, 126,
127, 129, 135, 150–51, 152, 161,
171, 173
"Sad Song, A" VI 59
"Sad Winter in the Land of Can.
Lit." V 323
Sa'di VI 228
Saga of Billy the Kid, The VIII
379–80
Saga of Eric the Red X 122
Sagas of Vaster Britain: Poems of
the Race, the Empire and the
Divinity of Man II 28–29
"Said the Phoenix . . ." VII 146
Sail-boat and Lake IV 32, 33, 38
"Sailing to Byzantium" X 40
Sailor (bissett) VIII 39, 89, 99

"Sailor" (Page) VI 248, 249

"Saint Antoine Street" V 306

"Saint Catherine Street" X 37

"Saint Denis, L.C., 1837–8" I 194

Saint John Telegraph-Journal VII 82, 83

"Saint Reat and the Four Winds of the World" VIII 315, 317

"Saint Yves between the Rich Man and the Poor Man, Tréguier Cathedral" IV 48

Saint-Denys-Garneau, Hector de VI 254 VII 223

"Saints and Others" V 321–22

"Saint's Apprentice, The" VII 109

"Salad" VIII 288

Salinger, J.D. VIII 92 IX 192

Salutin, Rick X 267

Samson Agonistes I 83, 90

"Samuel Hearne in Wintertime" X 288, 311

Sanctuary: Sunshine House Sonnets II 100

Sandburg, Carl III 20, 30, 46–47 V 80, 98, 240, 250 VI 91

Sandler, Linda VI quoted 103

"Sandman, The" IX 251

Sandwell, B.K. V quoted 87 VI quoted 98

Sanford and Merton I 167

Sangster, Charles I 7, 8, 10, 11–12, 13, 14, 16, 75, 81, 85, 104, 107, 137, 138, 142 II 8, 13 IV 10

Santayana, George II 78, 84–85, 97–98, 99, 108 quoted 98, 107, 213 VII 287–88

Sapir, Edward VII 225

Sappho VII 263

Sappho lyric XXII II 117–18

Sappho: One Hundred Lyrics II 88, 100, 117–18

Saraha IX 207

Sartor Resartus V 82, 98, 240, 250

Sartre, Jean Paul II 219 VII 254, 266 IX 192

Saskatchewan X 257

"saskatchewan" VIII 61

Satie, Eric VII 198

"Satiric Novel in Canada Today, The" V 65

Saturday Night II 245 III 26 IV 18, 71, 75, 78, 101, 207 VI 98, 222 IX 190, 194, 195, 197, 216

Saturday Reader, The I 161

Saturday Review, The I 84

"Saturday Sundae" IV 207

Saul: A Drama in Three Parts I 15, 77, 78, 79, 80, 81, 83, 84, 86, 87, 88, 89, 90, 91, 92–98, 100, 101, 102, 168

Saul and Selected Poems, Including Excerpts from Jephthah's Daughter *and* Jezebel: A Poem in Three Cantos I 89

Saussure, Ferdinand de VIII 45

Savage Fields: An Essay in Literature and Cosmology VIII 374 IX 190–91, 197–200, 209, 218–19, 222 n.50

"Saving Grace, The" VI 154

"Saws Were Shrieking, The" III 177

Say Yes V 281, 290, 295, 315, 320, 327 n.49

"Scamander" VI 203

Scarlet Letter, The III 25, 38

"Scene at Lake Manitou, A" II 250, 256, 258

"Scenes from a Stereoscope" VII 212

"Scenes from the Lives of the Saints" VIII 315, 316

Schaeffer, Frank VI 224

Schafer, R. Murray VIII 28, 271

Schiller, Friedrich von VIII 24, 373
"Schizophrenic" VI 247
Schlegel, August Wilhelm von VIII
   73, 280
Schlegel, Karl Wilhelm Fredrich
   von VIII 73, 280
Schoemperlen, Diane VI 234
"Scholarly Disagreements" VII 153
Scholes, Robert VII 273
"School Globe, The" VII 215
"School of Hygiene" VI 312 n.33
Schroeder, Andreas IX quoted 195
Schultz, John Christian I 124, 125,
   126, 145
Schultz, Gregory P. IV 77–78
Schwartz, Delmore IV 129
Schwartz, Louis IV 175
Schwitters, Kurt VIII 37, 40, 269
Scobie, Stephen IV 182 VI 36 VII
   266, 267, 272–73, 283, 285, 308
   n.122 VIII 12, 275, 281 quoted
   35, 39–40, 242, 269, 272, 274,
   276–77, 282, 284–85, 288, 298,
   304, 307–08, 309, 312 X 24, 27,
   28, 29, 31, 32, 34, 37, 41, 46
   quoted 26, 56 n.54, 57 n.57
Scorpio and Bull VII 288–89
Scotsman in Canada, The II 29, 61,
   62
"Scott" X 383
Scott, Andrew V quoted 161
Scott, Colin A. II 35–36 quoted 35
Scott, Duncan Campbell I 10, 11,
   12, 169 II 7, 8, 9, 11, 12, 16–17,
   19, 21–22, 23, 28, 29, 38, 82,
   135, 143, 144, 146, 150, 171 n.1,
   200, 201, 202, 224 III 1, 21, 23,
   24, 26, 114 IV 7, 10, 32, 177,
   178, 179, 234 V 1, 280 VI 253
   VIII 121 IX 3, 88, 217 quoted 217
   X 11

Scott, F.R. III 2, 3, 5, 6, 12, 112,
   116, 150, 151, 166, 171 quoted
   150 IV 5, 6, 7, 8, 11, 12, 13, 17,
   18–22, 24, 32, 36, 38, 69, 72, 78,
   80, 104, 110, 124, 126, 127, 231,
   232, 234–35, 236, 240, 254, 262
   V 2, 78, 79, 80, 84, 91, 93, 101,
   112, 240 VI 9, 10, 88, 91, 92, 93,
   105, 223, 229, 247, 283 VII 17,
   28, 140, 223, 253, 255, 265, 300
   n.21, 304 n.70 VIII 120 IX 1, 3,
   19, 88, 105, 116 X 23, 37, 192
Scott, Frederick George II 240 IV
   173, 178, 179, 180, 196 VI 86
Scott, Gail VIII 190
Scott, Sir Walter I 83, 167 V 173 VI
   278 VIII 306
"Scott Hutcheson's Boat" VII 158
"Scott's Drowned Poet" II 247
"Scream, The" VII 158
Scribner's Magazine II 136, 236
"Sculptor, The" VII 164
" 'sculptural energy is the /
   mountain' / gaudier-brzeska" VIII
   213–15
"Sculpture of Poetry, The: On Louis
   Dudek" V 90
"Sea, The" V 97–98
Sea and the Mirror, The VIII 296
"Sea Cliff" IV 250, 251
Sea Garden IV 235
"Sea Haven, The" VIII 189
Sea Is Also a Garden, The VII 252,
   255, 266, 269–70, 280, 288, 300
   n.14, 305 n.91 VIII 296
"Sea of Crises, The" IX 240, 257–59
"Sea of Faith" IV 215
"Sea of Tin Cans, The" X 34
"Sea Things" X 251
"Sea-Cathedral, The" III 139
Seagull on Yonge Street VIII 84

"seagull on Yonge Street" VIII 84

Seamon, Roger VII 270

"Search, The" V 164

Search for America, A: The Odyssey of an Immigrant V 108

"Search for an Undiscovered Alphabet" VII 210

"Searching and Sounding" VI 30, 56, 57, 59–60, 62

Searching Image, The V 77, 101, 102

"Seascape" VI 173

"Seasons" VI 173

Season's Lovers, The V 280–81, 286, 306–08, 310

"Season's Lovers, The" V 320

Second Century Anthologies of Verse, The IX 189

"Second Hand, The" VII 263

"Second Letter" VII 223

Second Scroll, The IV 126, 129, 133, 134, 158–59 V 282, 287

Second Silence, The V 280–81, 289, 317

"Second-degree Burns" IX 261

Secord, Laura I 150

"Secret of Old Trees, The" V 302

"Secret Rose, The" IV 242

"Secret Sleeper, The" VI 193, 194

Secular Love VIII 365, 370, 371, 393–400

Sedgewick, G.G. V 27 VII 262

"See the World Clearly" III 96

Seed Catalogue X 13, 14, 73, 74, 76

"Seed Catalogue" X 80, 96, 99, 105, 107, 110–11, 113, 114, 121, 129, 130, 140, 141, 150–51, 162, 166, 167, 168, 173

"Seeing Me Dazed" X 301

"Seeing the Bear" X 134

Seferis, George X 140, 284

Segal, J.I. V 279

Seizin Press VI 174

Selah IX 232

"Select Samaritan" IV 36

Selected Essays (Eliot) VI 48

Selected Essays and Criticism (Dudek) V 78, 98, 120

Selected Poems (Atwood) IX 77 n.68

Selected Poems (Dudek) V 78

Selected Poems (Gustafson) VI 89, 102, 163 n.87

Selected Poems (Purdy) VII 137, 143

Selected Poems (Scott) IV 174, 217

Selected Poems, The (Souster) V 7, 245

Selected Poems: Beyond Even Faithful Legends (bissett) VIII 15

Selected Poems 1954–65 (Webb) VII 256, 270–71, 272

Selected Poems 1956–1968 (Cohen) X 22, 29, 45–46

Selected Poems of Dorothy Livesay 1926–1956 III 63, 68

Selected Poems of E.J. Pratt III 150

Selected Poems of Sir Charles G.D. Roberts II 198

Selected Stories of Raymond Knister III 22

Selections from Canadian Poets I 171 II 8, 13

"Self Epitaph" IV 83

"Self Reliance" II 213

"Self-Portrait from the Year 1952" V 270 n.53

Seliger, Charles VI 225

"Selves, The" VI 261

Semiotics of Poetry X 33

"Sempre" V 163, 164

"Sense of Angels, The" VI 255–56

Sensible, The VIII 135, 137

"Sensible, The" VIII 146

"Sensuous Imagery of Shelley and Keats, The" VI 86

"Sentence" X 99

"Sentimental Journey" VI 173

Separations IX 136, 142, 152–56, 167

"September" VII 213, 220

"September Street" VI 44

"Sequel" IV 88

"Sequence of Songs, A" IV 124

Sequences VI 107, 163 n.87

"Seraphim" VI 261

Serinette VII 197, 208

Service, Robert W. I 91 IV 72 X 284

"Sestina (1964)" VI 63

Seton, Ernest Thompson II 199, 225 n.3

Setter, John J. I 126

"Set-Ups" VI 203–04, 205

Seven Pillars of Wisdom IX 263, 265

"Seven Poems for Duncan" III 86

"Seventh Letter" VII 222

Seventy-one Poems for People VIII 168–69

Sewanee Review, The II 35 IV 130 VI 87

Sex & Death VII 171–74

Sexton, Anne IX 22, 44

"Shadow, The" V 221 n.95

"Shadow Beach" VIII 170

"Shadow Voice, The" IX 36–37

Shadow-Maker, The IX 232, 233, 237–38, 240, 241, 245, 249–56, 259

"Shadow-Maker, The" IX 254–55

"Shadows and Substance" VI 303

"Shadows There Are" IV 247, 248, 253

Shah, Idries VI 256 quoted 256, 257

Shaine, Merle VI 27, 66 n.10

Shake Hands with the Hangman: Poems 1940–52 V 261

Shakespeare, William I 9, 25, 61, 80, 82, 83, 84, 94, 98, 120, 133, 136, 137, 139, 141, 146, 147–48, 167, 187 II 140, 253, 258 III 114, 127, 131 IV 79, 102, 128, 131, 139, 206, 247, 248 V 106 VI 67 n.22 VII 262 X 37, 39, 113

"Shakespeare's Sonnets" X 325, 328, 330

Shamanism: Archaic Techniques of Ecstasy VIII 76

"Shamballah" II 104, 116

"Shape of Prayer, The" VII 276, 287

Shapes and Sounds: Poems of W.W.E. Ross III 6, 9, 163, 165, 169, 170, 171, 175, 180, 181

Shapiro, Karl IV 23, 129, 202

"Shark, The" III 125–26 X 343

Sharman, Vincent III 119, 142

Shattered Plinths, The V 159, 193–96

Shaw, George Bernard III 123 quoted 123 V 150, 213 n.16 VII 80, 202

Shaw, Neufville IV 176, 202 VI 223, 232 VII 304 n.70

Shaw, W. David VII 211, 213

"She Considers Evading Him" IX 71 n.39

"She Is" V 33, 41

"She Reaches Out" X 300

Shelley, Mary IX 71 n.46

Shelley, Percy Bysshe I 82, 95, 133, 136, 139, 141, 167 II 30, 37, 38, 41, 139, 140, 142, 160, 162, 166, 170, 197, 221, 224, 239 quoted 166 III 65, 131 IV 128 V 20 VI 90, 147, VII 201 VIII 6, 23, 24, 27, 73, 114, 125 IX 8, 19, 205

"Sheltered Garden" IV 250–51, 277 n.101

Shepard, Odell II 124 n.65 quoted 81, 89

Shepheardes Calender, The III 9

Sherman, Joseph IX quoted 238

Shikatani, Gerry VIII 281

Shining People of Leonard Cohen, The X 22

"Ships of St. John, The" II (1902) 110; (1921) 116–17

"Shit" V 221 n.93

Shivaree VII 197, 224–25

Shklovsky, Victor VII 307 n.112 VIII 278 X 173

"Shopping at Loblaws" VII 165

"Shore" IV 92–93

"Short History of X County" VII 151

Short, Sad Book, A VIII 150, 153

Short Stories of Thomas Murtha III 26

"Short Story, A" VIII 164

"Shout, The" VII 177

Show Me Death III 21

"Show the Way, England" II 33

Shrive, Norman I 15, 129, 133, 134, 137, 151 n.1, 152 n.14 quoted 8, 120, 128, 129–30, 131, 134, 137, 145, 146

"Shropshire Lad, A" III 26

Shrouding, The (Kennedy) III 26 IV 5, 17, 70–71, 73, 74, 75, 76, 77, 78–79, 80, 84, 86, 87, 88, 91, 93, 94, 95, 97, 99, 100, 103, 109, 110 IX 192

"Shrouding, The" (Livesay) III 75 IV 73, 246

Shucard, Alan VII 93

"Sibelius Park" IX 214

"Sibyl, A" IX 35–36, 52–53, 71 n.43

"Sick, The" VI 248

Sidney, Sir Philip III 169

Siebrasse, Glen VIII 130

Sift in an Hourglass VI 8, 100–01, 105, 131

Sifton, Clifford I 129

"Signal" IV 189–90

Signature IV 174, 211–12, 215, 216

"Signature" IV 206

"Signboard in Soho, A" VII 111, 113

"Significance of Lampman, The" II 149

Signpost III 12, 61, 64, 67, 74, 78, 94

"Signpost" III 74, 89

"Signs and Portents" V 179, 197, 199, 201

"Signs on a White Field: Klein's *Second Scroll*" V 282, 287

"Silence" (Layton) V 222 n.97

"Silences" (Pratt) III 114, 128

"Silences, The" (Mandel) X 237–39

Silent Ancestors, The: The Forebears of E.J. Pratt III 121

"Silent Poet Craves Immortality, The" X 120

"Silent Poet Eats His Words, The" X 120, 123

"Silent Poet Sees Red, The" X 120

"Silent Poet Sequence, The" X 105, 116, 120–23, 150

"Silk Factory" IX 177–78

Sillers, Pat IX 70 n.27

"Sillery, L.C., 1648" I 194

Silver, Jack VIII quoted 201–02, 229

Silver Wire, The VIII 135, 137

"Silverthorn Bush" IV 16, 55–56

Silverthorn Bush and Other Poems, The IV 32, 39, 57

Simcoe, John Graves II 238

Simms, Norman X quoted 204

"Simon: finis" VI

Simpson, Colin IX 265

"Simulation" X 249

Singer, I.J. IV 129

"Singing Girl" IV 93

"Singing Head, The" X 288, 305, 306

"Sinner, The" V 198

"Sir Charles G.D. Roberts" (Pacey) II 198

Sir Charles G.D. Roberts: A Biography II 197

"Sir Pompey" VII 214

"Siren Song" IX 48

"Sister Mary Cecilia" VII 114

"Sisters" VI 250

Sisters of Mercy X 22

"Sitting" VII 266, 287

Sitting in Mexico VIII 125, 135

Sitwell, Edith IV 13, 39, 103, 245, 246 VI 91 VII 198, 204, 211–12, 212–13, 213–14, 216, 233

Sitwell, Osbert VI 91

Sitwell, Sacheverell VI 91

"Six Years" III 102 n.80

"Six-Quart Basket, The" V 6–7, 256

"Sixth Letter" VII 222

Sixth Sense, The: Individualism in French Poetry, 1686–1760 IV 31

"Skaters, The" IV 56–57

"Skeleton by an Old Cedar" VII 169

"Skeleton in the Grass" V 35

Skelton, Robin III 70–71, 72, 74 quoted 71 IV 181, 182 VI 103–04, 108 quoted 101, 104, 106, 107 VIII 113 IX 26, 27–28, 70 n.27 quoted 27

"Sketch: Cement Worker on a Hot Day" VI 59, 60

"Sketch: End of a Day: or, I as a Blurry" VI 50

"Sketch: From Train Window (Leamington to Windsor) in March" VI 72 n.92

"Sketch: Thaws" VI 44, 63

"Sketches of a Lemon" X 125

"Skin Boat" VIII 397–98

"Skyscraper and Bird" V 258

"Skyscraper Tower" III 183

"Skyscrapers" III 183, 184

"Sleep" X 387

"Sleep Is the Silence Darkness Takes" IX 163

"Sleeper" (Page) VI 250

"Sleeper, The" (MacEwen) IX 250–51

"Sleeper, The" (Page) VI 247

Sleeping Lady, The X 340, 344, 346, 373–75

"Slideshow, The" IX 20, 31

"Sliverick" VI 50

Slonim, Leon II 247, 271 IX 235

"Slug in Woods" V 49

"Small Poems for the Winter Solstice" IX 60, 67

"Small Rain, A" V 102

"Small World" VI 258

"Smalltown Hotel" V 40

Smart, Christopher VIII 279 X 192, 202, 257

"Smelling Your Blood" X 298

Smith, A.J.M. I 12, 14, 28, 29, 30, 61, 86, 87, 133, 135, 140, 142, 151 n.1, 173, 181, 190, 192 quoted 12, 86–87, 135, 181, 190, 192 II 11, 22, 149, 246, 247–49, 252, 265 quoted 11, 149 III 2, 3, 6, 14, 26, 65, 68, 71, 76, 112, 116, 164, 165, 166, 167, 171, 172, 173, 174, 177, 178 quoted 14, 68, 167 IV 5, 6–7, 8–9, 10, 11–15, 16, 17, 18, 19, 20, 21, 22,

24, 32, 34, 35, 38, 39, 57, 69,
72–73, 75, 78, 79, 80, 82, 83, 84,
85, 87, 88, 89, 91, 92, 93, 94, 99,
104, 110, 124, 127, 129, 134,
139, 159, 174, 175, 176, 177,
178, 179, 180, 181, 182, 185,
193, 198, 199, 207, 215 V 2, 37,
79, 85, 87, 91, 150, 154, 156,
158, 240 quoted 34, 37, 56, 84,
87, 156 VI 7, 8, 10, 21 n.6, 34,
36, 69 n.37, 69 n.39, 87, 88, 91,
92, 93, 101, 105, 156 n.5, 156
n.7, 223, 229, 231, 232, 233–34,
247, 249, 281, 284, 285, 286,
287, 288, 296, 301, 302, 304
quoted 8, 10, 35, 42, 46, 68
n.28, 100, 231, 233, 252, 265
n.9, 286, 301 VII 7, 17, 137,
140, 255, 260, 261, 269 VIII
120, 272 IX 1, 3, 19, 88, 97, 194
X 94
Smith, Goldwin I 25, 146 II 190
Smith, I. Norman III quoted 64
Smith, Joseph VII 125
Smith, Kay VI 282
Smith, Patrick Keeney V 160 X 116,
124
Smith, Rowland X 30
Smith, Steven VIII quoted 263
Smith, Stevie VI 33, 50, 292
Smoked Glass VII 83, 92–93, 95,
118–22
Smoking Mirror VIII 160
"Smoking Mirror" VIII 160–61
Smuts, J.C. III 115, 120
"Snake, The" X 343, 371, 372
"Snake Charmers" X 243
"Snake Trying, The" III 9
"Snapshot" VII 109
"Snow" II 40–41, 42, 44 VI 29, 31,
38, 46, 71 n.73

Snow, C.P. V 112
Snow, Michael X 244
"Snow at Roblin Lake" VII 161
"Snow Buntings" IX 109–10, 111
Snow Queen, The VIII 208, 210
"Snowfall" III 31 VI 110, 261
Snowflakes and Sunbeams II 28, 29,
40–48, 53, 67
"Snowman, The" VI 254
"Snows of William Blake, The" V
321
" 'So Deadly Silent': The Resolution
of Pain and Fear in the Poetry of
Lampman and D.C. Scott" II
175 n.44
"So you're the kind of vegetarian"
X 49
"Social Notes" IV 197
Social Organization and the Secret
Societies of the Kwakiutl Indians,
The VIII 221
Social Planning for Canada IV 174
"Socrates" VII 253, 301 n.35
"Soil in Smoke" III 21
"Soirée of Velvel Kleinburger" IV
127, 138, 139, 140–46, 161 n.14
"Soldiery" III 182, 183
Solecki, Sam V 212 n.56 VIII quoted
13, 371, 395
"Solemn Land, The" III 168
Solidarnosc: Prelude VI 89–90
"Soliloquy of an Amoeba" V
95–96
"Soliloquy to Absent Friends" IX
106, 107–09, 110
"Solitary Confinement" VII 301
n.35
"Solitary Woodsman, The" II 197,
215
"Solstice Poem" IX 55
Solway, David V 151

"Some Afterthoughts on *Contact* Magazine" V 250, 269 n.51

"Some Critics Are Music Teachers" VII 197

"Some Final Questions" VII 290–91

"Some of Farmer Stebbin's Opinions" I 40, 41–42

"Some There Are Fearless" VI 249

"Someone Who Used to Have Someone" V 321, 327 n.51

"Something" X 322,

"Something Apart" IV 247

"Something Other than Our Own" IX 172

"Something to Write About" VII 78, 79, 82, 98

"Somewhere in Argentina" X 369–70

"Somewhere in my trophy room" X 49

Sommer, Richard V 159 quoted 159

"Somnia" VIII 134

"Son of the Sea, A" II 111

"Son-and-Heir" IV 255–56

"Song" (Cohen) X 37

"Song" (Kennedy) IV 75, 80

"Song" (Lampman) II 153

"Song" (Lee) IX 213–14

"Song" (Mandel) X 234

"Song against Constancy, A" IV 241

"Song and Dance" III 89

"Song but Oblique to '47" VI 43

"Song for Canada" I 191, 198

"Song for Simeon, A" VI 55

"Song — God Bless the Dominion" I 194

"Song: Lay Down" IX 193

"Song . . . Much of It Borrowed" VI 260

"Song of a Frightened Jewish Boy" V 192–93

"Song of Hiawatha, The" I 65 n.56

Song of Leonard Cohen, The X 23

"Song of North York between Sheppard and Finch, A" V 302

"Song of Seasons" IX 192

"Song of the Arrow" I 33–34

"Song of the Flaming Sword" VI 31

"Song of the Fox" IX 48

"Song of the Happy Shepherd" IV 81

"Song of the Hen's Head" IX 48

"Song of the Impermanent Husband" VII 158

"Song of the Wandering Aengus, The" IV 242

"Song of the Worms" IX 48

Songes en équilibre, Les VI 179

"Songs for the Soldiers" I 63 n.20

Songs from a Room X 22, 31, 42

Songs of Experience VI 190–91, 192

Songs of Innocence VI 37, 190–91, 192

Songs of Leonard Cohen X 22, 31

Songs of Love and Hate X 22, 31

Songs of the Common Day, and Ave: An Ode for the Shelley Centenary II 197–98, 206

Songs of the Great Dominion: Voices from the Forests and Waters, the Settlements and Cities of Canada I 85, 161 II 225 n.5, 236

Songs of the Sea Children II 117

"Songs of the Transformed" IX 26, 30, 40, 47, 63, 69 n.8

"Sonic Horses" VIII 21

"sonik prayr" VIII 76

"Sonnet for Ontario" III 64, 75

"Sonnet in Time of Affliction" IV 135–38

Sonnets (Heavysege) I 78, 80, 85

Sonnets (W.W.E. Ross) III 163, 169, 171, 172

"Sonnets Semitic" IV 138

Sonnets to Orpheus VIII 400

"Sonnets, Written in the Orillia Woods, August 1859" I 11, 184–87, 193

Sono Nis Press VI 90, 156 n.9

"Sons & Divinations" VIII 319–20, 328–29

"Sons and Lovers" VII 155–56

Sons of Captain Poetry, The VIII 13, 265, 366

Sonthoff, Helen VII 269–70, 272 X 203

Sophocles IV 31 VII 262

"Sorcerer, The" IV 247

Sorestad, Glen X 8, 200

Sorfleet, John II 15, 22, 92, 93, 94, 97

"Sorrow of Stones, A" VI 303

"Sorrows of Saint Orm, The" VIII 315, 316–17

Sort of Ecstasy, A: Poems New and Selected IV 238

Sosa, Roberto VIII 169

soul arrow VIII 61, 62–63, 64, 70

"Soul, Geologically, A" IX 42–43

"Sound of the Birds at Dawn, The" VII 110

Sound Poetry: A Catalogue VIII 275

"Sounding the Name" X 154, 155, 165

"Sounds Carry" VI 59

Sourkes, Cheryl VIII 246

Souster, Raymond III 2, 6, 9, 73, 163, 175 IV 59 n.25, 236 V 2–3, 4, 5, 6–10, 11, 12, 21, 34, 77, 82, 85, 86, 87, 93, 96, 112, 124, 152, 207 n.4, 280 quoted 6, 8, 77 VI 92, 93, 223 VII 23, 26, 28, 49, 84, 85, 86, 87, 140 VIII 8, 121, 122, 123, 125, 127, 132, 134, 159, 189, 264 IX 2, 86, 87, 91, 121, 234, 235 X 191, 228

"Souster's Lament" V 252–53

"Souster's Vision of Life Is So Consistent" V 246

"Sousterre" VIII 160

"South" VII 163

Southam, Anne VIII 28

Southey, Robert I 136

"Souvenir du Temps Perdu" IV 14, 263

Soviet Poems: Sept. 13 to Oct. 5, 1976 VI 89, 142

Sowton, Ian V 289, 306, 307 IX 146 quoted 146–47

"Spain" III 80

"Span" VI 32

"Spanish B.C." VIII 134, 137

"Speaking about Death: *Blues for Mentor Williams*" IV 264

Specimens of the English Dramatic Poets Who Lived about the Times of Shakespeare I 82

Spector, Phil X 23, 31

"Speeches for Dr. Frankenstein" IX 22, 39–40, 72 n.47

"Speleologist" VI 61

Spencer, Herbert III 115

Spender, Stephen II 12, 17, 249 III 4, 12, 65 IV 6, 13, 21, 74, 177, 204 V 1, 2, 31, 79, 240, 250 VI 88, 90, 228, 229 VII 198 IX 8

"Spending the Morning on the Beach — Ten Related Lyrics" X 166, 167, 168, 172, 174

Spenser, Edmund I 120, 135, 170, 175, 181, 187, 193 III 10, 169, IV 124, 134, 162 n.23 VII 200–02 VIII 280 X 118

Spettigue, D.O. IX 94 quoted 94
"Sphere" III 7–8
Spicer, Jack V 91
Spice Box of Earth, The X 16, 21, 26, 37–42, 44–47
"Spider Blues" VIII 386
Spinoza, Benedict de IV 131, 133, 145, 146, 147 V 197
Spirit of Solitude, The: Conventions and Continuities in Late Romance VI 174, 175, 176–77, 192, 208–09, 210 n.4, 213 n.36, 213 n.37, 214 n.48
"Spirit River" II 273, 275
"spirit ship, th" VIII 85
Spoon River Anthology III 29
Spreading Time: Remarks on Canadian Writing and Writers, Book I: 1904–1949 III 27, 28
"Spring" IV 246 VI 249
"Spring Flame" IV 196, 214
"Spring Harvest" X 99
"Spring in the Igloo" IX 35
"Spring on Mattagami" II 250, 258, 276–77
"Spring Poem" IX 47, 76 n.65
"Spring Song" III 179–80 VII 154; (1968) 154
"Spring-Flooded Ditches" III 40
"Spring-time" X 36
"Squatter, The" II 215
"Squatters, 1946" VI 248
Squire, J.C. III 115
"St. Anzas: basis/bases" VIII 339
St-Denys Garneau & Anne Hébert: Translations/Traductions IV 174, 218
"St. John" II 224
"St. Lawrence and the Saguenay, The" I 161, 173, 175–82, 184, 185, 192, 193

St. Lawrence and the Saguenay and Other Poems I 12, 160, 163, 169, 170, 171, 174, 175, 182–84, 190, 191, 192–93
St. Nicholas Hotel, The VII 196
"St. Valentine Is Past" V 33
"Stab" VIII 135, 146
Stalin, Joseph V 31, 183, 184, 188 IX 94
Stand of Jackpine, A VII 25, 35
Standard Dictionary of Canadian Biography II 192
"Standing" VII 287
Stanley, George VIII 126
Stansbury, Joseph I 15
"Stanzas Written on First Looking into Johnston's Auk" IV 263
"st*r" VIII 295
stardust VIII 62
"Stars" VII 103
"Stars over Evil Houses" IX 103
"stars turn their noble stories, The" X 45
"State of Sonora" V 47, 48, 60
"Statement" VI 229
"Statue in the House" X 233
"Stay in This Room" X 303–04
Stead, Robert J.C. X 5
Stedman, Clarence II 195, 225 n.4
"Stefan" VI 259
Stegner, Wallace X 199
Stein, Gertrude VII 277 VIII 11, 21, 23, 25–26, 91, 168, 193, 268, 271, 274, 307, 319 quoted 26, 314 X 133
Steinberg, Donna V 213 n.60
Steinberg, M.W. III 69 IV 133
Steiner, George X 245
Stendhal (Marie Henri Beyle) III 11 VIII 11

"Stenographers, The" VI 242, 244, 246–47, 248

Stephens, Donald II 92–93 quoted 82, 93

"Steps of Love" VIII 134

Stereoscope VII 232

"Stereoscope, The" VII 232

Sterne, Laurence VIII 7, 153

Stevens, Peter III 29, 30, 45, 69, 120, 128, 166, 168, 170, 172, 178, 179 quoted 29, 70, 166, 170, 172, 179 IV 39, 78, 79, 87, 89–90, 99, 100, 109, 184, 240, 243 V 89, 160 quoted 17, 89–90 VI quoted 107 IX 91 quoted 25, 91 X 346 quoted 206, 345

Stevens, Wallace II 269 IV 33, 194, 234, 235, 241, 245 V 104, 282 VI 94, 104, 128, 131, 148, 154, 227, 228 VII 263–64, 274, 276 VIII 13, 25, 114, 369, 373 quoted 151, 165, 170 IX 20, 69 n.3, 76 n.62, 87, 99, 102 quoted 18, 59 X 284, 291

Stevenson, O.J. II 90

Stevenson, Robert Louis II 109, 243 VI 278

Steveston VIII 14, 190, 197, 199, 200, 201, 202, 205, 206, 220, 224–29

Steveston Recollected: A Japanese–Canadian History VIII 14, 190, 225

Stewart, George I 168, 181, 190 quoted 181, 190

Stewart's Literary Quarterly Magazine I 161, 168

Stich, K.P. II 247

Sticks and Stones VII 196, 203–04, 207, 227–29

"Still" (Birney) V 5

Still (Nichol) VIII 311

Still, Robert IV 184

"Still Hunting" IX 167–68

"Still ist die Nacht" VI 213 n.36

"Still Life" VI 291, 292

"Still there are wars and crimes of war" VII 271

Still Water VIII 11, 265, 294

"Stills" VIII 301

Stockdale, J.C. I 75, 89 quoted 89

"Stocktaking on the Day of Atonement" V 187

"Stoic and Hedonist" II 163

"Stoics, The" III 129

Stoker, Bram VI 198

"Stone" IV 206

Stone Bird, The IV 209 VII 178–80

"Stone Hammer Poem" X 14–15, 96, 104, 113, 123, 128, 158

Stone Hammer Poems: 1960–1975, The X 13, 73, 99–103, 105–06, 129, 134, 173

"Stone's Secret" VI 32, 59, 65

"Stoney Ridge Dance Hall" VII 104

Stony Plain X 193, 199, 200, 204, 243–54, 255

Stoppard, Tom VII 277

"Store Seeds, The" VI 40, 72 n.92

"Stories of Snow" VI 232, 249, 251, 252

"Stories on a String: It All Started in London, Ontario in the mid-1960s (Part I)" VII 195

"Storm" II 170 VI 303

Storm Warning VIII 32

"Story" X 36

Story, Norah I 88

"Story of an Affinity, The" II 147, 164, 168–69, 171

"Story of Isaac" X 38

Story, She Said, The VIII 232–33

Story So Far, The VIII 126

Stouck, David VII 144–45

Strafford I 83

"Stragglers, The" X 72

*Strait of Anian, The: Selected
    Poems* IV 163 n.43 V 28, 35–36

"Stranded Ship, The" II 215

Strange Fugitive IV 106

Strange Grey Day This VIII 19

"Stranger Song, The" X 45

"Strangers, The" VII 180

"Strawstack, The" III 24

"Stray Dog, near Ecully" VI 52

"Street Opera" VIII 238

"Streetcar" VI 52

"Streetlights" X 236

Strength of the Hills, The IV 32

Strickland, Lakefield I 21

Strickland, Robert I 21

Strickland, Samuel I 21

Stringer, Arthur III 167

Stromberg-Stein, Susan V 75

"Strong Yellow, for Reading
    Aloud" VI 49, 65

Student Christian Movement IV 173

Studhorse Man, The X 72

Studies in Canadian Literature VI
    38 VIII 36, 37

Studies in Canadian Literature
    series VI 37

*Studies in Pauline Eschatology, and
    Its Background* III 111, 131

"Study of Poetry, The" II 141

"Style" II 143, 167, 168 X 43, 48

"Style of Byron's *Don Juan* in
    Relation to the Newspapers of
    His Day, The" VI 27, 31, 38, 44,
    47, 50, 51, 57, 59, 72 n.91,
    73–74 n.117

"Subjective Eye" VI 249

"Substitutions" VI 196

Suckow, Ruth III 20, 26 IV 103

Sufi poets VI 13, 225, 228, 234,
    249, 256, 257

Sufis, The VI 256

al-Suhrawardi VI 228

"Suicide Notes" X 365

Suit of Nettles, A III 9, 28, 31 VII
    15, 195, 201, 203, 204, 205–06,
    207, 211, 213, 219–22

"Suite for Ann, A" X 263

"Suite of Lies" VII 251, 299 n.8

Suknaski, Andrew V 29, 34 VII 138
    VIII 30 IX 140, 145, 175 X 8, 194,
    199, 206

Sullivan, Sir Arthur V 44

Sullivan, Rosemary III 72 VI quoted
    19 IX 146 quoted 8, 146

"Sumach" III 40

"Summer" VII 103

"Summer Acres" VI 16, 277,
    288–89, 306

"Summer Camp" IV 36, 190, 199

"Summer in the Street" V 306

"Summer Is a Poem by Ovid" VIII
    367

"Summer Resort" VI 244–45

"Summer Romance" VII 300 n.14

"Summer Solstice" VIII 126, 131,
    148, 149–50, 152, 153, 165, 167

"Summer Song" IX 213–14

"Summer Storm, A" II 263

"Summons to Vagabonds" VII 145

"Sun, The" VII 300 n.14

Sun and the Moon, The VI 223,
    225, 231, 236–43 VII 195, 196,
    224

*Sun and the Moon and Other
    Fictions, The* VI 225

*Sun Has Begun to Eat the
    Mountain, The* IX 162

"Sun in the Garden, The" VI 147, 148

Sun Is Axeman, The IX 86, 87, 91, 93, 99, 103, 104–10, 112, 114, 116

"Sun, Moon, and Stars" I 182

"Sun, Wind, and Snow: The Poems of Dorothy Livesay" III 12, 64, 72

"Sunbathers" V 191

"Sunbeams" II 44–45, 46, 49

sunblue VI 18, 20, 28, 31, 32, 36, 39, 44, 48, 49, 50, 57, 58–64, 65, 67 n.21, 70, n.61

"Sundance" VII 175–76

Sundance at Dusk VII 141, 171, 175–77

"Sunday Poem, The" VIII 133

Sunday Water VII 257, 266, 305 n.84

"Sunday Water" VII 250, 280, 297

"Sundogs, The" VII 216

"Sunflowers" V 217 n.82

"Sunstroke" VIII 145

"Surfaces" III 91

Surfacing VI 241 IX 29

"Surrealism in the Service of Christ" IV 258

Surrealist poets V 4

Surrey, Philip V 283

"Surrogate" VI 199, 203, 204

Survival: A Thematic Guide to Canadian Literature VI 177–78 VIII 33, 173 X 384

"Survivors, The" V 316

Sutherland, Annie I 21

Sutherland, Audrey VII 265

Sutherland, Betty (later Betty Layton) V 170, 180, 215 n.67 VII 265

Sutherland, Fraser VII 138

Sutherland, John II 137, 148–49,

155 quoted 137, 148 III 116, 117–18, 119, 132 quoted 118 IV 8, 15, 38, 40–41, 132, 153, 176, 234, 236, 238, 260 V 5, 19, 76, 77, 79, 84, 145, 152, 154, 170, 182, 238, 240, 241, 242, 244, 280, 281, 314, 315 quoted 5–6, 154, 242, 244 VI 9, 87, 118, 156 n.6, 222, 223, 231–32, 232–33, 249, 265 n.8, 281 VII 85, 204, 213–14, 259–60, 261, 265 IX 86, 190

Swados, Harvey X 72

"Swamp Alder" VI 211 n.16

Swann and Daphne VI 279, 285, 304–06

Sward, Robert VII 145

"Sweeney Comes to McGill" IV 104

"Sweet Light Strikes My Eyes, The" V 205

Swift, Jonathan III 122 VIII 95, 151 IX 13, 60, 158

"Swift Current" IV 249–50

"Swimmer, The" V 145 IX 252–53

"Swimmer's Moment, The" VI 19–20, 32, 43, 53, 56, 258

"Swimming" VII 252

"Swimming Lesson" VI 300

Swinburne, Algernon Charles I 12, 83 II 13, 37, 96–97, 189, 197, 258 IV 76 X 17, 29, 373

"Swing, The" VIII 135, 139

Swinging Flesh, The V 187

Sykes, W.J. II 36, 249 quoted 36

"syllable's discarded / to reveal a real breast // 'the rest is history', a" VIII 297

"Syllables [*via* Sanskrit]" X 329

Symbolist poets IX 140

Symbolists, English II 83

Symbolists, French II 13–14 VI 11,
226–27, 227, 230
Symbols of Transformation IX 253
Symons, A.J.A. VIII 12
Symons, Arthur II 80 X 17
Symons, Julian VI quoted 156 n.11
"Sympathy" V 304
"Synagogue in West Palm Beach" V
223 n.102
"System of Ethics" IV 45
S/Z VIII 46–47

T.E. Lawrence Poems, The IX 12,
232, 262–66
T.O. Now: The Young Toronto
Poets IX 190, 193
"TTA 10:" VIII 304
"TTA 12:" VIII 304
"TTA 42:" VIII 304
"Tagged" IV 36
Tait, Michael I 88 quoted 88 II 38
VII 202, 206–07
Take the Big Picture VII 197, 233
"Taking Place" VIII 230
Taking Sides: The Collected Social
and Political Writings V 220
n.92, 225 n.106
"Takkakaw Falls" V 41–42
"Talisman in Seven Shreds" IV 146
Talking VII 257, 272, 275, 276,
277, 284
"Talking Doorknobs" V 110
"Tall Man Executes a Jig, A" V
14–15, 16
"Tall Suns, The" VI 254
"Tall Tale, A" VII 266, 296
Tallman, Ellen VIII 122
Tallman, Warren V 150 quoted 150
VIII 8, 21, 28, 92, 121, 122, 147,
189, 192, 204, 271 quoted 43 X 9
"Tallness and Darkness" V 299

Talman, James J. VII 226
Talmud I 25 IV 128, 158, 159, 163
n.35 V 170, 203
Talon VIII 264 IX 135, 137
Tamarack Review, The V 78, 121,
239 VI 34, 224, 262, 279, 280,
283, 285, 301, 302 VII 85 IX 136,
194, 232 X 21, 286
"Tamed Birds" V 194, 223 n.100
"Taming, The" III 92
"Taming of the Dragon, The" IX
237–38
Tanabe, Takao X 281, 282, 294
"Tantramar Revisited" II 19–20,
197, 207, 217, 223–24 IX 205
"Taormina" II 222
"Tapered Green Gowned Lady, A"
X 381
"Tapeworm" VI 211 n.16
Tasks of Passion: Dennis Lee at
Mid-Career IX 191, 196–97,
200–01
"Taste of Space, The" IV 263
Tate, Allen IV 235
Tawney, R.H. IV 173, 197
Tay John IX 235
Taylor, Bayard I 75, 76, 77, 78, 81,
85, 171 quoted 77, 78, 171
Taylor, Charles IX quoted 206
Taylor, Michael VI quoted 38
"T-Bar" VI 250, 251
"Tears, Idle Tears" IV 92
Technology and Culture: Six
Lectures V 78, 123, 124, 125
"Technology Is Spreading" VI 65
"Tecumseh" I 194
Tecumseh, a Drama I 8, 119, 128,
131, 132, 136, 137, 145–48, 149,
151, 152 n.13, 168
Tecumseh, a Drama, and Canadian
Poems I 130, 145, 148–50

Tecumseh, a Drama, and Canadian Poems; Dreamland and Other Poems; The American Bison; Through the Mackenzie Basin; Memoirs and Reminiscences I 132

"Teleological" IV 185, 199–200

Tempest, The I 136 X 37

"Temporizing in the Eternal City" VII 172

"Temptation" VII 109

Ten Canadian Poets IV 239

Ten Elephants on Yonge Street V 259

"Ten Miles in from Horsefly" IX 152, 153

"Ten Thousand Pianos" VII 177

"Ten Years and More" V 318

"Ten Years at Play" VII 196, 202, 206, 224

Tennyson, Alfred, Lord I 11, 25, 28, 35, 83, 89, 96, 102, 133, 136, 139, 140, 141, 167, 187–88, 190, 193 II 13, 37, 78, 82, 89, 142, 150, 158–59, 162, 168, 170, 197, 236, 239 quoted 159 III 3, 76, 114, 115 IV 10, 20, 76, 92, 176, 194, 247, 258, 268 V 145, 152 IX 205

"Tent Rings" VII 163–64

"Tenth Letter" VII 223

Teoria da poesia concreta VIII 28

"Tercentenary of Quebec, The: 1608–1908" II 277

"Terribly awake I wait" X 49

Terror and Decorum VII 198, 202, 206, 224

"Terror and Erebus: A Verse Play for Radio" IX 232

"Terrorists" V 197

Tessera VIII 190, 249

"Testament" IV 71, 247

"Testimony of a Tent Preacher" VII 96

"Tethers, The" VI 261

"Teufelsdröckh Concerning Women" V 219 n.87

Thackeray, William Makepeace V 109 VI 278

"Thackeray and the Profession of Letters" V 76

"That There Is No Relaxation" X 290, 325

"That Year on Salisbury Street" VII 114

"That Yellow Prairie Sky" X 72, 73

" 'The Poetry of Earth': A Note on Roberts' Sonnets" II 202

"The stars are glittering in the frosty sky" I 107

"The Young Ravens That Call upon Him" II 209

"Them Ducks" VI 263

"Theme and Variation" (Kennedy) IV 108

"Theme and Variation" (Wilkinson) VI 293

"Theme and Variations" (Wilkinson) VI 312–13 n.33

Theme and Variations for Sounding Brass VI 89, 104, 142

"Then" VI 61

"Then, If I Cease Desiring" X 299

Theocritus VIII 23

"Theology" V 190–91, 201

"Theory of the Image in Modern Poetry, The" V 82, 93, 124

"There Are Delicacies" V 54

"There Are Some Men" X 46

"There Is No One Here Except Us Comedians" X 230

"There Is No Such Thing as Going Too Far" VII 257

"There Is Only One of Everything" IX 51, 52–53

"There Was a Time When Children Died" VII 119

"There Was an Old Woman from Wexford" VII 79–80

"There Were No Signs" V 204

There's a Trick with a Knife I'm Learning to Do VIII 365, 375, 389–91

"These Are Yours" X 312

"These Heroics" X 37, 43

"These notebooks, these notebooks" X 44

"These Times" V 299, 300

Thesen, Sharon VII 272, 275, 309 n.135 VIII 126 quoted 237–38

They Are Returning III 113

"They Go Off to Seek Their Fortunes" VII 93, 114

"They Might Have Been Zebras" VI 258

"They Return" VI 200

Thibaudeau, Colleen VII 215 VIII 31

"Thief Hanging in Baptist Halls" X 223

"Thin Garden, The" IX 251–52

"Thing Is Violent, The" IX 246

" 'Things' in Space: Mystic Missiles, Flying Sorcerers, Etc.: A Valedictory Article" V 111

"Things of the World" V 320–21

"Things We Talked About, The" V 318

Things Which Are, The VII 82, 85, 90, 91–92, 101

"Third Eye, The" VII 216, 222, 224, 237 n.43

"Thirteen Ways of Looking at a Blackbird" X 285

"Thirty Below" IX 162

"Thirty Miles in from the Coast" IX 162

"This Canadian Poetry" III 66, 68

"This Form" III 173, 181

"This Frieze of Birds" VI 254

"This Is a Photograph of Me" IX 25, 33, 37, 55, 57, 66, 76 n.57

"This Is Another Spring" VI 249

"This is the only poem" X 44

"This is the poem we have been waiting for" X 47

"This Is the Song" X 300, 301

"This Is What I Wanted to Sign Off With" VII 125–26

This Magazine IX 68 n.1

"This Man of April" IV 76

"This Northern Mouth" IX 252

"This Page My Pigeon" V 33

This Quarter [Paris] III 10, 20, 27

Thomas, Audrey III 14 VIII 162, 173, 195

Thomas, Dylan IV 23, 177, 202 V 2, 80, 282 VI 15, 29, 40, 43, 92, 229, 281, 282, 283, 284, 290 VII 147, 150, 263 IX 20, 21, 76 n.64, 193 X 39, 208

Thomas, Edward III 7, 11, 76

Thomas, Peter X 85, 88, 100 quoted 89, 111

"Thomas Moore and Sweet Annie" IV 263

Thompson, David X 257

Thompson, E.P. IX 219

Thompson, Eric IX 25, 194 quoted 25, 194

Thompson, Francis II 216

Thomson, Edward William II 135, 170, 243 III 23

Thomson, James II 18

Thomson, Tom VIII 154 IX 208,
209 X 102–03

Thomson, Virgil IX 69 n.12

Thoreau, Henry David II 79, 84,
112 VI 227, 302

"Those Damned Visionary Poets
(Les Poètes Maudits
Visionnaires)" V 111

"Thou Didst Say Me" V 319–20

"Thoughts on a Narrow Night" VI
144

Thousand and One Nights, A IX
252

"Three Cast with the I Ching" IX
119

"Three Days after Crisis in Cuba"
IX 149–50

"Three Emily's, The" III 64, 67, 88

"Three Feathers, The" VI 242

"Three Gold Fish" VI 258

"Three Haiku on a Literary
Theme" VII 279, 287

"Three Pilgrims, The" II 147

"Three Poems about Poets" VI
298

"Three Poems for My Teacher" V
314

"Three Sonnets in Sequence" IV
101–02

"Three Western Tales" VIII 309–10

"Through Clear Crystal" VI 152

Through the Looking-Glass IX 252

Through the Mackenzie Basin: A
Narrative of the Athabasca and
Peace River Treaty Expedition of
1899 I 130, 152 n.14

Through the Vanishing Point VIII
275

"Through Way, The" V 307

"Thyrsis" IX 205

"Tiamut" IX 239

"Tidewater Burial" X 98

"Tigerlily" IX 192

"Tigers Know from Birth" VI
15–16, 298–99

Tillinghast, Richard VI quoted 36,
39

Time X 29

"Time and Again" VIII 148

"Time Is Tiger" VI 293

"Time of the Fictitious 'I,' The" IX
102

"Time of the Fire, The" VII 101

Times Literary Supplement, The IX
136 X 29

"Tin Roof" VIII 370, 395, 399

"Tintern Abbey" II 211

"Tirade by Way of Introduction"
VII 44,

Tish V 4, 243 VII 6, 139 VIII 5, 8,
119–20, 122, 123–26, 133, 134,
137, 189, 192, 197, 264, 369 IX
137 X 9, 281

Tish poets III 72 VI 230

Titanic, The III 112, 116, 120,
139–41 IX 192

Titans III 112, 131, 132, 133

"title untitled" VIII 298

"To — " (Mair) I 141

"To . . ." (Webb) VII 287

"To a Cat-Shaped Ashtray" VII 146

"To a Millionaire" II 18

"To a Morning Cloud" I 140

"To a Pioneer in Canadian Studies;
and to All in Such Pedantry" VI
65

"To a Psych-Neurotic" VI 293

"To a Robin in November" II 30,
35, 41–43, 44, 46

"To a Sad Daughter" VIII 397–98

"To a Skylark" II 41

"To a Teacher" X 38

"To a Zen Buddhist Who Laughs Daily" VII 278, 282

"To Autumn" I 140

"To Be a Healer" V 307–08

"To Certain Friends" IV 212

"To Chaucer" II 156

"To Emmaus" VI 63

"To Eve in Bitterness" IX 114

"To Friends Who Have Also Considered Suicide" VII 287

"To Give Intuition a Certitude" VI 131–34, 163 n.92

"To Henry Vaughan" IV 14, 263

"To His Coy Mistress" IV 216, 263

"To Hold in a Poem" IV 243

"To I.P.L." X 37

"To Irving Layton, on His Love Poem to Mrs. Jacqueline Kennedy, Then First Lady" IV 263

"To Islands Rowboats Stand On" VIII 286–87

"To Jacques Ellul" VI 74 n.124

"To Jay Macpherson on Her Book of Poems" IV 263

"To My Children" X 223, 224–25

"To My Photograph" I 142–43, 144

"To Not Know When It Is the Worst Is Worst" VI 52

"To Professor X, Year Y" VI 41, 50

"To R.E." V 214 n.65

To Say the Least: Canadian Poets from A to Z VI 225

"To Souster from Vermont" V 245

"To Swindon from London by Britrail Aloud/Bagatelle" V 43

"To the Indian Pilgrims" X 48

"To the Outlaw" IX 12, 134, 136, 138–39, 141, 155

"To the Prophetic Soul" II 152–53

"To the Secret City: From a Winnipeg Sketchbook" VII 217

"To the Spirit of Song" II 216

"To the Victims of the Holocaust" V 222 n.97

"To Those Concerned" VI 110

"To William Carlos Williams" V 103

"Today" IX 55–56

"Toll of the Bells, The" III 124

Tolstoy, Leo III 11

Tom Jones I 120

Tombeau des rois, Le VI 179

"Tombeau des rois, Le" IV 218

Tommy Fry and the Ant Colony X 340

"Tomorrow's Past" IV 45

Top Soil X 340, 341, 346, 347

"Top Soil" X 340

"Toponymy" VI 111, 113

"Topsoil to the Wind" VI 296

Toronto Arts and Letters Club III 115

Toronto Daily Star III 62 V 238

Toronto Evening Telegram, The I 24, 26, 29, 32, 33, 34, 40, 54, 59

Toronto Globe, The I 24, 29, 34, 59, 124, 125, 130, 153 n.14 II 17, 28, 136, 143, 193, 237 quoted

Toronto Globe and Mail, The III 71 IX 142, 145 X 193

Toronto Mail, The I 22, 25, 34, 47, 52, 54

Toronto Mail and Empire, The III 117

Toronto Miscellany I 35

Toronto National, The I 26, 29, 34, 36, 40

Toronto Star, The IX 142

Toronto Star Weekly III 26

"Toronto the Golden-Vaulted City"
V 306

Tostevin, Lola Lemire VIII 281

"Totems, The" IX 38

"Toth" VIII 305

Touch, Selected Poems 1960–1970
VIII 133, 139

Touch to My Tongue VIII 14, 203,
204, 206, 240, 245–49

"Touching, The" III 92

"Toughest Mile, The" X 72

"Tourists" V 306

Tourneur, Cyril VI 100

Tovell, Vincent IV 184

Towards a View of Canadian
Letters: Selected Critical Essays
1928–1971 IV 10, 262

Towards the Last Spike III 2, 5,
113, 148–50

"Tower Lullaby VI 292

Tower of London, The VI 279

"Tower of Song" X 51

Toye, William IX 166

"Toys, The" II 252

Trace: The Guide to the Little
Magazines V 131 n.78

Tracing the Paths: Reading ≠ Writing The Martyrology VIII 281

"Tradition and the Individual
Talent" IV 76, 243–44

Tragical Historie of D. Faust VI 213
n.40

Traherne, Thomas IV 10 VI 15, 281
quoted 281

"Trail" VIII 133

"Trail of Bread, The" VI 261

Traill, Catharine Parr I 21, 22, 57,
58, 59 II 136 IX 88

"Trails" VIII 224

"Train Wreck" X 191, 209

"Trainride, Vienna-Bonn" IX 62

"Train-Window" IV 57

"Trans Canada" IV 208

"Transcendentalist, Mystic,
Evolutionary Idealist: Bliss
Carman, 1886–1894" II 15

Transcendentalists, American II 31,
51, 83–84, 213

"Transformation" VI 205

"Transient" VII 159

"Transients" VI 51

"Transistor" V 45

Translating Translating Apollinaire
VIII 303

"Translations from the Japanese
('Kolto' — Lafcadio Hearn)" III
180–81

Transparent Sea, The V 88–89

Traps VII 197, 207

"Travel" X 46

"Traveller, Conjuror, Journeyman"
VI 255, 267 n.30

"Traveller's Palm" VI 258

Treasury of Canadian Verse, A I
75

Treaties of Canada with the Indians
of Manitoba and the North-West
Territories, The IV 217

"Treaty-Trip from Shulus
Reservation" IX 150–51

"Treblinka Gas Chamber" VII 301
n.35

"Tree" III 177, 185 n.12

"Trees at the Arctic Circle" VII 151,
164

Trehearne, Brian IV 39

Très riches heures IX 89

Trial of a City (play) IV 180 V 28,
36–37, 42, 44, 51

Trial of a City and Other Verse V
28–29

Trilling, Lionel V 81, 82 VII 265

Trio VII 16, 254, 263, 269, 272, 281, 308 n.117 X 189, 191, 203, 208–14
"Trip from the City" V 306
"Triumph of Art, The" VII 59
Trojan Women, The (1979) IX 232
Trojan Women: The Trojan Women by Euripides and Helen and Orestes by Ritsos (1981) IX 232
Trotsky, Leon V 3, 31, 62
Trout Fishing in America X 379
"Trout Pond, The" VII 41
Trouvailles: Poems from Prose IV 174, 217
Trower, Peter VII 138
"Troy Town" VIII 367, 375, 377–78
"Truant, The" III 121, 129, 130, 141
Trübner & Co. (publishers) I 160
"True Desire, The" X 48
True Eventual Story of Billy the Kid, The VIII 12, 265, 272, 276
"True Eventual Story of Billy the Kid, The" VIII 309
"True Life, The" II 163
"True Romances" IX 60–62
True Stories IX 59–68, 75 n.57
"Truth, The" II 161
"Tuesday Night" VIII 134
Tufu X 140
Turnbull, Gael V 255 VII 16, 265 X 191
Turner, Frederick Jackson IX 94
"Turning Loam" III 19, 20
Turvey: A Military Picaresque V 28, 32, 36, 49, 60–62, 63
"*Turvey* and the Critics" V 36, 39
Tutuola, Amos VI 302
Twain, Mark (Samuel L. Clemens) VII 78 VIII 95

Twayne's World Authors Series VI 105
Twelfth Night III 127
Twelve for Christmas IV 32
Twelve Landscapes VI 90
Twelve Letters to a Small Town VII 195, 205–06, 222–23
Twentieth Century Canadian Poetry V 50
"28/10/76" IX 121
Twenty-four Poems V 77, 102
"XXII Sonnets" IV 125
Twigg, Alan III 72 VII 145 VIII 37
"Twilight" IV 247
"Twilight Hymn" I 177–78
"Twilight of the Gods" VI 295, 296
"Twin Heads" VII 152
"Twin Masks" VII 296
"Two, The" IV 33
"Two Aspects of the Moon" IX 242
"Two Birds, The" IV 247
"Two Canadian Poets: A Lecture, 1891" II 16, 137, 152
"Two Dream Songs for John Berryman" X 254
"Two Heroes" VIII 309
"Two Mayday Selves" VI 44, 60
"Two Miles Away" IX 56
Two Novels VIII 274, 307
"Two Part Exercise on a Single Image" X 219
"Two Pears: A Still Life" VII 264, 276
Two Police Poems VIII 135, 139
"Two Rivers" II 187–88, 224
"Two Selves, The" VI 56
"Two Sides of a Drum, The" IV 247, 268
"Two Songs" I 54–55
"Two Strangers" VII 101, 106
"Two Trees" V 303

"Two Versions of Sweaters" IX 43

"Two Versions: 1. Poetry, 2. In Situ" VII 264, 287

"Two Visitors from Utah" VII 125

Two-Headed Poems IX 29, 30

"Tyger, The" X 343

"Typists" VI 244

"Typographer's Ornate Symbol at the End of a Chapter or Story, The" VI 49

Tzara, Tristan VIII 23, 37, 40

U.S.A. V 62

Ubyssey, The (Univ. of British Columbia) V 27

Uher, Lorna 136, 169 quoted 169

"Ultimatum" VI 111

Ulysses IV 126, 129, 158 V 62 VI 9 VIII 268 IX 175

"Umbrella Poem" VI 204–05

"Unable to Hate or Love" VI 248

"Unabsolved" II 53–54, 67

"Unborn Things" IX 165–66

Unborn Things: South American Poems IX 135, 136, 143, 163, 164–66, 167

"Unbroken Lineage" VI 40

"Uncertainties" V 317 VII 175

"Uncle Ford on Côte des Neiges" VII 155

Uncle Louis VIII 160

"Uncle Louis" VIII 160, 161

"Uncle Nathan, Blessed Be His Memory, Speaketh from Land-locked Green" X 357–58

"Uncle Nathan Poems, The" X 357

Uncollected Acorn, The VII 25, 66

Uncollected Poems of Irving Layton 1936–59, The V 161, 214 n.64

Under the Ice VII 82, 90, 91, 101

Under the Thunder the Flowers Light Up the Earth IX 4, 86, 88, 89, 90, 92, 109, 111, 115–22, 123

Under the Volcano VIII 370

Underhill, Evelyn IX quoted 243–44

Underhill, Frank IV 174

"Understanding Snow" V 295–96, 297

"Undertaker's Anthology" IV 73, 94

"Unfinished After-Portrait, or, Stages of Mourning" VI 54

"Unhappy People, The" VII 121–22

"Unicorn" VI 305

"unicorn song" VIII 51

Union League Civic and Arts Foundation Prize IX 68 n.1

Unit of Five V 76, 77, 79, 87, 96, 97, 239, 244, 250, 251, 254 VI 223, 231

Unit of Four VIII 303

"Unitas" III 92

"Universe and I, The" VII 60

Universe Ends at Sherbrooke and Queen, The VII 29

University Game, The IX 201

"University of the Air" VII 255

University of Toronto Quarterly I 86, 87 III 171 IV 260 V 154 VI 97, 149, 180 IX 194, 197 X 88

"Unknown City, The" II 216

"Unless the Eye Catch Fire" VI 13, 262, 263–64

"Unnamed Lake, The" IV 179

Unquiet Bed, The III 63, 69, 74, 89, 93

"Unquiet Bed, The" III 92

"Unquiet World" V 299

"Unseasoned" VI 72 n.94

"Unsleeping, The" II 214

"Unspeakable" (Avison) VI 39, 49, 58

"Unspeakable, The" (MacEwen) IX
   253
Untermeyer, Louis II quoted 88 IV
   74, 87, 91
Untitled Novel, ca. 1905 II 247,
   275–77
"Unwavering Eye, The" V 186
"Up and Down of It, The" VI 292
"Up Her Can Nada" V 53, 55
"Uprooting, The" III 97
Upward, Allen II 263, 281 n.48
"Urban Tree" VI 59
Urquhart, Donald I 23
Urquhart, Tony VII 195
"Us Artists — before Public Was, or
   Grants; or Can Litter" VI 65
"Use" IX 64
Use of Poetry and the Use of
   Criticism, The VIII 164
Ustick, Michael VII 93–94
UU, David VIII 28, 30, 269

"Vacuum Cleaner Dream, The" IX
   258
"Vagabond" IV 241
"Vagabond Song, A" II 113–14
Vagabondia poets, American II 82,
   115
"Vagabonds, The" II 112–13
"Vain Comfort" IV 241–42
"Vain Shadow, The" II 271
"Val Marie" X 208, 209, 211–12,
   214
"Valediction, A: Forbidding
   Mourning" I 32
Valéry, Paul VI 227 n.32
Valleau, Allen Keith VI 267 n.32
"Vampires" VII 123
Van Duyn, Mona V quoted 88
Van Gogh, Vincent VII 254 IX 202
Van Sickle, John V 110

van Wilt, Kurt V 160, 204
"Vancouver Lights" V 19–20, 28 VI
   116
Vancouver Poems VIII 14, 197, 198,
   199, 201, 220, 221, 222–24
Vancouver Province IX 143
Vancouver Sun, The VII 135 IX
   143
Vapour and Blue — Souster Selects
   Campbell: The Poetry of William
   Wilfred Campbell Selected and
   Introduced by Raymond Souster
   II 30 V 238
"Variations" IV 29
Variations & Theme IV 29, 32
"Variations on a Seventeenth
   Century Theme" II 258
"Variations on a Theme" VI 301
"Variations on a Tree" III 91
"Variations on the Word Love" IX
   64
"Variations on the Word Sleep" IX
   64–65, 76 n.64
Varieties of Religious Experience VI
   27
"various kinds of doubles:, the" X
   263
Various Persons Named Kevin
   O'Brien VII 80, 83, 96–97,
   99–101, 113
Various Positions X 23, 31
Varley, Frederick H. III 112, 168
Varney, Ed VIII 269
Varsity, The (Univ. of Toronto) II 27
   V 280
"Vashti, the Queen" I 50, 52, 65
   n.64
Vaughan, Henry IV 10, 235, 246 VI
   281, 287 IX 203
Vendler, Helen IX 59, 75 n.55, 76
   n.62 quoted 38, 75 n.55

"Vengeance Is Mine" II 273–75
Venus X 165
"Verandah, The" VI 251–52
"Verigin" X 297
"Verigin, Moving in Alone" X 285, 306
"Verigin III" X 297
Verlaine, Paul II 13 VIII 6
Vernon, John VIII quoted 282
Verses of the Sea III 113
"Version One" VIII 292
"Vesper Star, The" I 22, 47–48, 49
"Vexata Quaestio" V 181
Via Borealis II 237, 238
"Victoria" VI 262
Victoria (Queen of England) II 63
Victoria Daily Times VII 254
"Victoria (Jubilee Ode, A.D. 1897)" II 63–64, 67
Victoria Times-Colonist IX 146
"Vie de château" IV 218
Viereck, Peter VII 198
"Vigil" V 169, 213 n.63
"Vigil of Sorts, A" VIII 134
"Vikki" V 214 n.63
"Vilanelle [plus I]" VII 151
Villa-Lobos VII 277
"Villanelle for Our Time" IV 201
Villon, François IV 102 V 150
Virgil III 151 IV 128 IX 113
"Virginia Woolf" VI 296
Virgins and Vampires X 340, 346, 365–70, 371
Virgo, Sean VIII 30
Vision, A IX 198
Vision Tree, The VII 257, 272, 308 n.117
Visitants, The V 281
"Visiting" VI 198, 205
"Visitor, The" VII 120

"Vitus Bering" V 50
"Vivia Perpetua" II 168, 169
Vivid Air, The: Collected Stories VI 156 n.8
Voaden, Herman VII 203
"Voice and Persona in Carman and Roberts" II 222
"Voice of God, The" I 182
Voices IV 235 VI 87, 92
"Voices of Women" (Feeling the Worlds: New Poems) III 94
"Voices of Women" (The Phases of Love) III 94
"Voltigeurs of Chateauguay, The" I 194
"Voluptuaries and Others" VI 45, 52, 54, 56, 57
Voorhis, Ernest II 171 n.1
"Votaries of April" VII 146
Voyage au bout de la nuit IX 141
"Voyage Begins, The" IV 48–49
Voyage of the Mood X 339, 345
"Voyageur" VI 260
"Vultures" IX 63

"W.L.M.K." IV 20, 190, 198
"Wabamum" X 252–53
Wachtel, Eleanor VII 252, 302 n.43
Wacousta! VII 196, 197, 207, 231–32
Waddell, Katherine II 17, 136, 151, 163
Waddington, Marcus III 24, 30–31 quoted 19, 20, 25, 30–31
Waddington, Miriam III 68 quoted 68 IV 132, 161 n.14 V 2–3, 4, 16–17, 240 quoted 3–4, 16, 17 VI quoted 233 VII 28, 90, 140, 265 X 195
Waddington, Patrick V 152 quoted 152

Wagner, Linda IX 69 n.15 quoted 69 n.15

Wah, Fred IV 261 VIII 120, 121, 122, 162, 163, 168, 193, 195, 277, 281, 369 quoted 192, 196, 278 X 9, 81, 132, 148 quoted 84, 173

"Waiter! . . . There's an Alligator in My Coffee" X 354

"Waiting for Her" VII 103

"Waiting for the Poem to Come Through" V 264–65

"Waiting Room, The" III 102 n.80

"Wake Island" V 50

"Waking" VI 249

"Waking and Sleeping: Christmas" VI 64

"Waking in the Dark" III 92

"Waking Up" VI 52

Waldron, Gordon II 92, 142 quoted 87

Waley, Arthur III 181 IV 177, 194, 197

"Walk, The" III 177, 186 n.12 VI 93

"Walk in Yoho Valley, The" VI 128

"Walk on Wellington Street, A" VII 166

Walker, Horatio II 236

Walking Death V 261, 270 n.53

"Walking to Bellrock" VIII 391

Wallace, Joe VII 30 IX quoted 213

Wallace, Lew VIII 380

Waller, Edmund IV 181

Walsh, Ernest III 20 quoted 20

Walsh, William IV 33, 34, 39 VI 286 quoted 286–87

Walton, Izaak X 379

"Wanted — Canadian Criticism" IV 8–9, 84, 232, 244

Wanton Troopers, The VII 84

"War" I 26 III 182, 183

"War and the English Intellectuals" V 59

"War Cloud, The" I 194

"War Cry" VIII 120

"War Lord in the Early Evening" VI 258, 260

"War Machine" VIII 384

"War Winters" V 42

Warhol, Andy V 55

Warkentin, Germaine III 120, 125, 129 quoted 125, 129 IV 183, 184, 234, 261, 262 VII 198, 204, 205, 206, 208–09

Warland, Betsy VIII 191, 203, 206

"warm place to shit, a" VIII 92–93

"Warm Wind" X 313

Warren, Robert Penn VI 33

"Warren Pryor" VII 101

Warwick, Ellen D. IX 239 quoted 239, 240

Washington Weekly Chronicle I 75

Waste Land, The III 168 IV 73, 95, 128, 133, 139, 141, 143, 146, 147, 148, 151, 152, 176, 180, 182, 194, 196, 268 V 59 VI 90, 176, 180 IX 34, 36, 46, 47, 74 n.54, 75 n.55 X 36, 37, 293, 343, 358, 377

"Watching the Old Man Die" IV 264

"Water" IV 209 IX 263

Water and Light VII 250–51, 252, 257, 258–59, 264, 272, 285, 288, 292, 296–98, 305 n.84, 308 n.116–17 X 131

"Water and Worship: An Open-Air Service on the Gatineau River" VI 61, 62

"water falls in yr mind nd yu get wet tooo, th" VIII 63

"Water Lily, The" II 264–65, 274

"Waterlily, The" I 34
"Waterlily and Multifoliate Rose: Cyclical Notions in Proust" VII 256
"Watershed" VI 40, 72 n.94
"Water-Truck, The" IX 152, 153
"Watkwenies" II 256
Watson, Homer I 14
Watson, Scott VIII quoted 64, 76
Watson, Sheila V 260 VIII 162, 173, 195, 271 quoted 372–73 IX 193, 235 quoted 222 n.50 X 78, 113
Watson, Wilfred VI 48 VII 201 IX 20
Watt, F.W. II 150 quoted 150 IV 183, 184 V quoted 158–59 X quoted 345–46
Watters, Reginald IV 40
Waugh, Evelyn VII 198
Waves IX 145
"Way of Cape Race, The" III 129
"Way to the West" V 52, 53
Way with Words, A VIII 162, 163
Wayman, Tom V 290–91, 309, 311, 312 quoted 291, 312 VII 141
"We All Got to Die" IV 69, 106–07, 109
"we ar made for loving nd sharing" VIII 90
"We Are Seven" I 140
"We Are Not Poor, Not Rich" VI 29, 62
"We Don't Like Reminders" IX 42
we sleep inside each other all VIII 21, 31, 41
"Weakness" VII 102–03
"Wealth" I 26
"Weather" (Souster) V 265
"Weather, The" (Newlove) X 325, 330, 331
Weaver, Robert III 68 quoted 68 VII 198, 256 X 27

"Weaver, The" II 147, 153
Webb, Phyllis VI 178 VII 5, 12, 16–17 VIII 8, 19, 195, 296 quoted 242 IX 20, 87, 91 quoted 3, 87, 88, 91 X 131, 191, 192, 295, 302, 325
Webster, John IV 11, 248 VI 15, 100, 281
"Wedlock" III 88
"Wednesday at North Hatley" VI 136
"Weed Seeds near a Beaver Pond" IX 75 n.57
Week, The I 21, 165 II 78, 136, 144, 190, 195
"Weight, The" IX 174–75
Weir, Lorraine IV 133 VI 211 n.15, 211 n.18, 214 n.48 quoted 17–18 IX 73 n.50
"Welcome to these lines" X 44, 47
"Welcome to you who read me today" X 47
Welcoming Disaster VI 17, 18, 174, 175, 176, 180, 184–86, 190, 193, 195–207, 209, 212–13 n.35, 213 n.36, 213 n.40, 213 n.42, 214 n.47
"Well, The" VI 203
"Well Done, Clan Campbell" I 194
Weller, Hilda X 70
Wells, Charles I 89
Wells, H.G. IV 188, 192 VII 80
Wells, Henry W. III 143 quoted 143
"Well-Tempered Clavier, The" IV 54
"Well-Travelled Roadway, The" X 305
"Wendigo" VIII 137
Wenek, Karol V 94
"we're at the graveyard" VIII 386
"Were-Wolves, The" II 35, 49–50, 67

Wesley, Charles I 167

West, David I 30 X quoted 87

West, Paul V 50, 81 VI 182–83 quoted 182

"West Coast: 1943" III 83–84, 85

West Coast Review IX 135, 145

West Window: The Selected Poetry of George Bowering VIII 160

"Westminster Abbey" V 191

Wetherald, Ethelwyn I quoted 61 IV 30

Whalen, Philip VIII 192

Whalen, Terry II 22, 38 quoted 38 VIII quoted 160, 161

Whalley, George VIII 366–67 IX 85

"What Colour Is Manitoba?" VII 119

"What Do Poets Want with Gold?" II 152

"What Do You Want, What Do You Want?" X 310

"what does mean mean" VIII 57

"what faith" VIII 63

"What Falada Said" VI 201–02, 204, 205, 213 n.42

"What Happened" IX 38–39

"What I'm Doing Here" X 46

"What It Was —" VII 159

What Matters: Writing 1968–70 VIII 205, 215–20

"What the Angel Said" V 322

What the Crow Said X 73, 144

"What the Thunder Said" IV 148

what we have VIII 89, 94

"Whatever Else Poetry Is Freedom" V 157, 180

what's so big about GREEN? V 29–30, 38, 54

"What's So Big about Green?" V 33

"Wheel, The" V 166

"When" IV 47

"When icicles hang . . ." I 141

"When It Is Over" IX 213–14

"When I Uncovered Your Body" X 39

"When I Went Up to Rosedale" IX 196

"When Mary the Mother Kissed the Child" II 226 n.15

"When Thought of Her" IV 241

"When Visitors Come I Go" VIII 135

When We Are Young V 240, 250

"When We Are Young" V 253

"When Wound Is Fresh" VI 295

"When You Are Old" IV 242

"Where Are You" X 306

"Where Cliffs Reflect, Cower" VI 295

"Where Has the Glory Fled" V 197

"Where Is the Voice Coming From" VIII 173

"Where the Moment Is" VII 151

"Where the North Winds Live" V 305

"While as yet no leaves may fall" VI 67 n.21

"Whip-Poor-Will in North Woods" III 40

"Whirlwind, The" I 182

Whiskey Jack, The VII 25, 66

White, Gleeson II quoted 87

White, Howard IX 144

White, T.H. VI 302

"White Cat" III 29, 34–35, 47

"White Cat v" X 298

"White Coffin, The" VIII 155

"White Dwarfs" VIII 384, 386

"White Goddess, The" VII 104–05

"White Margaret" II 168

White Narcissus III 11, 21, 23, 25, 38

White Pelican III 63 IX 193

"White Philharmonic Novels" X 329–30

White Savannahs, The IV 5, 76, 130, 179–80, 237

Whiteman, Bruce III 171 V 5 quoted 6 IX 92 quoted 92 X quoted 87

Whiteman, Neil IX 144, 145 quoted 144

"Whither Do You Wander?" VII 217

Whitman, Walt I 25, 61, 134 II 79, 82, 84, 162, 240 III 65, 177 IV 11 V 80–81, 85, 96, 113, 115, 116, 150, 282 VI 181, 182, 183, 227 VII 138, 267–68 VIII 114, 120, 125, 132, 144, 147, 282 X 6, 81

"Whitman's Barbaric Yawp" V 80–81, 95

Whitridge, Margaret Coulby II 143, 171 n.1

Whittaker, Herbert VII 207

Whittier, John Greenleaf I 172

"who cud have predictid anee uv ths remembr what it was" VIII 29

"Who Drops Plummet" VI 117

"Who Killed Cock Robin?" VI 296

"Who Will Give Me Back" V 194

Whole Bloody Bird, The: Obs, Alphs & Pomes V 186, 196, 200

"Whom I Write For" V 191

"Whose Murderous Shadow, Then?" VI 303

"Why a New Poetry Magazine" V 110

"Why Do Ye Call the Poet Lonely?" II 152

"Why I Happen to Be Free" X 57 n.68

"Why I Should Care about the World" V 304–05

"why i write like ths poetree is for communikaysyun" VIII 93–94

"Why You Can't Teach Creative Writing" V 65 n.21

Wicken, George II 143, 143, 151, 177

"Widower, The" VII 155

Wiebe, Rudy III 85 VIII 173 X 78, 112, 257

Wiggle to the Laundromat IX 10, 191

Wijngaard, Juan IX 191

Wilbur, Richard VII 138

"Wild Birds" IX 168

"Wild Dogs" IX 156–57, 160

Wild Grape Wine VII 143, 165–69

"Wild Grapes and Chlorine" VIII 147

"Wild Horses" IX 152, 153, 155–56, 157

"Wild Peculiar Joy, A" V 205–06

Wild Peculiar Joy, A: Selected Poems 1945–82 V 147

Wild Thing VIII 11, 265

Wilde, Oscar I 14 IV 13, 102 VI 242 X 11, 17

"Wilderness Gothic" VII 168

"Wilderness Stone" III 75

Wilfred Campbell: A Study in Late Provincial Victorianism II 37

Wilkinson, Anne III 13 IV 236, 262 VI 7, 14–16 quoted 15 IX 20

Will to Power V 217, n.79

"Will to Win" IV 206

Will Ye Let the Mummers In? VII 84, 88

"William Wilfred Campbell" (C.A. Scott) II 35

Williams, H.G. IV 30

Williams, Jonathan V 207 n.4

Williams, William Carlos II 12, 262 III 29, 185 quoted 185 IV 235, 236, 261 V 1, 6, 13, 51, 80, 91, 104, 150, 156, 207 n.4, 241, 242, 250, 254, 255, 256, 258, 259, 262, 266, 268 n.41, 269 n.51, 292, quoted 13, 239, 292 VI 88, 92, 94, 95, 128, 154 VII 29, 86, 87, 103, 107, 109, 109, 138, 200, 267, 304 n.78 VIII 8, 121, 125, 127, 135, 159, 172, 173, 189, 192, 194, 203, 271, 296 IX 20, 87, 92, 102, 108, 124 n.11, 234 X 16, 81, 109, 232, 251, 287, 291, 292

Williamson, Janice VIII quoted 203–04, 247–48

Willinsky, A.J. VI 27

Willison's Monthly II 246 VI 86

Willmot, Rod VI quoted 36

Wilson, Daniel I 12, 146, 170, 172, 199 quoted 170

Wilson, Edmund V 101

Wilson, Milton II 247 III 28, 31, 133, 134–35, 150 quoted 28 IV 146, 239 V 88, 149, 157–58, 160, 289 quoted 10, 59, 88, 289 VI 19, 35, 71 n.82, 173, 180, 181–82 quoted 35, 36, 181, 182 VII 41, 42, 44, 91, 92, 204, 206, 209, 221, 269 VIII quoted 134 IX quoted 237, 238 X 26, 28 quoted 27, 203, 205

Wilson, Robert X 86, 92–93

Wilson's Bowl VII 251, 257–58, 266, 270, 271–72, 281, 285–86, 291, 293, 294–95, 302 n.42, 306 n.98

"Wilson's Bowl" VII 261, 271, 296

Wimsatt, William F. VII 268

"Wind at Djemila, The" X 221

"Wind Chimes in a Temple Ruin" V 65 n.25

Wind in a Rocky Country VII 82, 90, 101

"Wind of Early Spring, The" VII 213

"Wind Our Enemy, The" III 66

"Wind that Lived in a Lane, The" IV 104

"Windfall" IV 190

Windfalls for Cider: The Poems of Raymond Knister III 22, 23, 27, 31, 33, 42, 48

"Window-Piece" IV 56, 57

Windsor Border Cities Star, The III 19

"Winemaker's Beat-Étude, The" VII 165

"Wings" VIII 155 IX 177

"Winnipeg as a Chess Game" VII 218

Winnipeg Childhood, A III 63, 67, 96–97

"Winnipeg Zoo, The" X 105, 122–26, 129, 131, 161, 169

"Winter" I 141

"Winter Birds" X 100

"Winter Boarders" VII 45–46

"Winter Fields, The" II 20

"Winter Lady" X 45

"Winter, / moving" VIII 230

Winter of the Luna Moth X 340, 341, 343, 356–59, 363

Winter of Time, The V 250, 269 n.44

Winter Prophecies VI 90, 148

"Winter Scene" VI 110

"Winter Sketch, Rockcliffe, Ottawa" VI 289–90, 305

Winter Sun VI 7, 19, 27, 31, 32, 34, 35, 38, 39, 40, 41, 51, 52, 54–55, 59, 64, 74–75 n.132 VIII 298, 371 IX 20

Winter Sun/The Dumbfounding: Poems 1940–66 VI 28

"Winter Walking" VII 158

"Winter's Night, A" II 41, 42, 44

"Winwod" X 361–62

"Wisdom of Old Jelly Roll, The" IV 264, 265

Wiseman, Adele IX 234

"Wishing Star, The" I 47, 48, 49

Witches' Brew, The III 112, 115, 131, 134 X 342, 368

Witching of Elspie, The II 238

"With April Here" II 222

"With Sweetest Heresy" IV 243

"With the Money I Spend" V 219 n.87

"With Undiminished Fire" V 211 n.40

"With Whom Should I Associate" X 299

"Without Benefit of Tape" III 93

"Without Words" VIII 137

"Witness Poetry" VI 111

"Witnesses, The" IX 163

Wittgenstein, Ludwig VIII 45 X 333

Wolf Willow X 199

"Wolfe" I 198

Wolfe, Gen. James I 178

Wolseley, Col. Garnet Joseph I 126–27

"Woman Being Born, The" X 43

Woman on the Shore, The VII 10

"Woman Skating" IX 43

Woman's Eye: 12 B.C. Poets III 66

"Women's Issue, A" IX 62

"Women's Jail, The" V 311–13

"Wonder: A Street-Car Sketch" VI 63

"Wonderful Country" V 299

Wood, Gayle IX 69 n.15 quoted 69 n.15

Wood, Susan X quoted 292

Woodcock, George I 30, 61, 89–90, 173 quoted 90 II 143 III 64, 72, 74 quoted 12, 64, 72 IV 6–7, 14–15, 38, 239, 262–63 V 37–38, 39–40, 150, 157, 158, 289 quoted 20, 37, 39, 40, 150, 156, 158, 289 VI 17, 21 n.6, 108, 212 n.28 quoted 108, 158 n.31, 285 VII 138, 141, 143, 261, 270, 272, 274, 293–94 VIII 38 quoted 35–36, 371 IX 7, 94 quoted 3, 4, 7–8, 87, 94, 95, 143, 144 X 32, 197

"Woodcutter's Hut, The" II 160–61

Woodhouse, A.S.P. VII 199

Woodsworth, J.S. IV 174, 217

"Wooing, A" I 44–47, 65 n.56

"Wooing of Gheezis, The" I 65 n.56

"Wooing of Monsieur Cuerrier, The" II 270

Woolf, Douglas VIII 162

Woolf, Virginia III 64 VII 198, 202, 249, 257–58, 280, 282, 302 n.41 VIII 193 X 78

"Word, The" III 182 VI 50, 57, 62 VII 109

"Words, The" X 316

"Words Failing" VI 198

"Words for a Resurrection" IV 90, 110

"Words for an Anthem" I 194

Words of My Roaring, The X 72

"Words Said Sitting on a Rock Sitting on a Saint" VII 35

Wordsworth, William I 11, 14, 133,

136, 139, 140, 167, 170, 176, 177, 183, 197 II 9, 13, 14, 30, 43, 97, 139, 140, 142, 148, 152, 156, 162, 168, 194, 197, 200, 208, 211–12, 239 quoted 69 n.32, 70 n.33, 208, 211–12 III 81, 83, 169 IV 41, 43, 85, 176, 213 V 48, 88, 106 VI 30, 48, 53, 74 n.130, 99, 287, 294 VII 262, 263–64, 307–08 n.112 VIII 6, 114, 132, 135, 142, 144, 149, 164, 172, 173, 304 quoted 150–51 IX 54, 159, 171, 201 X 80

"Work in Progress" VI 259 VIII 296

"Working and Wearing, The" VIII 144

"Work-Up, A" VI 43

"World Egg, The" X 351

"World Mother (Scotland), The" II 62, 67

"World Still Needs, The" VI 30, 50, 52

Worldly Muse, The IV 263

"Worthwhile Visitations" VI 12, 21 n.6, 85, 91, 96

Wreford, James VI 223

"Wrestler, The" II 215

"Writer and the H-Bomb, The: Why Create?" V 32–33

"Writers and Writing" X 194

Writers Union of Canada IX 2, 17, 68 n.1

Writing VIII 339

"writing is" VIII 91

Writing Life, The VIII 120

"Writing West: On the Road to Wood Mountain" X 193

"*Writings of Saint And, The*" VIII 313

"wun uv th first time iud evr got publishd" VIII 89

"wundrfulness uv th mountees our secret police, th" VIII 96–98

Wundt, Wilhelm III 115

Wuthering Heights VII 199

Wyatt, Thomas VIII 390 X 373

Wycherley, William I 99

Wylie, Elinor III 77 IV 11, 17, 74, 78, 80, 83, 84, 85, 87, 90, 97, 100, 105, 109 VI 286

Yale University Press VI 174, 214 n.48

"Yard, The" V 183

Yates, Frances VIII 373

"Ye Poet and His Ideal" II 216

Yearbook of the Arts in Canada, 1936, The IV 98

Years, The V 259

Yeats, William Butler I 140, 148 II 17, 80, 242, 252, 261, 262 III 23, 66, 73, 116 quoted 23 IV 10, 72, 79, 80, 81, 124, 231, 232, 234, 235, 237, 241, 242, 243, 246, 250, 252–53, 261, 262, 266 V 2, 150, 151, 282 VI 10, 47, 91, 93, 95, 96, 100, 101, 108, 154, 157 n.17, 227, 243, 303, 305–06 quoted 143, 176 VII 44, 50, 138, 170, 200, 200–02, 221–22, 254, 259, 263, 294–95 VIII 73, 114, 149, 172, 369 IX 20, 31, 124 n.11, 159, 192, 198 X 24, 190, 198, 201, 208, 211, 221, 251, 293 quoted 40

"Yeats Unconquered" VII 221

"Yellow Bear" X 307

"Yellow People in Metamorphosis, The VI 258

"Yeoman, Ann" I 29, 30 quoted 30

Yes V 85–86

"Yes" (Livesay) III 82

"Yes and No" IV 207

Yesterdays IX 211

"Yet What If the Survivors" V 222
n.97

Yogi and the Commissar, The IV
202–03

"Yonge Street Minstrel" X 228

York University Poet's Award IX
136

You Are Happy IX 5, 26, 30, 31,
46–54, 69 n.8

"You Are My Country & Western,
Lullaby" X 160

"You Are My Never" V 319

"You Are the Model" X 41

"You Begin" IX 58

"You Can Climb Down Now" IX
213–14

"You Can See" X 300

"You Cannot Do This" IX 247

"You Can't Get There from Here"
VII 124–25

"You Know" X 302

"You Live Like a God" X 46

"You Must Marry the Terror" X
150

*You Shall Be As Gods: A Radical
Interpretation of the Old
Testament and Its Tradition* V
220 n.97

"YOU SURE LOOK FUNNY WHEN
YOU WRITE" VII 250

"You Told Me" X 313

Young, David VIII 162

Young, Ian IX 193

"Young Girls" VI 250, 251

"Young Man, A" X 314

Young Traveller, The VII 223

"Your Plays Are Like Movies —
Cinemascope Ones" VII 196

"Yours" IV 189

Youth's Companion II 136

"Ypres: 1915" VII 111–12

"Zambia" (*The Colour of God's
Face*) III 63, 66, 69, 89–90

"Zardust and Selima" I 145

Zend, Robert VIII 28

Zend-Avesta I 25

Zezulka, J.M. VI 38, 50, 67 n.22,
71 n.82

Zichy, Francis IV 11, 17, 18 VI 38,
46 quoted 38, 46 VII 34–35

Zieroth, Dale IX 140

Zimmerman, Susan III 70, 75

Zitner, S.P. VI quoted 159 n.45

Zocalo VIII 14, 233–37, 239

Zonailo, Carolyn VIII 30 IX 144

Zoraster I 145

"Zorba the Jew" V 201

Zukav, Gary VIII 66

Zukofsky, Celia VIII 304

Zukofsky, Louis V 255 VIII 193, 304

*Zygal: A Book of Mysteries and
Translations* VIII 304–06